REVIVAL ANSWERS
TRUE and FALSE
REVIVALS

Genuine or Counterfeit

DO NOT BE DECEIVED

• • • • • • • • • • •

DISCERNING BETWEEN
THE HOLY SPIRIT
AND THE DEMONIC

Mathew Backholer

Revival Answers, True and False Revivals, Genuine or Counterfeit: Do not be Deceived, Discerning Between the Holy Spirit and the Demonic

Copyright © Mathew Backholer 2013, 2016, 2017 - ByFaith Media **www.ByFaith.org** - All Rights Reserved.

Scripture quotations unless otherwise stated are taken from the Holy Bible, the New King James Version (NKJV). Published by Thomas Nelson, Inc. Copyright © 1982 by Thomas Nelson, Inc. Used by permission. All rights reserved.

Also used is the Authorised Version (AV), first printed in 1611 and also known as the King James Version (KJV).

All rights reserved. No part of this publication may be reproduced, stored in a retrieval system, or transmitted in any form or by any means – electronically, mechanically, photocopying, recording, or any other (except for brief quotations in printed or official website reviews with full accreditation) without the prior permission of the Publisher, ByFaith Media – (Mathew Backholer) – **www.ByFaith.org**. Uploading or downloading this work from the internet (in whole or in part) is illegal, as is unauthorised translations. For requests for Translation Rights, please contact ByFaith Media.

References to deity are capitalised. As is the nature of the internet, web pages can disappear and ownership of domain names can change. Those stated within this book were valid at the time of first publication in January 2013.

ISBN 978-1-907066-15-3 (paperback)
ISBN 978-1-907066-25-2 (eBook ePub)

British Library Cataloguing In Publication Data. A Record of this Publication is available from the British Library.
First Published in January 2013 by ByFaith Media in association with www.RevivalNow.co.uk. Updated in January 2016 and August 2017.

- Jesus Christ is Lord -

Contents

Page		Chapter
5.	Preface	
7.	Revival – The Facts	1
13.	Evangelism and Revival	2
17.	Revivals in the Bible	3
21.	Revival Related Scriptures	4
25.	What Does Revival Do?	5
28.	The Abnormal and Normal Church	6
34.	The Pendulum Swing of Revival	7
41.	The Beginnings of Revival	8
46.	The Characteristics of Revival	9
53.	Reoccurring Experiences in Revival	10
59.	The Church and Revival	11
63.	The Community in Times of Revival	12
69.	Educational Establishments in Revival	13
73.	Evangelism and Missions During Revival	14
77.	Physical Phenomena	15
83.	Conviction and Confession of Sin	16
87.	Conversion and Dealing with the Past	17
91.	The Supernatural of Revival	18
99.	Persecution – Verbally and Physically	19
104.	The Old and the New Wine	20
109.	Divine or Demonic – True and False	21
113.	Enemies of the Cross	22
118.	False and Counterfeit Revival	23
124.	The Dangers of Revival	24
132.	Nurturing Revival	25
136.	Wisdom and Discernment	26
140.	Deception and Rejection	27
146.	God's Rules and His Laws	28
149.	Human Emotions	29
153.	Handling Physical Phenomena	30
157.	Foolish Excess and the Demonic	31
159.	Rebellion Against the Holy Spirit	32
163.	A Variety of Human Personalities	33

Contents

Page		Chapter
169.	The Tongue and Social Networks	34
173.	Fresh Water or Salt Water	35
179.	Regeneration and False Converts	36
185.	The Devil's Deception	37
189.	You Shall Know the Truth	38
191.	Analysing Revivals	39
195.	Self and Full Surrender	40
198.	Personal Revival	41
201.	Pathway to Revival	42
206.	Steps Towards Revival	43

Appendices A-E
212. (A) Revival Memorabilia and Products
217. (B) Why Revivals are Chronicled
219. (C) Contention of the Evangelical Revival (1739-1791)
221. (D) Kentucky Revivals (1800s) – Physical Phenomena
222. (E) What to Pray For

Additional Information
223. Sources and Notes
229. ByFaith Media Books
231. ByFaith Media DVDs

Preface

"...It shall come to pass afterward that I will pour out My Spirit on all flesh. Your sons and your daughters shall prophesy, your old men shall dream dreams, your young men shall see visions; and also on My menservants and on My maidservants, I will pour out My Spirit in those days" (Joel 2:28-29).

The word 'revival' means many things to different people and frequently the word 'revival' is thrown around like confetti, causing one group to believe one thing, and another something else. One church says, "We are going to have a revival!" Another prints posters stating 'Revival meetings on Tuesday and Friday at 7:30pm.' Some conferences declare come and 'Receive an impartation of revival!' or 'A touch of revival.' An evangelist declares, "I am going to (such and such a town) to have a revival." An elder declares, "We are going to have a prayer meeting for revival every Saturday night." A ministry declares, "Come to our meetings and meet with God to receive an anointing!" No wonder there is so much confusion with varying views, opinions, statements and declarations flying about.

BUT WHAT IS THE TRUTH?

What is revival and how can we tell the genuine from the false, the true from the spurious? With many preachers claiming to *have* 'revival' and some wanting to impart *it* into your life, and with many churches and conferences claiming that *they will* have revival, so come and be touched – what is the truth? Why is there so much hype, exaggeration and distortion when we can have the real thing, a visitation from God as He rends the heavens and pours out His Spirit for His great name's sake! Is it cheap fakes peddling for cheap sakes whilst wishing for higher stakes? What about the genuine preacher who has erred, or the false preacher or prophet who has come as a wolf in sheep's apparel? Have you been misinformed or at times duped by the extravagant claims of a flamboyant and energetic preacher or evangelist?
Revival Answers, True and False Revivals will answer these questions and many others so that we can discern between the genuine and the counterfeit and not be deceived, as we see the

workings of the Holy Spirit compared to the demonic. The author has not dwelt or largely focussed on the negative, but neither has it been ignored, or omitted. If you teach the truth, error will expose itself and this book contains much biblical truth and historical facts. We will keep our feet firmly rooted on the Rock, Christ Jesus as we dig deep into the Bible and delve into Church history to allow the truth and facts to speak for themselves.

Some Christians are pessimists of revival believing, "It is not for today," but is this biblical? The Scriptures declare otherwise. God says, "I will pour out My Spirit…" (Joel 2:28a) and the work of the Holy Spirit still continues. The 'promise of the Father' is still available (Acts 1:4) and we must all receive our own Pentecost, power for victorious Christian living (Acts 1:8).

There is a huge difference between God's dynamics and the demonic, the Holy Spirit and the satanic, between light and darkness, good and evil. However, history records that even people who had faithfully and persistently prayed for revival rejected it when it came because they misunderstood the workings of the Holy Spirit. It was not at a time or in a form how they had expected or anticipated. Some have rejected revival because of the physical phenomena, or written off a move of God because of the negative aspects of a minority. Even R. T. Kendall of Westminster Chapel, London, UK, said, "I have prayed for revival all my life, but I wonder if I will recognise it when it comes? Will I be able to cope with the packaging in which God sends it?"[1]

Some have even been so brazen to say, "If that is revival, I don't want it in *my* church," all to the detriment of their congregation. They have rejected the Holy Spirit and missed revived Christians, saved sinners and restored relationships, all for the glory of God.

Charles H. Spurgeon said, "He [God] *can* bless us as He wills and He will bless us as He wills. Let us not dictate to God. Many a blessing has been lost by Christians not believing it to be a blessing, because it did not come in the particular shape which they had conceived to be proper and right."

'God is greatly to be feared in the assembly of the saints and to be held in reverence by all those around Him' (Psalm 89:7).

Chapter 1

Revival – The Facts

'The works of the Lord are great, studied by all those who have pleasure in them' (Psalm 111:2).

What is Revival?
Revival is a visitation of the Holy Spirit, a quickening, a bringing to life. It is God rending the heavens and coming down, the hills melting like wax before His presence. It is water being poured out on the thirsty and floods on the dry ground. It is a turning from darkness to light, from the power of Satan to God, a casting off of the works of darkness; thus the light of the world (Christians – Matthew 5:14-16) burns brighter and thus aids the Church to be without spot or wrinkle until the glorious day of His appearing.

The apostle Paul declared '…always pursue what is good both for yourselves and for all' (1 Thessalonians 5:15) and 'the manifestation of the Spirit is given to each one for the profit of all' (1 Corinthians 12:7). Revival, God's Spirit being poured out, is for the reviving of Christians and the benefit of the Church. The Holy Spirit will in turn move hardened sinners to fall before the living God and to call upon His name, because whoever calls upon the name of the Lord will be saved, and there is no other name (Jesus Christ) under heaven given to men by which they must be saved.

Henry C. Fish in *Handbook of Revivals* wrote: 'Until the Spirit be poured out from on high' (Isaiah 32:15) saints are neither quickened nor sinners saved. The effective cause in all revivals is the life-giving, light-imparting, quickening, regenerating and sanctifying energy of the Holy Spirit, converting the hardened sinner and reclaiming the backslidden and dormant believer.'

Dr. Martyn Lloyd-Jones speaking on revival said, "Suddenly they are aware of this presence, they're aware of the majesty and the awe of God. The Holy Spirit literally seems to be preceding over the meeting and taking charge of it, and manifesting His power and guiding and leading them, and directing them. This is the essence of revival."[1]

Revival is generally 'localised' amongst a Church, community or town where many individuals share a common experience of the Holy Spirit descending in their midst, or 'national,' amongst a large people group, or nation where multitudes share the common experience of the presence of God. A localised revival is a quickening from the Holy Spirit, a visitation from Him, when Christians are revived, but a national revival is where not only Churches, communities and towns are revived, but a people group or nation is transformed and becomes a habitable praise of God.

Revival is essential for the life and well-being of the Church. Revival glorifies God, vindicates His name, exalts Jesus Christ, gives the Holy Spirit His rightful place in the Church, raises the high and holy standard of the body of Christ and saves sinners who become part of the Church.

To Revive – to Quicken, to Live

The word 'revival' comes from the Latin word 'revivere' meaning to live, to return to consciousness, to reawaken or a renewal of fervour, 'but strictly speaking, it means to bring to life again, to reanimate...' so wrote G. J. Morgan in *Cataracts Of Revival.*

The Greek word for revival is anazōrpureō, which means to stir up or rekindle a fire which is slowly dying, to keep in full flame. It is used metaphorically when the apostle Paul wrote to Timothy, '...Stir up the gift of God which is in you...' (2 Timothy 1:6).

Welsh revivalist, Christmas Evans who spanned the eighteenth and nineteenth centuries wrote: 'Revival is God bending down to the dying embers of a fire just about to go out and breathing into it until it bursts once again into flame.'

A. Skevington Wood in *And With Fire* noted that 'revival [in the Holy Bible] is throughout associated with varying forms of the root hāyā, to live. The general sense of the verb usually (though not uniformly) translated "to revive" is to quicken, to impart fresh life [as in Ecclesiastes 7:12, wisdom "giveth life" to them that have it].' Whilst 'a whole series of usages suggest the idea of recovery or restoration [as in Genesis 45:27, Jacob their father "revived"].' Wood also noted: 'In Hosea 14:7 it is used with reference to grain, and they shall "revive as the corn" ' and Joab "repaired" the rest of the city (1 Chronicles 11:8), another connotation of revival. 'On many occasions, forms of this selfsame root appear in passages, which relate to resuscitation from physical death' as in 1 Samuel 2:6 and "maketh alive"...and "bringeth up."

In the book of Psalms, the same verb relates to personal or communal revival. The note in *Hebrew-English Lexicon* by Brown Driver and Briggs states: 'To revive the people of Jehovah, by Jehovah Himself, with fullness of life in His favour' as in to "quicken me" again (Psalm 71:20) and "quicken us," and we will call upon

Your name (Psalm 80:18-19). 'They are abundantly satisfied with the fullness of Your house and You give them drink...' (Ps. 36:8).

The Words 'Revival' and 'Awakening'
The word 'revival' first came into the English language in 1702; the standard definition being: an awakening in or of evangelical religion. Sometimes the concept of revival is referred to as: a quickening, a spiritual awakening, a visitation, the Holy Spirit descending or a Pentecost etc.

The word 'awakening' first came into the English language in 1736, when Jonathan Edwards published a letter referring to a 'general awakening' amongst his parishioners at Northampton, Massachusetts, New England, during 1734-1735, when virtually the whole town was converted. In the context of Edwards' letter, it meant: an awakening of conscience among the people.

The word 'revival' is not in the majority of Bible translations. Because of this, there are some who would say revival does not exist; or cannot happen, but that is like someone claiming that cars do not exist because the word 'car' or 'motor vehicle' is not found in Holy Writ. The words: Trinity, rapture, missions and soteriology (the doctrine of salvation) are also not found in the Holy Bible – but would we deny the validity and essential truths of their doctrines?

In 1384, John Wycliffe, an Oxford professor, completed the first translation of the Holy Bible in the English language. It had been translated from the Latin Vulgate and was written by hand. With this translation, new words came into the English vocabulary, with about one thousand Latin words being added; whilst other biblical words were thought up to express theological terminology including: sanctified, justified and atonement. No Christian would be foolish to claim that there was no 'atonement' because it was not in the English language prior to the 1380s. Jesus was the Lamb of God who was slain before the foundation of the world; so conversely, we cannot say that the word 'revival' has no credence for today because it is not found in the majority of Bible translations. 'Until the Spirit is poured upon us from on high, and the wilderness becomes a fruitful field...' (Isaiah 32:15).

In the Old and the New Testament, by direct word of inspiration, 'revival' is recorded by inspired inference and the concept is clearly seen in the lives or events of individuals and groups. We have revival Scriptures; verses from the Word of God, which have been prayed through and pleaded by multitudes of people through the centuries who have acted on the promises (and conditions) of God and seen revival in their church, community, town or nation. There are thousands of books on the subject of revival in the English language alone; many of which document accounts of revival or are biographies of revivalists. The author during his time of research has come across more than one thousand revivals and awakenings throughout the world and has merely scratched the surface.

John D. Drysdale, principal of Emmanuel Bible School, (in the 1930s), at Birkenhead, UK, wrote: 'A revival is a renewed interest in religion, after indifference or decline. A revival is a reanimation from a state of languor and decline. A revival is a period of religious awakening. A revival is restoration to consciousness of life. A revival is voluntary, and determined return to first things, and a whole-hearted honouring of God as Creator, Jesus Christ as our Lord and Saviour, and the Holy Ghost as our Sanctifier.

'A revival, in the first instance, has to do with God's people. Then when the unsaved see God's people taking Divine things seriously, they become alarmed about their sin, and their rebellion against God and many of them are won to God. A revival is...a manifestation of the mighty power of God in turning men and women of every walk of life from their sins, to a life of God-glorifying, and whole-hearted sacrifice and service towards our fellows.'[2]

What is Revival For?

Revival is the Church (a group of Christians and not a building) being saturated with God – it is primarily intended for the Church so that they can be revived into a true, proper and correct relationship with God and one another. From this, revival begins to affect those who are outside of the Church to a lesser or greater degree. Theologically and historically, the river of revival begins amongst the Church, but will naturally flow outwards and bring to life those who are dead in their trespasses and sins (non-Christians) because God has no pleasure in the death of the wicked. During times of revival, Christians get revived before sinners get converted because this is a spiritual law of revival.

The quickening and reviving of Christians is 'floods being poured on the dry ground' (Isaiah 45:3). Christians get on fire for God and have renewed consecration and zeal. The Holy Spirit comes to refine, purify and to wash clean, 'a refiners fire and like fullers soap...He will purify...and purge them as gold and silver that they may offer to the Lord an offering in righteousness' (Malachi 3:2-3). Once Christians have been quickened then a visitation of the Holy Spirit on the community or beyond is possible and very probable as long as the Church keeps praying, seeking and pleading for God to 'rend the heavens' (Isaiah 64:1) and come down – as the Holy Spirit descends to 'convict the world of sin, and of righteousness and of judgment' (John 16:8). God is 'mighty to save' (Isaiah 63:1) and 'He shall see the travail of His soul and be satisfied' (Isaiah 53:11). 'God has no pleasure in the death of the wicked' (Ezekiel 18:23) but 'desires all men to be saved and to come to the knowledge of the truth' (1 Timothy 2:4), because 'whoever calls upon the name of the Lord will be saved' (Romans 10:13 and Joel 2:32). God has promised, "I will pour out My Spirit on all flesh..." (Joel 2:28). 'No good thing will He withhold from them that walk uprightly' (Psalm 84:11b), because He is 'a sun and a shield; the Lord will give grace and glory' (Psalm 84:11a). God says, "I will yet for this be enquired of by the house of Israel to do it for them" (Ezekiel 36:37), and the dry bones shall live (Ezekiel 37), because God declares, "Before all the people I must be glorified" (Leviticus 10:3).

On very rare occasions, the exception and not the norm, revival can be for those who are completely dead in their trespasses and sins. This is what happened in the case of the city of Nineveh, who repented under Jonah's preaching (the reluctant revivalist), who declared, "Yet forty days, and Nineveh shall be overthrown!" It was also seen in the Samaria Revival under Philip the evangelist (Acts 8:5-8) and amongst the Angas Tribe in Nigeria in the 1930s.[3]

The Theology of Revival

In times of revival, the fundamental truths of Jesus' eternal Sonship, the virgin birth, His sinless life, His death, resurrection, ascension, second coming and the judgment (and heaven and hell); alongside repentance, the new birth, faith in Christ and total consecration are always preached.

A Christ-less, cross-less, blood-less message will result in spineless, defence-less and power-less churchgoers with the nickname Christian, because a fast food gospel message will result in biodegradable believers. The doctrine of any revival *will always* emphasise Christ crucified, the cross, the efficacy of Jesus' shed blood and the coming judgment. The message will lift up Jesus Christ, the Son of God and Saviour of the world. The first Bishop of Liverpool, J. C. Ryle said, "Without Christ crucified in her pulpits, a church is a little better than a dead corpse, a well without water, a sleeping watchman, a silent trumpet, a speechless witness, an ambassador without credentials, a lighthouse with no power, a messenger with no good tidings. Such a church is a stumbling block to weak believers, a comfort to infidels, a hot-bed for formalism, a joy to the devil, and an offence to God!"

Vinet, in *Outlines of Theology* wrote: 'If you learn in a general way that there has been a revival in a place, that Christianity is reanimated, that faith has become living, and that zeal abounds – do not ask in what soil, in what system, these precious plants grow. You may be sure beforehand that it is the rough and rugged soil of orthodoxy [the foundation of agreed belief], under the shade of those mysteries which confound human reasoning.... The revival has preached the total depravity of man and his powerlessness to save himself. The revival has preached salvation by grace and not by works, the necessity of the new birth in order to enter the Kingdom of Heaven and the absolute dependence of man in regards to God. The revival has preached the plenary and essential deity of Jesus Christ as well as His perfect and entire humanity; it has declared that God was in Jesus Christ, reconciling the world unto Himself; and that it is in Jesus Christ alone that we have remission of sins and access to the Father; and that whosoever abideth not in Him abideth in death.'[4]

Evangelist and revivalist, James A. Stewart of the twentieth century wrote: 'Revival is an assembly word. Any movement that fails to deliver the local church from its subnormal existence and raise it to a higher elevated position in its ascended Lord has no true marks of a New Testament Revival...Revival, as presented to us in the New Testament, is not so much an individual experience as a collective experience of a church of born again believers.'[5]

'Renewal is not revival. Local renewal meetings, as important and essential as they are, more often than not, only revive the Christians present and leave the local church untouched.' James A. Stewart wrote: 'God's way of revival is through renewals from within, so that our local churches become the centre of blessing.'[6]

If we understand the previous quotes by Vinet and Stewart it makes it easier to understand the difference between a revival and an outpouring, such as the Toronto Blessing (1994+) in Canada, the Sunderland Outpouring (1994) in England, and the Lakeland Outpouring (2008) in America, with a large emphasis on healing (the last section of chapter 27 covers the Lakeland Outpouring). The focus is largely on Christians who need to be renewed, refreshed or healed. They know the essential tenets of truth and thus live by them. However, we should all be regularly reminded of these wonderful and blessed essential truths of Jesus and His atoning sacrifice for fallen mankind, because Jesus is Lord!

Chapter 2

Evangelism and Revival

The Great Commission – Personal Evangelism

Jesus' parting words to His disciples, before He ascended into heaven revealed His most passionate desire to reach the lost – the Great Commission, "Go into all the world and preach the Gospel to every creature" (Mark 16:15) and "Go therefore and make disciples of all nations…" (Matthew 28:18). This very important message which was entrusted to them was to be passed on from generation to generation because Jesus came to 'seek and to save' those who are 'lost' (Luke 19:10) for 'there is no other name under heaven given among men by which we must be saved' (Acts 4:12).

God's love for mankind is immense and is documented in the most famous verse of the Holy Bible, John 3:16, 'For God so loved the world that He gave His only begotten Son, that whoever believes in Him should not perish but have everlasting life. For God did not send His Son into the world to condemn the world, but that the world through Him might be saved. He who believes in Him is not condemned, but he who does not believe is condemned already' (John 3:16-18).

The disciples were commissioned to preach and teach about the Kingdom of God; to proclaim the good news of salvation, to make disciples, to cast out demons, to heal the sick and raise the dead (Matthew 28:18-20 and Mark 16:15-18) – all in the mighty name of Jesus Christ. These commands of Jesus Christ are just as binding to us, as to the early disciples to whom Jesus spoke. They are passed from one generation to the next until every tribe and tongue has heard the glad tidings – 'as a witness to all nations' and then, and only then, will Jesus come again (see Matthew 24:14, Revelation 5:9 and 7:9). However, remember, that Peter in relation to the Day of the Lord (the end times), reiterated that we have our part to play – our responsibility and duty towards mankind. God is 'longsuffering towards us, not willing that any should perish but that all should come to repentance' and that we should be 'looking for and *hastening* the coming of the day of God' (2 Peter 3:9-12). This is when we fulfil our vital role in the Great Commission by personal evangelism, sharing the good news. We all need an anointing from God, power for evangelism, the baptism of the Holy Spirit, power for service (Luke 24:49 and Acts 1:5, 8). If the Church does not evangelise, it will fossilise! "I am the Lord, and besides Me there is no Saviour...you are My witnesses..." (Isaiah 43:11-12).

Evangelism or Revival

Revival is not evangelism and evangelism is not revival. In effective evangelism, God may bless the work and people will respond to the call of repentance and make a profession of faith. However, in revival there is an overpowering presence of God and regardless of any leaders present, or an appeal to get right with God, the people will be compelled by the Spirit of God to get right with Him. They will repent, forsake their sins, pour out their hearts to the Almighty and call upon the name of the Lord who is mighty to save. He shall see the travail of His soul and be satisfied.

In evangelism, the focus is on the evangelist or preacher, and many who profess Christ soon fall by the wayside. But in revival, the focus is on God, and the vast majority of those who profess Christ stay true to Him as abiding fruit.

J. Edwin Orr, twentieth century evangelist, revivalist and world renowned revival historian said, "In times of evangelism, the evangelist seeks the sinner, in times of revival the sinners comes chasing after the Lord."

Selwyn Hughes, founder of Crusade for World Revival wrote: 'Evangelism is the expression of the Church; revival is an experience of the Church. Evangelism is the work we do for God; revival is the work God does for us.'

James A. Stewart saw numerous revivals in Eastern Europe prior to 1939 and after World War II he saw revival in Norway (1947) and a move of God in Milldale Bible Conference (1966) in America. After more than three decades of ministry, he wrote: '...Revival results in a great wave of evangelism and ingathering of souls. Revival includes evangelism, but evangelism may not include revival. Evangelism always follows revival, but revival does not necessarily follow an evangelistic campaign. Evangelism seeks the resurrection of sinners who are dead in trespasses and sin. Revival is a spiritual quickening of the life of the redeemed.'[1]

On occasions, revival does break forth during evangelistic campaigns. The giants of evangelism such as Dwight L. Moody, Reuben Alexander Torrey, Wilbur Chapman, A. C. Dixon, James A. Stewart, Billy Graham, Carlos Annacondia and Luis Palau, all saw revival break forth on more than one occasion during their evangelistic campaigns. When Christians become revived, they will inevitably be more effective in personal evangelism, being burdened for the lost, and on fire for God.

Rev. William Haslam saw at least seven revivals and is most noted for the Baldhu Church Revival (1851-1854) in Cornwall, England, which began when the Anglican preacher got converted under his own preaching! He said, "Revivals – that is the refreshing of believers and the awakening of sinners – ought to take place wherever the gospel is preached in faith and power."[2]

Revival is Not Man-Made

Much of what is called revival is not, and 'indifference and opposition can come from a confusion of terms. There attaches to the word 'revival' what does not belong to it,' so wrote Henry C. Fish. Revival cannot be put together, manufactured or produced. If it can be planned, orchestrated and be turned on or off then it cannot be revival. Revival cannot be worked up, a man-made spark of fleshly wood shavings (Isaiah 50:10-11), but it needs to come down (Isaiah 32:15), Divine fire! (1 Kings 18:38-39). Revival is not an organised event, though out of an organised event, such as an evangelistic campaign or during effective evangelism, revival can break forth. The object of evangelism is to seek lost souls, whereas revival revives dry and weary souls, transforms saints, saves sinners and can change entire communities.

Evangelist Dr. Fred Barlow described revival as: 'Heaven-sent, Spirit-given, sin-convicting, soul-saving, politic-purging, society-redeeming and nation sparing....'[3]

One author wrote: 'This is revival from heaven! – When men in the streets are afraid to speak godless words for fear that God's judgment will fall! When sinners, aware of the fire of God's presence, tremble in the streets and cry for mercy! When, without human advertising, the Holy Spirit sweeps across cities and towns in supernatural power and holds people in the grip of terrifying conviction. When every store becomes a pulpit, every heart an altar, every home a sanctuary and every people walk carefully before God – This is revival!'[4]

The vast majority of Christians unnecessarily live and die without ever seeing a revival – this is a travesty and an indictment on the Church – because God has promised to give water to the thirsty and to pour floods on the dry ground (Isaiah 44:3) and He is not a man that He should lie!

Some people would say that in revival, there is no need for an altar call, (to call people to the front, to repent and to surrender to Christ) and that it should be reserved for evangelistic meetings. Many revivalists from revival Church history have been noted for their altar calls, enquiry rooms or after meetings. In some revivals, there is no altar call, as people get on their knees where they are and cry out to God for His mercy. During the Lewis Revival (1949-1952), in the Outer Hebrides, Scotland, UK, seventy-five percent of people were converted outside of a church building! People crying out under conviction of sin is also a Scriptural response – Peter preached at Pentecost and the people cried, "What shall we do [to be saved]" (Acts 2:37). After the supernatural earthquake, the Philippian jailor came trembling and fell before Paul and Silas and said, "Sirs, what must I do to be saved?" (Acts 16:30).

However, challenging the people to make a response or application to the message that has been preached is a Scriptural process (1 Chronicles 29:5b). Moses came down from Mount Sinai and saw the Israelites unrestrained and declared, "Whoever is on the Lord's side, let him come to me" (Exodus 32:26). Joshua declared, "Choose this day whom you will serve..." (Joshua 24:15). Elijah challenged the people, "How long will you falter between two opinions? If the Lord is God, follow Him; but if Baal, then follow him" (1 Kings 18:21). Many are invited to the Great Supper at the end of the age and we are to 'go into the highways and hedges [byways] and compel them to come in' that God's 'house may be filled,' but many will make lame excuses (Luke 14:15-24).

During the Congo Revival (1953-1957) a missionary wrote to the Worldwide Evangelisation Crusade and stated that the Holy Spirit had descended on the 'hard and dry district' amongst the Meje tribe. From the Egbita centre she wrote: 'God has done in a few days things we had never seen in twenty years of labour, but one realises too that nothing has been lost of all the efforts of sowing and reaping. It is as though the Lord has reaped in a day.'[5]

Oswald J. Smith wrote: 'The greatest need of the world and the Church today is a mighty manifestation of the Spirit of God. Before the days of [Charles] Finney revivals [prior to 1821] there were only 200,000 church members in the United States. When Finney ended his ministry [he died in 1877], over three million had joined the churches. The greatest days of the Church have been the days of revival. Nothing can take its place. The best that man can do does not meet the need. Only as God comes upon the scene in revival power are the problems solved.'[6]

Gamaliel, a teacher of the law before the Council at Jerusalem said, "...keep away from these men [Peter and the other apostles] and let them alone; for if this plan or this work is of men, it will come to nothing; but if it is of God, you cannot overthrow it – lest you even be found to fight against God" (Acts 5:38-39).

Chapter 3

Revivals in the Bible

'One generation shall praise Your works to another and shall declare Your mighty acts' (Psalm 145:4).

Old Testament Revivals
1. From the godly line of Seth men began to call on the name of the Lord (Genesis 4:26) – they saw their need which was an awakening of this group of people.
2. King Asa became King of Judah and did what was right in the eyes of the Lord. He banished the male and female prostitutes from the land and removed all the idols. He commanded his people to seek the Lord God of their fathers and to observe the Law and the commandments (1 Kings 15:9-15 and 2 Chronicles 14:1-15).
3. The prophet Elijah had a spiritual battle on Mount Carmel, before King Ahab and the four hundred and fifty prophets of Baal and four hundred prophets of Asherah. Once the true altar was prepared; a complete offering was given and Elijah called upon his God and the fire fell! The people fell on their faces crying out, "The Lord He is God! The Lord He is God!" And revival broke out (1 Kings 18:20-40).
4. Jehoiada the priest made a covenant between the Lord, the king and the people that they should be the Lord's people. They also tore down the temple of Baal (2 Kings 11:17-18 and 2 Chronicles 23:16-21).
5. King Hezekiah of Judah reopened and repaired the house of God which had been shut up and neglected for many years. He made a covenant before God and the house of God was cleansed and sanctified. A big Passover festival was held and all the idols, wooden images, high places and false altars were smashed, cut down and destroyed. The temple worship was reinstated and the Levites got their jobs back (2 Kings 18:1-8 and 2 Chronicles 29-31).
6. Evil King Manasseh of Judah as a captive in Babylon, humbled himself before God who permitted him to return to Jerusalem. He removed the idols and foreign gods, repaired the altar of the Lord and commanded the people

of Judah to serve the Lord God of Israel (2 Chronicles 33:12-16). BUT there was still *consequences for his sin which another generation reaped* (2 Kings 24:3-4).
7. King Josiah (whose father and grandfather were evil) saw revival in Judah, when the Book of the Law was found and he acted upon it – by repenting and humbling himself before God. King Josiah, the elders and the people of Judah made a covenant before the Lord to obey His commandments. The temple of the Lord was cleansed, and all the false altars and temples of idols were destroyed and they celebrated with a huge Passover festival (2 Kings chapters 22-23 and 2 Chronicles chapters 34-35).
8. Jonah was called to preach in Nineveh, to the notorious cruel Assyrians, but fled from the call of God. Eventually the prophet Jonah preached in this large pagan city, shouting, "Yet, forty days and Nineveh shall be overthrown!" The people of Nineveh believed the Word of the Lord. The king commanded his people to humble themselves, cry mightily to God and turn from their evil ways. God saw their humility and contrition, and judgment was avoided which upset Jonah! (The book of Jonah).[1]

The Bible does record many instances of God, the Lord, Angel of the Lord (see Judges 2:1) or the glory of the Lord coming or descending upon the earth: The Lord came down upon Mount Sinai in fire (Exodus 19:18-20). Moses, Aaron and 72 other people saw the God of Israel on Mount Sinai and they ate and drank (Exodus 24:9-11). The pillar of cloud descended to the tabernacle door when Moses went there (Exodus 33:9-11). Moses saw the glory of God from a cleft in a rock (Exodus 33:18-23). The cloud covered the tabernacle and the glory of the Lord filled it (Exodus 40:34-38). The glory of the Lord, a cloud filled the temple during the dedication ceremony under King Solomon (2 Chronicles 5).

New Testament Revivals
1. John the Baptist called the people to a baptism of repentance for the remission of sins and told them to bear fruits worthy of repentance. They came to him for baptism and confessed their sins. He told them of the One who was to come (Mark 1:4-5 and Luke 3:1-18).
2. Jesus was the promised Messiah, the Saviour of the world and was the Anointed One (Luke 4:18-19). At His baptism He was filled with the Spirit and returned from His forty

days in the wilderness in the power of the Spirit (Luke 4:1, 14). He preached the Kingdom of God with signs and wonders following confirming the message and thus proving He was the Promised One (Matthew 11:2-5 and Luke 8:25). The people flocked to hear His teaching (and to be healed) and Jesus had periods of perpetual revival in various cities.
3. The Holy Spirit fell on the Day of Pentecost and people began to speak in tongues. Peter preached and about three thousand people were cut to the heart, being under conviction of sin. They believed on the Lord Jesus Christ, repented of their sins and were baptised in the name of Jesus (Acts 2).
4. Peter and John preached and around two thousand people were added to the Church (Acts 4:1-4) – five thousand less three thousand from the Day of Pentecost.
5. Through the hands of the apostles many signs and wonders were performed and multitudes became believers in Christ Jesus (Acts 5:12-14).
6. The number of disciples of Jesus multiplied greatly in Jerusalem including many of the priests (Acts 6:1-8).
7. Philip went down to Samaria, preaching with miracles following and multitudes with one accord heeded what he said and became followers of Jesus. There was great joy in that city (Acts 8:5-8).
8. Peter visited Joppa and raised Dorcas from the dead; as this fact became known throughout Joppa, many believed on the Lord Jesus (Acts 9:36-43).
9. Peter and some brethren went to Caesarea and preached at Cornelius the centurion's home. The Holy Spirit fell upon those gathered, they spoke in tongues and were then baptised (Acts 10:23-48).
10. Some of the disciples of Jesus (not the twelve) preached at Antioch to the Hellenists and a great number believed and turned to the Lord (Acts 11:19-21). When news of this revival reached the church at Jerusalem they sent Barnabas to assist in the work and more people were added to the faith (Acts 11:22-24).
11. The apostle Paul and friends preached to the Jews in the synagogue in Antioch at Pisidia. Many of the Jews and devout proselytes followed the teaching of Jesus Christ. The Gentiles then begged that they also may hear this preaching on the following Sabbath and almost the whole

town came to hear. This upset the elders of the city, but the Word of the Lord spread throughout that region (Acts 13:14-50).
12. The disciples preached in the synagogues at Iconium and both Jews and Greeks believed. Signs and wonders were performed and the city was divided against the Jews and the apostles (Acts 14:1-4).
13. Paul and the apostles travelled; the churches were strengthened in the faith and the Church increased in numbers daily (Acts 16:1-5).
14. Paul and Silas went into the synagogue in Thessalonica and preached. A great multitude of devout Greeks and many of the leading women followed them, which led to a riot, as people said, "These who have turned the world upside down have come here too" (Acts 17:1-9).
15. Paul and Silas were sent to Berea and they preached in the synagogue. Many believed, both Greeks and prominent women of the city, but Jews from Thessalonica stirred up the crowd and another riot began! (Acts 17:10-15).
16. Paul preached on Mars Hill, in the midst of the Areopagus in Athens to the pagans, some mocked, but others joined them and believed (Acts 17:22-34).
17. Paul, Silas and Timothy travelled to Corinth and spoke at a house meeting of Justus who lived next door to the synagogue. Crispus the synagogue ruler and his entire household believed along with many of the Corinthians. They stayed there for six months, teaching the new converts (Acts 18:7-11).
18. Paul taught in the school at Tyrannus for two years and all who dwelt in Asia (Minor) heard the Word of the Lord, both Jews and Greeks, but some were hardened and spoke evil of the Way (Acts 19:8-9).
19. In Ephesus, after hearing and seeing the power of God working through the apostle Paul, fear fell on the Jews and Greeks. Jesus was magnified; many who had believed on Jesus Christ publicly confessed their sins and those who had practised magical arts publicly burned their occult books (Acts 19:11-20).
20. Paul was shipwrecked on the Island of Malta. Many people were healed under his ministry including the leading citizen of the island (Acts 28:1-9). There is no recorded mention of conversions, but undoubtedly there were as they thought he was a god (v6) and Paul always preached!

Chapter 4

Revival Related Scriptures

God's Spirit and the Glory of the Lord
- Thus says the Lord, "And it shall come to pass afterward that I will pour out My Spirit on all flesh; your sons and your daughters shall prophesy, your old men shall dream dreams, your young men shall see visions; and also on My menservants and My maidservants I will pour out My Spirit in those days" (Joel 2:28-29).
- The Lord said, "But truly, as I live, all the earth shall be filled with the glory of the Lord" (Numbers 14:21).
- 'Surely His salvation is near those who fear Him, that glory may dwell in the land' (Psalm 85:9).
- '...The Lord will arise over you and His glory will be seen upon you' (Isaiah 60:2).
- 'For the earth will be filled with the knowledge of the glory of the Lord, as the waters cover the sea' (Habakkuk 2:14).

Covenant-Keeping God – Conditional Promises
- "If My people who are called by My name will humble themselves, and pray and seek My face, and turn from their wicked ways, then I will hear from heaven, and will forgive their sin and heal their land" (2 Chronicles 7:14).
- "If you will keep My commandments and execute My judgments, then will I do it!" (1 Kings 6:12), AV.
- "Ask of Me, and I will give You the nations for Your inheritance" (Psalm 2:8). This is the Father speaking to His Son, but we can also pray it because the Great Commission is the Church's responsibility and God has no pleasure in the death of the wicked.
- "Ask Me of things to come concerning My sons, and concerning the work of My hands command ye Me" (Isaiah 45:11), AV.
- "I will yet for this be enquired of by the house of Israel to do it for them" (Ezekiel 36:37), AV.
- 'The Lord is not slack concerning His promise...but is longsuffering towards us, not willing that any should perish but that all should come to repentance' (2 Peter 3:9).

God's Vindication and for His Glory
- God said, "By those who come near Me, I must be regarded as holy; and before all the people I must be glorified" (Leviticus 10:3).
- The twelve memorial stones were set up, 'That all the people of the earth may know the hand of the Lord, that it is mighty, that you [the Israelites] may fear the Lord your God forever' (Joshua 4:24).
- God said, "For My own sake, for My own sake, I will do it; for how should My name be profaned? And I will not give My glory to another" (Isaiah 48:11).
- 'O Lord, though our iniquities testify against us, do it for Your name's sake; for our backslidings are many, we have sinned against You' (Jeremiah 14:7).
- 'Not unto us, O Lord, not unto us, but to Your name give glory, because of Your mercy, and because of Your truth. Why should the Gentiles say, "Where now is their God?" ' (Psalm 115:1-2).
- '[The] Gentiles...glorify God in the day of visitation' (1 Peter 2:12). See also Ezekiel 36:22-23 and Romans 15:9a.

The Holy Spirit and God Descending
- 'Until the Spirit is poured upon us from on high and the wilderness becomes a fruitful field, and the fruitful field is counted as a forest' (Isaiah 32:15).
- Thus says the Lord, "For I will pour water on him who is thirsty, and floods on the dry ground; I will pour out My Spirit on your descendants and My blessing on your offspring" (Isaiah 44:3).
- Thus says the Lord, "Rain down, you heavens, from above, and let the skies pour down righteousness; let the earth open, let them bring forth salvation, and let righteousness spring up together. I the Lord have created it" (Isaiah 45:8).
- 'Oh, that You would rend the heavens and come down! That the mountains might shake at Your presence...to make Your name known' (Isaiah 64:1).
- 'For behold the Lord is coming out of His place; He will come down.... The mountains will melt under Him, and the valleys will split like wax before the fire, like waters poured down a steep place' (Micah 1:3-4).[1]
- 'He shall come down like rain upon the mown grass, like showers that water the earth' (Psalm 72:6).[2]

- 'Bow down Your heavens, O Lord, and come down; touch the mountains and they shall smoke' (Psalm 144:5).
- "Not by might nor by power, but by My Spirit," says the Lord of hosts (Zechariah 4:6).

God's Merciful Nature and Reviving
- The Lord said, "If My people who are called by My name will humble themselves, and pray and seek My face, and turn from their wicked ways, then I will hear from heaven, and will forgive their sin and heal their land" (2 Chronicles 7:14).
- '...But You are God, ready to pardon, gracious and merciful, slow to anger, abundant in kindness and did not forsake them' (Nehemiah 9:17).
- 'The eyes of the Lord are on the righteous and His ears are open to their cry' (Psalm 34:15).
- 'Will You not revive us again...?' (Psalm 85:6).
- '...Revive me in Your way' (Psalm 119:37b).
- 'Revive me, O Lord, for Your name's sake! For Your righteousness' sake...' (Psalm 143:11).

Holiness Scriptures
- 'Who may ascend into the hill of the Lord? Or who may stand in His holy place? He who has clean hands and a pure heart, who has not lifted up his soul to an idol, nor sworn deceitfully. He shall receive blessing from the Lord and righteousness from the God of his salvation. This is Jacob, the generation of those who seek Him...' (Psalm 24:3-6). See also Psalm 15.
- 'Sow for yourselves righteousness; reap in mercy; break up your fallow ground, for it is time to seek the Lord, till He comes and rains righteousness on you' (Hosea 10:12).
- 'Let the words of my mouth and the meditation of my heart be acceptable in Your sight, O Lord, my strength and my Redeemer' (Psalm 19:14).

Contemplation, Confession and Forsaking Sin
- 'I acknowledged my sin to You and my iniquity I have not hidden. I said, "I will confess my transgression to the Lord" and You forgave the iniquity of my sin. Selah. For this cause everyone who is godly will pray to You' (Psalm 32:5-6a). See John 9:31, God hears those who do His will.

- 'If I regard iniquity in my heart, the Lord will not hear' (Psalm 66:18). See also Isaiah 59:2.
- 'One who turns away his ear from hearing the law, even his prayer shall be an abomination' (Proverbs 28:9).
- 'Search me, O God, and know my heart; try me, and know my anxieties; and see if there is any wicked way in me, and lead me in the way everlasting' (Psalm 139:23-24).
- 'Let us search out and examine our ways, and turn back to the Lord; let us lift up our hearts and hands to God in heaven. We have transgressed and rebelled.... You have covered Yourself with a cloud that prayer should not pass through' (Lamentations 3:40-42a, 44).
- 'He who covers his sins will not prosper. But whoever confesses and forsakes them will find mercy' (Proverbs 28:13). See also Leviticus 5:5, Acts 19:18 and James 5:16.
- Does our heart condemn us? Is our conscience pricked with unconfessed sin because we have not kept God's commandments and therefore we are not pleasing in His sight? (1 John 3:21-22).
- Confessions of our sins, the sins of our forefathers and our nation's sins are paramount (Exodus 20:5-6, Judges 2:6-19 and 1 John 1:9). We need to make sure that we are right before God. Unless we deal with the sins of the past it is impossible to move forward into all that God wants for us.

Our Responsibility

- Obey the precepts as revealed in the Holy Bible! 'One who turns away his ear from hearing the law, even his prayer shall be an abomination' (Proverbs 28:9).
- Jesus must be at the centre of our lives, we need to be living a God-glorifying lifestyle, walking in holiness. God said, "Be holy, because I am holy" (1 Peter 1:16).
- We must abide in God so that we can bear fruit for His glory (see John 15:1-11, 1 John 3:6 and 1 John 3:24).
- We must be fully submitted to the Father's will, having offered our bodies as a living sacrifice, which is our reasonable service (see Romans 12:1-2, Galatians 2:20 and 2 Corinthians 5:15). Walk in the Spirit (Galatians 5:25).
- Jesus said, "Blessed are those who hunger and thirst for righteousness for they shall be filled" (Matthew 5:6). Are we hungering and thirsting for more of God? Will He not fill those who ask? (Luke 11:5-13). Obey God (Acts 5:32).

Chapter 5

What Does Revival Do?

'Restore us, O Lord God of hosts; cause Your face to shine and we shall be saved' (Psalm 80:19).

Revival does a thousand and one things and this chapter brings to the fore the essence of revival and includes statistics from revivals of what God has done in the past in different centuries, in many nations on different continents.

Revival and the Trinity
- Glorifies God.
- Exalts Jesus Christ in praise, love and adoration.
- Gives the Holy Spirit His rightful and due place within the Church.

Revival and People
- Revives Christians and brings that which was stale or dying back to life and vigour.
- Brings the brethren into a correct relationship with God and one another; restores relationships.
- Converts sinners, produces saints and draws the backsliders back into the family of God.
- The way of revival is costly and humiliating. It includes dear and costly repentance, often with its exacting demands of open confession (Mark 1:4-5) and restitution (Luke 19:5-10). Leaders above all must not shrink back from paying the price.
- It re-emphasises the liberating release from the guilt and power of sin by cleansing in the blood of Jesus Christ.

Revival and the Church
- Transforms, strengthens, unifies, revives, renews and makes strong the Church, the body of Christ, but it may also divide and even split congregations.
- Brings to light that which was in darkness and exposes sin and motives of the heart.

- Produces an increase of godly sincere repentance, reconciliation and restitutions (Luke 19:5-10).
- Brings a greater emphasis on the cross of Calvary and the efficacy of the blood of the Lamb that was slain to take away the sin of the world.
- Revival upsets some professors of Christianity who are not living up to its high and holy standards. It also condemns and reveals the secrets of others.

Revival and Christian Ministry
- Raises up more lay-workers and thrusts forth more labourers into the harvest field. See Matthew 9:35-38.
- Calls more individuals from secular employment into full time Christian ministry. The intakes at Bible Colleges / Seminaries, mission agencies and other ministries increase as more Christians heed the call of God.
- Brings into being new ministries and occasionally new mission agencies and / or humanitarian works.
- Christian ministries become more fruitful and effective for the Kingdom of God.

Revival and Educational Institutions
- Strengthens Bible Colleges and Training Centres etc., and sometimes leads to founding new ones.
- Revolutionises institutions of learning; often founding them and they owe a great debt to revival. This was best seen in America during the eighteenth and nineteenth century when many, now prestigious institutions were founded by Christians for godly education. See, chapter thirteen, Educational Establishments in Revival.

Revival and the Community
- Can transform families, places of employment, churches, communities, people groups and islands.
- National revivals or awakenings can transform a nation and uplift society at large. In the past this had brought about social welfare and changes which have been enshrined in law. This was most clearly seen in the Evangelical Awakening (1739-1791) and the fruit of reform that flowed into nineteenth century Britain. Revival elevates society and can change the moral character of a nation, truly transforming it from within.

After George Whitefield had preached in Philadelphia, New England, America, in 1739, the American philosopher, Benjamin Franklin said, "It was wonderful to see the change made by his preaching in the manner of the inhabitants of Philadelphia. From being thoughtless or indifferent about religion, it seemed as if the whole world were growing religious."

In October 1742, Rev. William Halley of Muthil, (shire of Perth), Scotland, UK, was witnessing a revival which was birthed out of the Cambuslang Revival (1742). In a letter he wrote: 'The arrows of the Almighty King are still flying thick amongst us, and wounding the hearts of His enemies, and laying them down groaning at the feet of the Conqueror, crying under a sense of guilt and the frightful apprehension of wrath, and thirsting after a Saviour.'[1]

William C. Conant, in reference to the First American Great Awakening (1735-1760) wrote: 'It cannot be doubted that at least 50,000 souls were added to the churches of New England out of a population of about 250,000, as it is estimated; which makes the remarkable proportion of twenty percent of all inhabitants – a fact sufficient to revolutionise, as indeed it did, the religion and moral character, and to determine the destinies of the country. But this was not all. Perhaps as many converts were made within the churches as without them; and this, as every experienced Christian knows, is a change of double moment to the Church, at once adding strength and removing the most depressing of all burdens. Not less than 150 new congregational churches were established in twenty years.'[2]

An eyewitness from Bicester during the 1860 Revival in England said, "It is not asserting too much to say that a greater number of sinners have been converted to God in Bicester, and within eight miles of it, during the last ten months than have made an open profession of religion during the last two hundred years!"[3]

During the Pingtu Revival (1931-1933) which became part of the Shantung Revival (1930-1932) in north China, a missionary in a letter, dated, 15 July 1932, wrote: 'In the densely populated county of Pingtu, Shantung [Province], where the revival began and the churches have become greatly revived, there are now villages in which every family has one or more saved persons, and in some villages nearly everyone has accepted the Lord. Is this not glorious news to all who love the Saviour!?'[4]

In 1952, during a revival in Brazil, in an interior city, the churches gained more additions in a month than in the previous decade.[5]

Chapter 6

The Abnormal and Normal Church

Thus says the Lord, "Rain down, you heavens, from above, and let the skies pour down righteousness; let the earth open, let them bring forth salvation, and let righteousness spring up together. I the Lord have created it" (Isaiah 45:8).

Abnormal and Normal Church

The majority of churches do not reflect the true representation of Christianity as revealed in the New Testament; the Church should be different than a social club and God must be glorified. This is why we need revival.

James A. Stewart wrote: 'Coldness, deadness and backsliding are abnormal and the Church will never become normal until she sees revival. The glorious splendour of the Church which shines out as a result of revival is the true standard our Lord has set up in the New Testament, and this is what He expects to see among His redeemed ones at all times.... A subnormal and backslidden Church is an insult and a disgrace to a holy and powerful God.'[1]

A Bible College student who had heard of several localised revivals in a number of Bible Colleges / Institutes wrote in his diary: 'I dedicated myself to pray persistently that the whole body of Christ might be made spiritual. At present it is far below normal. I find no basis in the Word for expecting those who are Christians to be subnormal! It is my duty to *claim* with thanksgiving the Church's possession of her privilege in Romans 8! May God make us spiritual, deliver us from conscious sin, and make us ever more conscious of sin!'[2]

Bishop Handley Moule in his description of the normal Church said, "It is nothing less than the supreme aim of the Christian gospel that we should be holy; that the God of peace should sanctify us through and through our being; that we should walk worthy of the Lord unto all pleasing ['fully pleasing Him' Colossians 1:10]. It is the insatiable desire of the soul which has truly seen the Lord, to be made fully like Him by His grace.

"...To displace...self from the inner throne and enthrone Him; to make not the slightest compromise with the smallest sin. We aim at being entirely willing, nay, definitely to will, to know with ever keener sensibility what is sin in us, that it might be dealt with at once by the Holy Spirit. We aim at nothing less than to walk with God all day long; to abide every hour in Christ, and He and His words in us; to love God with all our heart, and our neighbour as ourselves, to live that in no conventional sense, 'no longer to ourselves, but to Him who died for us, and rose again' [Romans 12:1 and Galatians 2:20]....'[3]

The Antidote is Revival
On 28 September 1935, J. Edwin Orr began a world tour to circumnavigate the globe. He travelled to America, Canada, Australia, New Zealand and South Africa. For the two preceding years he had travelled extensively around Britain, Eastern and Western Europe, into Soviet Russia and as far away as modern-day Israel and saw localised revivals in many countries. After World War II, J. Edwin Orr, a preacher and revivalist, became known as a world renowned revival historian. He wrote: 'No one will suggest that the spiritual poverty and smug self-satisfaction...is the ideal of the Lord for the body of Christ. The antidote is revival, and revival must always be the will of God. To refuse to pray for revival (as hopeless) is like impudently telling the Lord that His power is limited.'[4]

'Away with pessimism. It is the sin of unbelief. The pessimist says that revival is impossible. Such are seldom men of faith. They say that revival is impossible before Christ comes. While the Spirit of the Lord is among us, who dare tell Him what is possible and what is impossible. God forgive our unbelief. They will try to justify their statements from Scripture. Tell them all that I challenge them to produce one single verse which proves the impossibility of revival among God's people. [Orr had just seen localised revival breakout in three Bible Colleges / Institutes in America and three localised revivals in New Zealand – all in a space of three months!]. They will quote, "When the Son of man cometh, shall He find faith in the earth?" Faith is already missing in the earth, but what has that to do with the Church of Christ? Revival is a Church affair. They will quote that we are in the Laodicean Church. The Laodicean Church is the apostate, professing Church – and you and I have nothing more to do with it. The call in the days of Laodicea is, "If any man hear My voice, and open the door" – have not we responded to that? Then we are free from the curse of Laodicea. It is a snare of the evil one to make us despair. Revival is always possible to the obedient child of God....'[5]

'...O Lord, do not give Your heritage to reproach' (Joel 2:17b).

J. Edwin Orr wrote: 'One finds that the pessimist fulfils their own ideas in themselves. ['As a man thinks in his heart, so he is' Proverbs 23:7]. As soon as a man starts talking about the impossibility of revival, his own work is beginning to shrivel up ['According to your faith be it done unto you' Matthew 9:29]. The man who believes in revival is the man who sees results.'[6]

Max Warren in *Revival An Enquiry* wrote: 'The Church which is true to the Bible knows that sin is a deadly reality in its own life and therefore it must seek the Holy Spirit. When the Holy Spirit comes in sin convicting power, revival takes place and revival is inevitably disconcerting for all that is complacent and sinful in the life of the Church, as well as disturbing for much that is good but falls short of the best.'[7]

Dr. Robert C. McQuilken wrote: 'Let us not limit God in His workings, and let us not fail to be ready for new and great outpourings of the Holy Spirit in the closing days of this age. For the days are upon us when nothing will avail to break through the overwhelming power of the enemy, except supernatural power beyond what most Christians have not known anything about. If the Church was supernaturally blessed of God at its birth, who will say that, in the closing days of its witness here on earth before its translation, it will not be blessed in even a mightier way?'[8]

Leonard Ravenhill wrote: 'Without question, the greatest need of this hour is that the Church shall meet her ascended Lord again, and get an enduement that would usher in the revival of revivals just before the night of nights settles over this age of incomparable corruption.'[9]

In March 1962, Rev. Geoffrey R. King, gave the presidential address at the Annual Assembly of the London Baptist Association. In his closing statements he said, "It is revival that we need – the one thing that can save the situation in our land today, in the world today – the one thing that will really begin to meet the whole situation. For this we must seek, for this we must cry, for this we must wait upon the living God, earnestly, humbly, unitedly, desperately. Our eyes must ever be up to Him for this. Our hearts must ever be lifted up [towards Him] for this is the one and only thing which will really meet our tragic need. But, meanwhile, let us give ourselves assiduously to digging the ditches for the floodtide of quickening which the Lord in His gracious purpose will be pleased to send us. And, while we are intent upon the quickening and the blessing of God upon our labours, who knows if, in His sovereign mercy, He may suddenly rend the heavens and break through upon us with the great thing, the Divine intervention, the outpouring of the Holy Spirit's power, the visitation of God in our time?"[10]

Willis Hoover who founded the Methodist Pentecostal Church in Chile, during the 1909 Chile Revival said, "I believe that the true secret of this whole thing is that we really and truly believe in the Holy Spirit – we really trust Him – we really honour Him – we really obey Him – we really give Him free rein – we really believe that the promises in Acts 1:4-5 [baptised with the Holy Spirit] and Joel 2:28-29 [I will pour out My Spirit on all flesh] is for us."[11]

A friend once asked Evan Roberts of the Welsh Revival (1904-1905) for a message to the churches that were praying for revival. Closing his eyes for a moment, he prayed for guidance and then said, "They have the Word and they know the promise. Let them keep God to His promise, 'ask and ye shall receive.'"[12]

The Need of Revival:
1. God must be glorified, Jesus Christ must be exalted and the Holy Spirit needs to be given His rightful place within the Church. He is not a thing or an influence, but the Spirit of God, a Person.
2. The Church needs to be revived. It must be swept free and cleansed from sin. If revival does not start in the Church then how can it move outside the Church amongst the graceless?
3. The graceless need to receive the grace of God, sinners need to be surrendered to Him and in times of revival they are drawn as if by an unseen hand to call upon the name of the Lord and to turn from their wicked ways.
4. Revival quickens evangelism and aids discipleship, 'Warning every man and teaching every man in all wisdom, that we may present every man perfect in Christ Jesus' (Colossians 1:28). New converts are often the most passionate evangelists (Acts 4:20).
5. In times of revival, under the searchlight of the Holy Spirit, people are highly sensitive to sin, responsive to repentance and forsaking sin, and desire to live righteously before a holy God, acknowledging the difference between, 'The holy and the unholy, and causing them to discern between the unclean and the clean' (Ezekiel 44:23).
6. Revival can so change a person in a matter of hours, which would have taken a Christian counsellor years to produce much lesser results. Some are instantly delivered from demons.

Society Needs God
The Church needs revival and individual members of society need to forsake sin and embrace Jesus Christ or face the fires of

hell on judgment day. Revival elevates society and can change the moral character of a nation and transform a nation. In the past, this had brought about social welfare and changes that have been enshrined in law. John Ferguson in *When God Came Down* wrote: 'Politicians can make good laws, but they cannot make good people. The Holy Spirit not only shows people how they ought to live but can give them a new heart to enable them to obey Him (Ezekiel 36:25-27).'

- 'It is time for You to act, O Lord, for they have regarded Your law as void' (Psalm 119:126). The word of God, the Holy Bible and the precepts contained within have been disregarded and are often laughed at as archaic and made null and void by many of our government's laws.
- 'Justice is turned back, and righteousness stand afar off; for truth is fallen in the street, and equity cannot enter. So truth fails, and he who departs from evil makes himself a prey' (Isaiah 59:14-15). For most people, there is no moral absolute, no conclusive right from wrong, and as in the days of the judges of Israel, everyone does what is right in their own eyes (Judges 21:25), and those who try to live by the rules of God are mocked, often denounced and sometimes attacked.
- 'Woe to those who call evil good, and good evil; who put darkness for light, and light for darkness; who put bitter for sweet, and sweet for bitter!' (Isaiah 5:20). There is no fear of God; morals have been turned on their head by political correctness that people are unaware of what is right or wrong, whilst some deliberately try and pervert justice and truth. 'In that you say, "Everyone who does evil is good in the sight of the Lord, and He delights in them..." ' (Malachi 2:17). Others try to move the boundary stone of truth which our forefathers established and lived by (Proverbs 22:28).
- 'This is the way of an adulterous woman; she eats and wipes her mouth, and says, "I have done no wickedness" ' (Proverbs 30:20). There is no shame or remorse for breaking God's laws as people have hardened their hearts and seared their consciences as with a hot iron.
- 'You have wearied the Lord with your words; yet you say, "In what way have we wearied Him?" (Malachi 2:17). Many people who profess to know God try to make an all-inclusive religion. They claim that all roads lead to God and that all people are good. Yet the Bible declares that 'all have sinned and fall short of the glory of God' (Romans

3:23), and that there is 'none that is righteous' (Romans 3:10). The only way to God is through Jesus Christ (Acts 4:12), who 'is the Way, the Truth and the Life' (John 14:6).
- 'Open rebuke is better than love carefully concealed' (Proverbs 27:5). Many people (including Christians) shy away from denouncing sin or condone sin by not speaking out – the sin of silent omission (Isaiah 58:1). 'He who rebukes a man will find more favour afterward than he who flatters with the tongue' (Proverbs 28:23), and 'Those who rebuke the wicked will have delight, and a good blessing will come upon them' (Proverbs 24:25).
- 'Defend the poor and the fatherless; do justice to the afflicted and needy. Deliver the poor and the needy; free them from the hand of the wicked' (Psalm 82:3-4). Society does not always stand up for those who cannot defend themselves and Christians should always be at the forefront of this.[13] See Isaiah 58:6-14 & Matthew 25:35-46.

'Now the glory of the God of Israel had gone up from the cherub, where it had been to the threshold of the temple. And He called to the man clothed with linen, who had the writer's inkhorn at his side; and the Lord said to him, "Go through the midst of Jerusalem, and put a mark on the foreheads of the men *who sigh and cry over all the abomination that are done within it*"' (Ezekiel 9:3-4).

Jonathan Edwards saw revival in his church at Northampton, New England, during 1734-1735 and again in 1741-1742, and is known as one of America's greatest theologians. He wrote: 'God hath had it much on His heart, from all eternity, to glorify His dear and only begotten Son; and there are some special seasons that He appoints to that end, wherein He comes forth with omnipotent power to fulfil His promise and oath to Him; and these times are times of remarkable pouring out of His Spirit, to advance His Kingdom; such a day is a day of His power.'

'The Spirit of the Lord is upon Me because the Lord has anointed Me to preach good tidings to the poor; He has sent Me to heal the broken-hearted, to proclaim liberty to the captives, and the opening of the prison to those who are bound; to proclaim the acceptable year of the Lord, and the day of vengeance of our God. To comfort those who mourn in Zion, to give them beauty for ashes, the oil of joy for mourning, the garment of praise for the spirit of heaviness; that they may be called trees of righteousness, the planting of the Lord, that He may be glorified' (Isaiah 61:1-3).

Chapter 7

The Pendulum Swing of Revival

Thus says the Lord, "For I will pour water on him who is thirsty, and floods on the dry ground; I will pour out My Spirit on your descendants and My blessing on your offspring" (Isaiah 44:3).

How does God Work in Revival?

There are differing views amongst Christians as to how we can see revival. It relates to God's sovereignty, man's instrumentality and to what degree they are interconnected. However, the common denominator from all sides is that it is the Holy Spirit that does the work as the Spirit is poured out (Isaiah 32:15).

If we are only familiar with the more prominent national revivals such as the Great Awakenings of the eighteenth century in Britain and New England, America; the Fulton Street Revival (1857-1859) or the Welsh Revival (1904-1905) then our perception of revival, how it comes about, the effect it can produce and other factors will be narrowed. As Jonathan Edwards noted, who had seen Revival at Northampton, New England in 1734-1735 and 1741-1742, there is 'latitude of the Spirit in His methods of operation.' This is also seen in Scripture, in how and when the Holy Spirit came.

G. J. Morgan in *Cataracts Of Revival* wrote: 'In the hidden ledger of God there is a specific law where every revival works accordingly, and every law runs back to the source of all things, even the wise Lawgiver who planned, the Mind that thought, the Heart that felt – the God that purposed everything in the end to reach the goal of perfection.'

Sovereignty, Instrumentality and Responsibility

- Is it purely God's sovereignty? – If so, do we sit back and do nothing and merely enjoy the ride?
- Is it a combination of God's sovereignty, human instrumentality and our responsibility?
- Does man have any degree of responsibility; some Scriptural duties that have to be undertaken?
- Do we pray revival down or can it be worked up?
- Are there key Scriptures to pray and plead?

The Views of Revival
1. It is totally a sovereign work of God.
2. It is God's sovereignty coupled with man's responsibility. Man applies God's promises.
3. Anybody can have revival at any time as long as the conditions and promises have been appropriated.
4. To see revival, preach the pure gospel with unction (an anointing); exalt Jesus Christ, the efficacy of the blood, Calvary, man's sinfulness and the wrath and mercy of God.
5. For some Pentecostals, revival can mean a gathering of Christians who receive the baptism of the Holy Spirit (often receiving the gift of tongues, Acts 2:1-11, Acts 10:46 and 1 Corinthians 12), or when a number of Christians in a service or conference are prayed for (by a leader, minister or evangelist etc.) and are touched by the Holy Spirit.

The first three views are all part of the same swing of God's revival pendulum. The Holy Spirit descends in the day of visitation; reviving Christians and converting sinners. With point four, there are preachers who have such an anointing on their lives that regardless of their location, they see revival; it is as if they 'carry' the presence of God with them – 'glory carriers,' others see revival by extension. Often they will have had intercessors prepare the way before them, breaking up the spiritually barren ground, praying and believing for a reviving of Christians and a harvest of souls.

The fifth point reveals why many Pentecostal personalities are referred to as revivalists, not because people come under conviction of sin and get right with God (though many do), but because Christians are touched by the Holy Spirit when prayed for, often with the laying on of hands. However, this can be abused leading to a "bless me," self-seeking attitude. Whilst some leaders minister with a 'different spirit' (2 Corinthians 11:3-4), (often unknowingly), for financial gain or popularity, and a mixture of Divine and demonic can be present.

A sixth point is that some preachers primarily aim at seeing Christians revived so as to build up and elevate the Church; they promote a revival of religion. They preach the Word of the Lord; denounce sin and challenge the brethren to get right before God. The brethren acknowledge their guilt and respond in Spirit-led repentance and confession which leads to contrition and brokenness before the Lord. Christians are revived and this inevitably flows into a community and sinners get converted. This was J. Edwin Orr's method of ministry in the second stage of his world tour (from September 1935) where ninety percent of results were amongst believers, but he also saw ten thousand professions of faith in a single year!

God's Sovereignty and Human Responsibility

After the resurrection, Jesus sent His disciples to proclaim the good news as part of the Great Commission – "Go into all the world and preach the gospel to every creature" (Mark 16:15) and "Go therefore and make disciples of all the nations..." (Matthew 28:19). To see sinners converted and lives transformed is a Divine-human partnership – we are called to make disciples and to help, train and build up the body of Christ to the praise and glory of God. It is God's sovereignty coupled with man's responsibility and this is how we can see revival in the fullness of time.

In 1970, J. Phillip Hogan gave the presidential address to the Evangelical Foreign Mission Association (EFMA) and stated, "In Acts 5:32 we read, 'And we are witnesses of these things and so is also the Holy Ghost, whom God hath given to them that obey Him.' This indicates that the task of worldwide witnessing is a joint task. It is a cooperative endeavour between the Lord of the harvest and His Church made up of human vessels."[1]

Rev. William Haslam of the nineteenth century saw at least seven revivals. In *From Death Into Life* he wrote: 'Revivals – that is the refreshing of believers and the awakening of sinners, ought to take place wherever the gospel is preached in faith and power.'

The Divine-human Partnership Quotes

- John George Govan, founder of The Faith Mission, (Scotland), partook of several revivals at the end of the nineteenth century. He said, "Without God we cannot, without man He will not."
- Victor Ellenberger wrote *A Century of Mission work in Basutoland 1833-1933*. In reference to the Qalo Awakening (c.1912) in modern-day Lesotho, he wrote: '...The awakening of a whole district under the guidance of a missionary who had joined the mission rather late in life, is a veritable miracle of the power of God in conjunction with the faithful service of man.'
- James A. Stewart saw many revivals in Europe in the 1930s and 40s, and a local revival in 1966 in America. In his book, *Opened Windows, The Church and Revival* he wrote: 'God's sovereignty and man's responsibility never clash in the Word of God. In His inscrutable wisdom and

providence God has chosen to do His work in the world through His saints, and has so bound up His purposes with man that He limits His workings to man's obedience.'
- Duncan Campbell of the Lewis Revival (1949-1952), Scotland, in his book, *God's Answers, Revival Sermons* wrote: 'Let me say what I frequently say – that the God I believe in is a covenant-keeping God who is true to His engagements. 'If you will keep My commandments and execute My judgments, then will I do it!" (1 Kings 6:12).
- Norman Grubb, in the foreword to *Floods on Dry Ground* which documented the Imbai Revivals of 1935 and 1936 in the N. E. Belgian Congo, wrote: 'It clearly demonstrates that revival is not an act of Divine sovereignty apart from human cooperation, but the legitimate outcome of man's compliance with Divine conditions for revival.'
- John Ferguson in his book, *When God Came Down an account of the North Uist Revival 1957-58* wrote: 'God Himself is the source of revival, but it is equally true that His people are the channels through which revival comes...Matthew Henry wrote: 'When God intends great blessing for His people, He first of all sets them a-praying.' And these words bring human responsibility and Divine sovereignty together, where they belong.'
- Miss Eva Stuart Watt's in her book, *Thirsting for God* wrote: 'Let us realise that revival is not a miracle, but like other events, is brought about by fulfilling God's requirements for revival and paying His price.'
- Arthur Wallis in his book, *In the Day of Thy Power* wrote: 'The Word of God presents to us side by side the two foundation stones of every revival [Acts 1:4, 11, the brethren were united and in prayer] – the sovereignty of God and the preparedness of man. Because we cannot understand how they harmonise is no reason for emphasising one at the expense of the other.'
- Michael Howard has seen at least five revivals in various African countries during the 1980s and 90s. In *Tales of an African Intercessor* he wrote: 'No move of God or mighty revival is His sovereign act. God works and moves by the distinct cry of His people or is prevented by the distinct lack of their cry.'

Rev. C Perren in *Revival Sermons In Outline* wrote: 'Who can question the importance of human instrumentality in the salvation of men, when the Word of God so plainly declares, 'he that wins souls is wise'? 'They that turn many to righteousness shall shine as the stars forever and ever.' 'Let him know that he which converts the sinner from his error of his way shall save a soul from death and shall hide a multitude of sins.'

'While human agency is thus very plainly declared, we should ever remember that all man's work, however zealous and untiring; all his words, however eloquent; all combined forces of the professed people of God, apart from Divine sanction and aid, shall be powerless in bringing one soul to Christ or reinvigorating the Church. Such results are 'not by might, nor by power, but by My Spirit, says the Lord of hosts.' To attain success we must be 'labourers together with God,' labourers not idlers, labourers together with God, not equal with, but under and belonging to Him, in subordination to God as instruments in His hand.

'Great was the success of [Charles] Finney in revivals, and of his preaching it was said, "He preached God's word clear through and without flinching, never muffling the sword of the Spirit, he made it cut to the very marrow." These words may with equal force be applied to Jacob Knapp and Elder Swan, whose labours were blessed to thousands. Thus, in God giving the Word, and in man preaching it, there is a union of Divine and human agency, and without the knowledge of God's word there can be no revival.

'Divine and human agency in revivals is markedly seen in the efficacy of personal and united prayer. The history of revivals amply proves prayer to be the right arm of every great awakening. To quote Scripture in proof of the necessity and potency of such work would be to transcribe a great portion of the sacred Word.'[2]

Covenant-Keeping God and the Fullness of Time

God is a covenant-keeping God because Scripture declares, 'know that the Lord your God, He is God, the faithful God *who keeps covenant* and mercy for a thousand generations with those who love Him and keep His commandments' (Deuteronomy 7:9). 'God of heaven, O great and awesome God, You *who keep Your covenant* and mercy with those who love You and observe Your commandments' (Nehemiah 1:5).

Revival can be seen through God's sovereignty and man's fulfilled responsibility, (the Divine-human partnership), which is revealed in the fullness of time. All things are decreed in heaven (Psalm 119:89), but they have to be outworked on earth. It was Lewis A. Drummond who wrote: 'Prayer opens the door to the fullness of time.' The fullness of time is a series of synchronised events coming together as one, which unlocks and releases all that God has for that particular situation. It was the accumulation of Divine orchestrated events that fulfilled the prophecies of the Messiah: the conception of the forerunner, John the Baptist, the census which resulted in Joseph returning to his home town of Bethlehem, the Virgin Birth, the flight to Egypt and the death of Herod which enabled Mary, Joseph and a young Jesus to live in Nazareth, because 'when the fullness of time had come, God sent forth His Son...' (Galatians 4:4).

The fullness of time, waiting upon God (Jeremiah 14:22b) is revealed when we have prevailed in prayer like the persistent widow (Luke 18:1-8) because prayer is the prevailing key to answer. But we also have to be living a consecrated life, in obedience to the Master with a pliable and contrite heart.

Our Cooperation is Needed

There are times when revivals seem to be spontaneous manifestations of Divine power and there is no human agency at work; but behind spontaneous moves of God are intercessors; or at least one person who prayed the heavenly fire down, as did Elijah on Mount Carmel (1 Kings 18). '...As soon as Zion travailed she gave birth to her children' (Isaiah 66:8b).

In every revival there is an interblending between the Divine and human agencies. The prayer of the burdened heart is the key that unlocks the heavenlies imploring God to come down and revive His people. In seeing revival, God needs our cooperation and assistance as He chooses to work through human vessels. God had mercy on the inhabitants of Nineveh, but He did not send revival until Jonah went through the city calling the people to "repent" – and they did! Whilst God can create and gather the harvest without human instrumentality, it is unlikely. Rev. Duncan Campbell wrote: 'God is sovereign and will act according to His sovereign purposes – but ever keeping in mind that, while God is sovereign in the affairs of men, His sovereignty does not relieve men of responsibility.' At Pentecost (Acts 2), Peter preached!

Rev. John Smith, from the early nineteenth century wrote: 'The *mode* of the Divine working is dictated by sovereign wisdom; but the *degree* depends on the faith of the Church. God Himself determines whether He will descend as the dew upon Israel or as the burning flame; but it is for His people to decide whether He shall come upon the single fleece while the rest of the floor is dry, or whether the whole of the camp shall be surrounded and gladdened by the scatterings of angel food...'[3]

George Mitchell chronicled the life of evangelist and revivalist, Jock Troup, who was used in the East Anglia Revival (1921-1922) in England, which flowed into the Fishermen's Revival (1922) in Scotland. Mitchell wrote: 'It is helpful and healthy to learn from revival times that God's emphasis has been on holy people He has mastered, rather than clever methods we can master.'

The Cost of Revival and Leadership

The way of revival is costly and humiliating. It includes dear and costly repentance, often with its exacting demands of open confession (Mark 1:4-5) and restitution (Luke 19:5-10). 'Let the wicked forsake his way, and the unrighteous man his thoughts, and let him return unto the Lord and He will have mercy upon him; and to our God, for He will abundantly pardon' (Isaiah 55:7).

Revival proves an acceptable time to many and a day of vengeance for others! (Isaiah 61:2). Jonathan Edwards in 1741 noted that 'those who do not become more happy with it [a time of revival] will become far more guilty and miserable...When God sends forth His *Word*, it shall not return void; much less His *Spirit*. When Christ was upon earth in Judea, many slighted and rejected Him; but it proved in the issue to be no matter of indifference to them. God made all the people to feel that Christ had been among them; those who did not feel it to their comfort felt it to their great sorrow.'

Leaders above all must not shrink back from paying the price. Leaders can help promote a revival, hinder one, as well as quench it. Leaders can share with their congregation about revivals from history, from those in the Holy Bible right up to the present. 'Tell ye your children of it, and let your children tell their children, and their children another generation' (Joel 1:3).

A leader can help prepare for revival by preaching the truths of God's Word (the whole counsel of God), living what they preach and praying for God to rend the heavens and pour out His Spirit. The preaching of God's Word may not necessarily be what the people want to hear, but it is what they NEED to hear under the direction and unction of the Holy Spirit. Preaching must be focused on Jesus Christ, the cross, repentance, forsaking sin, full surrender and total consecration to Christ; as we are called to walk in the Spirit, be led of the Spirit and obey the Spirit. We are also called to take up our cross and follow the Master; and to put away all sin. Congregations need to work with their leaders, not against them. To get right with God and with one another, because where there is unity, God commands the blessing (Psalm 133).

Chapter 8

The Beginnings of Revival

The Lord said, "If My people who are called by My name will humble themselves, and pray and seek My face, and turn from their wicked ways, then I will hear from heaven, and will forgive their sin and heal their land" (2 Chronicles 7:14).

Prayer, Intercession and an Assurance of Revival
- Before a revival comes, faithful disciples of Jesus Christ will be praying and interceding for God to move His mighty hand and to pour out His Spirit from on high. They will plead the promises of God as contained within the Bible.
- It has been said by many a preacher that preceding revival, the word 'O' or 'Oh' is always used in passionate prayer, pleading and interceding as it comes from deep within, a heartfelt sigh. "If one sigh of a true Christian," said an old preacher "wafts the bark (sailing ship with three or more masts) to the desired haven, or stirs Zion's ship, how much more a gale or sighs breathed by hundreds of believers!"
- There will always be prayer and intercession before revival as revival always begins with a burden. This is Holy Spirit led prayer by someone, or a group who are standing before God on behalf of the land, see Isaiah 59:16a, Isaiah 62:6-7 and Ezekiel 22:30. '…The Spirit…for we do not know what we should pray for as we ought, but the Spirit Himself makes intercession' (Romans 8:26).
- Those with a burden become the watchmen who stand in the gap (intercession) on behalf of the land. To some they may appear to be going mad, like Jonathan Goforth of China or Evan Roberts of Wales, as they are so consumed and burdened with revival.
- Those with a burden would have long realised that personal revival always precedes a general revival. They would have got their own lives sorted out before they could expect God to move others *en masse* (all together).
- Genuine disciples of Jesus Christ will be grieved and burdened over the state of the weak impotent Church (Joel

2:17b), their sin-ridden community, city or country. They will be grieved that God is blasphemed and derided and is not being glorified as He should be (Ezekiel 9:4 and 21:6).
- They desire Jesus' name to be lifted high and flown as a banner across their land. They wish all Christians could enter into a living relationship with the Holy Spirit, to know Him and His convicting and guiding power as He leads them closer to Jesus.
- God frequently steps in at the last minute, at the darkest hour – if God did not step in with His mercy, then He would have to step in with His judgment.
- These disciples will be earnestly trying to live righteous, holy and God-glorifying lives. They will talk, read and *study revivals, awakenings and revivalists and encourage others to seek God for revival blessings. Because what He has done in the past He can do again. *See Psalm 111:2.
- Some will go through a period of agony in prayer / intercession '…As soon as Zion travailed she gave birth to her children' (Isaiah 66:8b), until they get an assurance that God will move in power and send the Holy Spirit. 'Those who sow in tears shall reap in joy' (Psalm 126:5). It is often a case of: 'Let us not grow weary while doing good, for in due season *we shall reap* if we do not lose heart' (Galatians 6:9). However, David Brainerd who saw revival amongst the North American Indians (1745-1746) had practically given up hope as he had his dreams dashed on too many occasions and then within days, revival came.
- This process of assurance is always after a period of intense intercession (Holy Spirit led prayer) which includes identification, agonising, which can incorporate: weeping, travail, pleading and groaning in the Spirit (Romans 8:26-28). This results in the assurance (spiritual authority), so that they know without a shadow of doubt that the victory has been won in the heavenlies and will soon be manifested physically through people's lives in their church or town. 'Forever, O Lord Your Word is settled in heaven' (Psalm 119:89), 'Our God shall come…' (Psalm 50:3).
- Missionaries and Church leaders on occasions have also had an assurance by the Spirit of God that revival will come. But, the Kuruman Revival (1829) in Namaqualand (in present day South Africa) amongst the Batlaping tribe of the Bechwanas, caught Robert Moffat and his fellow missionaries by surprise. It was a case of, 'The wind blows

where it wishes and you hear the sound of it, but cannot tell where it comes from and where it goes' (John 3:8). For the missionaries it was, 'This is the Lord's doing. It is marvellous in our eyes!' (Psalm 118:23).

- Some people know precisely when revival will come and have dates from the Lord, but this does appear to be the exception and not the norm. For Rees Howells in Rusitu, Gazaland (present day Zimbabwe), he only knew that revival was coming a day before on 9 October 1915. Pentecost broke out on the tenth and lasted for five years!

Anticipation and Assurance

William C. Burns, referring to the Kilsyth Revival (1839) in Scotland, UK, on 23 July 1839, wrote: 'Some of the people of God who had been longing and wrestling for a time of refreshing from the Lord's presence, and who had during much of the previous night, been travailing in birth for souls, came to the meeting, not only with the hope, but with well-nigh anticipation of God's glorious appearing.'

Charles Finney, from the nineteenth century wrote: 'There was a woman in New Jersey, who was very positive there was going to be another revival.' She spoke to the minister and elders to hold conference meetings but they ignored her request. So convinced was she that God was going to move that she employed a carpenter to make extra seats (benches) so that she could hold meetings in her home. 'She had scarcely opened her doors for meetings, before the Spirit of God came down with great power. And these sleepy church members found themselves surrounded all at once with convicted sinners...'

A few months prior to the Lewis Revival (1949-1952), two sisters in their eighties who had been persistently praying for revival into the early hours for months, knew that their prayers had been answered. One of them received a vision of a packed church in their community of Barvas. The parish minister was informed and for at least three months, prayer meetings for revival were held twice a week in a thatched cottage with church deacons and elders in attendance, whilst the sisters prayed at home. Rev. Duncan Campbell arrived in late 1949, after his first meeting, as the people were dispersing the deacon told him not to be discouraged, "God is hovering over; He is going to break through...He is coming. I hear already the rumbling of heaven's chariots wheels." About thirty people went into a cottage to pray and at 3am, God came down and swept in which set the community ablaze for three years!

Rev. David Davies and his wife Anne were used in the Congo Revival of the 1950s. In July 1953 they brought a native evangelist, Tomu from Lubutu, North East Belgian Congo (the place where revival first broke out in February 1953), to their large mission station at Wamba. On Thursday the sixteenth; the evangelist spoke from Exodus 19:11, 'Let them be ready for the *third day.* For on the *third day* the Lord will come...' and on Sunday the nineteenth, God came and revival continued for four years!

Steve Hill, a visiting evangelist to Brownsville AOG Church, Pensacola, America, told the congregation on Father's Day, 1995 that God was going to do something special and within two hours He did – revival lasted for five years! The church saw 3.5 million visitors from across the globe and more than 100,000 converts!

Our Responsibilities

God is not obligated to send revival if we have negated our responsibilities to 'be holy' (1 Peter 1:16), to 'walk uprightly' (Psalm 15:2) and we *must* have 'clean hands and a pure heart' (Psalm 24:3-6), because without holiness 'no one will see the Lord' (Hebrews 12:14). For our individual and corporate responsibility towards mankind see: Psalm 82:3-4, Isaiah chapter 58, Hosea 10:12, Amos 5:21-24, Matthew 5:1-12, 25:35-40 and Luke 9:13.

J. Edwin Orr wrote: 'If you want to serve God, "Present your body a living sacrifice, holy, acceptable to God" – it is your reasonable service (Romans 12:1). Jesus Himself said, "Why call Me, 'Lord, Lord,' and do not the things I say?" (Luke 6:46). He does not want the lip service of sentimental humbug; He wants the heart service of reasonable honesty. What is more, He needs it. "My son, give me thy heart..." (Proverbs 23:26). If the law required us to love the Lord with all our heart, we should not withhold it under grace. Full surrender is our reasonable service and "the love of Christ constraineth us" (2 Corinthians 5:14).'[1]

As long as we do not fail to fulfill our part, living up to God's high and holy standard, then God will not fail to fulfill His. This is not trying to twist the arm of God, being manipulative or being presumptuously arrogant. Our covenant-keeping God has declared, "If My people who are called by My name will humble themselves, and pray and seek My face, and turn from their wicked ways, then I will hear from heaven, and will forgive their sin and heal their land" (2 Chronicles 7:14). 'God is not a man that He should lie...has He said, and will He not do it? Or has He spoken, and will He not make it good?' (Numbers 23:19). "Behold I will do a new thing...I will even make...rivers in the desert" (Isaiah 43:19).

Arthur Wallis, in regards to Nehemiah's intercession for Jerusalem wrote: 'Nehemiah was able to prevail in prayer because he held God to be faithful and pleaded His promises. He reminded Him of what He had covenanted to do [Nehemiah 1:4-11] and pressed Him to fulfill it. This is a spiritual lever that never fails to move the Hand that moves the world.'

Praying for revival is taking God's promises as revealed in the written Word, the Holy Bible and presenting His own words to Him and seeking the fulfilment of those Scriptures, because He has promised – but it is foolhardy to pray these Scriptures whilst neglecting those which need to be lived out daily, e.g. "Be holy because I am holy." If we have not done our part, then we cannot expect God to do His. However, if we have done our part, then we can expect God to do His; though the timing and the method may be different than what we expect, as God says, "My thoughts are not your thoughts, nor are your ways My ways..." (Isaiah 55:8), but those of us who wait upon God 'will not be ashamed' or disappointed (Isaiah 49:23). Glory!

Just like the parable of the widow and the judge, 'men always ought to pray and not lose heart...' and 'cry out day and night' to Him (Luke 18:1, 7). And let us not forget the parable of the persistent friend who asked, sought, knocked and received, because God likes to give good gifts to His children (Luke 11:5-13). Therefore, 'be patient, brethren, until the coming of the Lord. See how the farmer waits for the precious fruit of the earth, waiting patiently for it until he receives the early and the latter rain' (James 5:7).

Miss Eva Stuart Watt, Home Secretary of the Sudan United Mission wrote: 'When He [God] finds Holy Ghost men willing to use Holy Ghost methods, things happen beyond the range of human effort or understanding. The Spirit of Truth has come to guide us into all truth and, if we are willing, [He] will teach us the truth about this mighty challenge.'[2]

In the spring of 1938, a teenage Arthur Wallis was at Moriah Chapel, Loughor; the birthplace of the Welsh Revival (1904-1905). He thought to himself: 'If God can achieve such mighty things in times of revival, and if the spiritual labourers of fifty years can be surpassed in so many days when the Spirit is poured out, why...is the Church today so satisfied with the results of normal evangelism? Why are we not more concerned that there should be another great revival? Why do we not pray for it day and night?'[3]

Chapter 9

The Characteristics of Revival

'Now when the Day of Pentecost had fully come.... Suddenly there came a sound from heaven, as of a rushing mighty wind, and it filled the whole house where they were sitting. Then there appeared to them divided tongues, as of fire, and one sat upon each of them. And they were all filled with the Holy Spirit and began to speak with other tongues as the Spirit gave them utterance.... "Cretans and Arabs – we hear them speaking in our own tongues the wonderful works of God." So they were all amazed and perplexed, saying to one another, "Whatever could this mean?" Others mocking said, "They are full of new wine" ' (Acts 2:1-4, 11-13).

Common Characteristics of Revivals
Some Christians when referring to manifestations may think of the demonic and the activity of the devil, the work of the antichrist. In this book, unless stated otherwise (or from the context in which it is written), the word manifestation(s) refer to physical phenomena, which come from the Spirit of God. Physical phenomena, bodily manifestations are not exclusive to times of revival, though they are greatly heightened during one. Some of the common characteristics of revivals are:
- When revival comes there will be a heightened awareness of God's presence as the Spirit descends on a church, chapel, hall, school, Bible College / Seminary, university, village, town, island, community or nation.
- Christians will be renewed, revitalised and revived, once they have examined themselves through the eyes of a holy God and put away their sin. The Church (individual members) will be cleansed, refined and purified under the spotlight of the Holy Spirit.
- Many non-Christians will be drawn to a church, chapel or mission hall where a meeting (heaven-sent revival) is in progress, as if by an unseen hand. Some of whom will have not been inside a church building for decades or if ever. Some will try to leave and will be unable too, as if a glass barrier or restraining hand is stopping them.

- People will be converted inside and outside of the church building (chapel, mission hall etc.) or wherever people meet, work or sleep. Some people will not even have had contact with a Christian, but the Holy Spirit will get a hold of them; at work, in the fields or on the road etc.
- There is a deeper reality of the cross of Calvary, the blood of Jesus, and what He has done for mankind, but especially for the individual (see Isaiah 53).
- God is no respecter of persons. People of all ages, from different social and political backgrounds of varying educational and economic levels get saved. Young children to the very elderly. A child of four or six can come under conviction of sin, just like an adult of eighty-four; though God will reveal sin (and Himself) in a way that each can understand.
- Converted teenagers become radical for Christ. They may not dress like us, look or talk like us, but they will press in for the deeper things of God and will not be ashamed of Jesus! The majority of these converts will stay true to God and be trophies of grace, lasting fruit, the next generation of leaders, evangelists and missionaries etc. Many will have a zeal which has not been tempered by maturity, but that is OK. We learn from our mistakes and we have all been young once.
- Many child converts of revival will have an unusual zeal for God, a capacity to pray and an anointing on their lives that can be quite mind boggling. With child-like faith and obedience to the Holy Spirit they can move in the gifts of the Holy Spirit without having any theology behind it. Child preachers (boys and girls) can come to the fore, though generally not many, and this also includes teenage girl preachers; Katie Booth of the Salvation Army and those from the Welsh Revival (1904-1905) whom God raised up.
- It is not uncommon to see 10%, 50% or virtually the entire village or town becoming Christians during a time of localised revival. This was seen during the Northampton Revival (1734-1735) under Jonathan Edwards where amongst 220 families, nearly 700 persons (virtually every adult) became converted. The greatest statistic for a country, of which I am aware, was 25% (of five million population) during the British Great Awakening (1739-1791). During times of repeated revivals this percentage can rise, as in Nagaland in north east India, where in 2006

it was reported that 99% of the population (under two million) were Christian (though this does include Catholics, and I am sure many nominal Christians), after revival broke out in 1949, 1952, 1956, 1966, 1967, 1972 and 1976.
- In revival, even nature itself seems more full of God!
- There will be a greater degree of Bible reading and an increase in the sales of Bibles and Christian literature and an increase in prayer, privately and corporately.
- Sabbath observances (one day of rest, which may or may not be on Sunday) will be more strictly observed; not out of compulsion or coercion, but out of a desire to please the Master and to get to know Him and His ways more.
- Those who are illiterate, even those who are elderly, will begin to learn to read so that they can read the Word of God for themselves, therefore the literacy rate in revival areas will be raised. This was perhaps best witnessed during the Second British Great Awakening (1859-1860), the Indonesian Revival (1964-1974), and in many developing countries.
- Many secular pursuits, hobbies, interests or even things that people enjoy, though not sinful in themselves are often disregarded for the greater price of the heavenly things above. Meeting with God is better than that which is good.
- In national revivals there will be a great upsurge of lay workers who will assist in the work. These workers as well as ministers will preach a lot more frequently. William Grimshaw of Haworth, England, was the first beneficed clergyman in northern England to exercise an unrestrained evangelical ministry. It began in 1742 and he would preach up to thirty times a week! For himself, he considered preaching twenty times over seven days a "lazy week."
- The press and frequently the secular papers alongside news websites, social media and bloggers will write about the move of God. Often they are open and honest, but some news reporters will always denounce it as fanaticism, hypnotism, emotional experience or some psychological trick, to pull in the masses. Good as well as bad reports will bring the unconverted closer to what is happening, as curiosity always gets the better of people, and as the old saying goes, 'There is no such thing as bad publicity!'
- There will also be those who have genuine concerns and are cautious, perhaps suspicious about what they see around them and are not immediately able to embrace the

move of God. Some never will. Whilst others will openly denounce it vehemently (which is very sad but very true).
- Sinners (and saints) will cause opposition and be critical of any move of God, especially in areas where Hindus, Muslims, Communists or Roman Catholics live. Often it is the demonic that stirs up the hatred and bitterness within individuals and groups. We could say that they are victims, as many have been taken captive by the devil to do his will.
- Where God moves, the enemy always tries to infiltrate and imitate to cause the good that is happening to be spoken of as evil. We must learn to discern between God's dynamic and the demonic.

The Holy Spirit in Revival
- The Holy Spirit, as the third Person of the Trinity will be honoured. He will not be seen as a "thing," "influence," or an "it," but as a Person, who brings conviction of sin, shows true righteousness, guides into all truth, gives direction and instruction and glorifies Jesus. The Holy Spirit can be 'resisted,' 'grieved' or 'quenched,' all of which is forbidden in Scripture, and we are commanded to be 'filled with the Spirit,' and He is 'given to those who obey Him.'
- Christians will be filled with the Holy Spirit (if not already) which is a separate and distinct experience from conversion. It can happen immediately or subsequent to conversion as the Holy Spirit cleanses them from all sin (via the application of the blood of Jesus Christ) and *can* deliver them instantly from past bondages and addictions.
- In many revivals there is often talk of the fullness of the Spirit (sometimes referred to as entire consecration, which can lead to entire sanctification). Whatever your preferred terminology, it is not that *you* have the Holy Spirit, but that the Holy Spirit has *you!* There is a world of difference which outworks itself practically into hourly and daily godliness.
- The Holy Spirit on occasions, can come in waves of revival power (touching some groups immediately whilst leaving other groups for other occasions), especially on mission stations, which in times past were considerably large (up to 100 acres), with hundreds of people and are often a community within a community. At the Ibambi Mission Station during the Congo Revival (1953-1957) the Holy Spirit came in three distinct waves. He first came upon the

station people, then the schools and then a few weeks later, He came upon the Central Bible School.
- The Holy Spirit will speak to individuals or bring them under conviction for certain acts or ways, which generally they would not respond to, if the issue was mentioned from the pulpit. The Holy Spirit by His loving conviction will make it known that God does not approve of certain things and that they must give them up. The stumbling block in their lives might not be 'open sin,' but 'secret sin,' or the motives of the heart and the reason why the believers do certain things. Perhaps it's pride to impress others, or overeating or overspending etc. as a way of self-comfort.
- Often in revival the Holy Spirit will set a person free instantly from alcoholism, smoking and other addictions, whom may have been bound by demonic forces – whilst at other times He will not *instantly* deliver them.
- Converts and revived Christians can receive fullness of joy in the Holy Spirit. Not just a few hours of joy whilst only at church, but a daily, weekly attitude of the fullness of joy, at work or at rest in His presence.
- The gifts of the Holy Spirit are always poured out in revival (to a lesser or greater degree), though from revival Church history it does appear that they have been more prominent since the Azusa Street Revival (1906-1909), leading to the rise of Pentecostalism and very prevalent after the Charismatic Renewal of the 1960s and 1970s.
- In times of revival there are more documented cases of people speaking in an 'unknown tongue' which *is known* to someone within the congregation. It could be as common as a European language of which the person speaking in tongues is completely unaware of, or a little known tribal dialect. This was frequently the case in the Dutch Presbyterian Church in Soe, on the island of Timor during the Indonesian Revival (1964-1974) and recorded at the Azusa Mission in Los Angeles, California, America.
- There can be spontaneity; inside and outside of meetings, anywhere and everywhere within the vicinity of the Holy Spirit. Spontaneity in prayer, worship, praise, testimony and sometimes preaching.
- On rare occasions, and for a period of the revival (from one day to two weeks), the Holy Spirit may not call anyone to preach, there could be no preaching at all, although this is the exception and not the norm. There may be lots of

praise and worship like what was seen at many of the meetings during the Welsh Revival (1904-1905) and the Azusa Street Revival (1906-1909). For the first two weeks during the Hwanghsien Revival (1932) in north China, there was nothing but confession of sin! A missionary wrote: 'Meetings lasted five or six hours at a time with nothing but confession of sin, one after another bringing out the hidden as well as the known sins of his life. So deep was the work that hours for eating and sleeping passed by unnoticed. And so 'judgment began at the house of God.' When sin was faithfully dealt with, and forgiveness received, many were baptised with the Holy Spirit. It is like the story in the book of Acts.'

William Booth was an evangelist who saw revival in Cornwall over an 18-month period during 1861-1862. Four years later he founded the East London Christian Mission, which in 1878 was renamed the Salvation Army. General Booth said, "Only God can take out of your heart the bad temper, pride, malice, revenge, love of the world, and all other evil things that have taken possession of it; and fill it with holy love and peace. To God you must look, to God you must go. This is the work of the Holy Spirit: He is the Purifying Fire; He is the Cleansing Flame."

Evangelist and revivalist, Rev. Lionel B. Fletcher stated that after his conversion, the greatest experience he ever had was when he realised that 'the mighty gift of the Holy Ghost was not only for men of the New Testament days, but was available for men today...the Christians birthright is the power of the Holy Ghost.' Whilst attending a conference in Sydney, Australia, (in which he fully gave himself to God at the after-meeting), Archdeacon Tress said, "God can only fill us to the extent that we yield ourselves to Him. If you yield yourself without reserve to God, you have the right to know that God gives Himself without reserve to you, and by faith you may claim the filling of the Holy Ghost."

Idols and Temples in Revival
- Where former heathen or animists worshiped idols of stone or wood, upon conversion they would smash their stone idols (or throw them into a deep lake) and burn their wooden ones. During the Shantung Revival (1930-1932) in north China, those who repented of their sins and put their faith in Jesus Christ took down their household gods, which had been worshipped for generations. See 2 Kings 23.

- Upon conversion, all fetishes (a charm embodied with demonic power), charms, amulets, spell books and various occultist paraphernalia will be destroyed which is an act of renouncing one's old ways and is often done publicly, see Acts 19:18-20 and 2 Kings 23:4, 16. During the Eggon Revival (1930s) in Northern Nigeria, former spirit worshipers, including spirit priests came and burned their fetishes and followed Christ. On 13 February 1960, during the Dani and Uhundi Revival (1957-1962) in New Guinea, 5,000 Dani and Uhundi, recent converts burnt their charms and 3,000 followed suit the next day!
- In the West, the idols of money, time-consuming hobbies or anything that takes priority over Christ have been disregarded as the flesh is crucified under the direction of the Holy Spirit.
- During the Florentine Revival (c.1493-1497) in Italy, at the bidding of Savonarola, the Florentine citizens threw onto the shelves of a giant wooden pyramid their books of magic, carnival masks and costumes, playing cards, dice boxes, the indecent books and pictures and many other things. This great pile was set on fire whilst the people sang hymns and was known as a 'bonfire of vanities.'
- If the majority of former heathen or animists villagers get converted, or most notably the chief of the village, they would often tear down the village temple or chop down the sacred groves. During the first five years of the Indonesian Revival (1964-1974), at least thirty temples were torn down. Destroying temples was also evident in African and Indian revivals, and during the Nagaland Awakenings of the 1950s, 60s and 70s.

Jonathan Edwards noted in 1741 that *The Distinguishing Marks of a Work of the Spirit* of God during revival are:
- It raises the esteem of Jesus.
- It operates against Satan's kingdom.
- There is a greater regard for Scripture.
- The Spirit of Truth guides into all truth and brings believers into the light whilst exposing the darkness.
- Believers have a spirit of love towards God and man.
- The attributes of 'love and humility' are the two most contrary to the devil [and Christians will exhibit these].

Chapter 10

Reoccurring Experiences in Revival

'That which has been is what will be, that which is done is what will be done, and there is nothing new under the sun' (Eccles. 1:9).

Reoccurring Experiences in Revival
- Prayer meetings begin to multiply and the numbers attending rise rapidly. The Kilsyth Revival (1839) had 39 weekly prayer meetings and the congregation of Ballymena during the 1859 revival in Ireland, held on average 16 prayer meetings each night! Also 12,000 of Newtownards inhabitants (33%) attended the union prayer meeting! In September, 20,000 gathered for an open-air prayer meeting in Armagh. In July, 10,000 gathered for prayer at the Maze Racecourse whilst in October, the attendance at the Maze Racecourse decreased from 10,000 to 500!
- Prayer meetings are instigated by children and teenagers, and united prayer meetings are held at different churches of different denominations. In days past and in various cultures it was common to have same sex prayer meetings so that there would be no appearance of evil and no cause of impropriety. (It also helps in confession of certain sins).
- The Holy Spirit through the ages has descended on schools, bringing children, teenagers and teachers alike into a saving knowledge of Jesus. Often it is like a ripple effect, moving from one classroom or floor to another. On occasions, this effect had travelled outside of the school gates and into the community.
- Youth are much more ready to run to extremes. Some religious affections (physical phenomena) are not gracious affections so noted Jonathan Edwards. There will always be imprudences, irregularities and a mixed multitude in revival meetings; you cannot denounce the whole because of a minority of discrepancies nor should you embrace everything you see or hear, or anyone and everyone.
- There are always some believers whose faces shine or radiate with the glory of the Lord, like Moses when he descended Mt. Sinai (Exodus 34:29-30). This could be a

revivalist, coming out of a prayer closet (Psalm 34:5a), or a new convert, rejoicing in his or her newfound salvation. This glowing or radiance can last for hours or a few days.
- The consumption of alcohol always drops. Pubs / drinking establishments in small communities or even larger towns may see a steep decline in business or go out of business completely. The owners of these establishments (and often the brewery owners) will be furious. Social drinking amongst Christians will decline as they will no longer want to prop up the devil's houses and dens of sin! Sometimes Christians do become drunk in the Holy Spirit and are unable to stand or become incoherent in their speech. This is not something to be sought, or to be ashamed of. God's work, done God's way will not lack fruit and He knows what He is doing. This was very evident in the Congo Revival (1953-1957) when people were 'intoxicated with joy' and 'drunk in the Holy Spirit' as several missionaries noted. I also witnessed it at the Brownsville Revival (1995-2000) when I visited in the summer of 1997.
- Regular Churchgoers (with the nickname Christian) who get converted will see the Scriptures in a new light. Often they see the Bible as a new Book, as doctrines and Scriptural truths come alive, jump off the pages and resonate within their spirit.
- Those who have been under deep agonising conviction of sin, having been 'stricken' by God (many of whom can appear to be in a coma or even dead, that is lifeless) and who had been evil or led dreadfully bad lives can get delivered from their demons, as well as being converted to Christ. It appears that the longer a 'stricken person' stays on the ground, immobile, the deeper the work of grace and the greater the deliverance that they receive.
- Revival Church history reveals that most 'stricken people' should be left to God, to fully allow the Holy Spirit to do His deep work in their lives. Trying to bring comfort, speaking 'peace, peace' when there is no peace can be disastrous, as they need to know their doomed state before they can receive His grace and abundant pardon. Their torment can go on for days or weeks, but when they are truly converted, it is a work of grace that is very deep and abiding.
- Prostrations can last for days; Church history records that in many of the revivals from previous centuries, people were left out in the open overnight or for several nights until

they came through to a saving knowledge of Christ Jesus. This may not be appropriate in the city centres in the twenty-first century, but people are still carried from meetings and driven to their homes or hotels etc.
- The conversion of others can promote 'hope,' but especially amongst friends or work colleagues who knew the converted person's former character and lifestyle. In their minds they may say, "If they can be saved, changed, or forgiven for their sins, then so can I."
- On a few occasions, as the preacher was speaking on the Judgment Day, lightning flashed across the sky, as in George Whitefield's day, and as witnessed at Rasharkin Presbyterian Church on 7 June 1859, when lightning filled the church and 500 people prostrated themselves on the floor and 100 came under deep conviction of sin!
- God's grace always reaches down to the worst of sinners. Even those who openly mock God (mock the revival and defy His laws) have been stricken by the Holy Spirit. Some get stricken with the grace of God (Jude 18-23), whilst others become stricken with His judgment (Psalm 73:18, Isaiah 66:15-16, Nahum 1:6, 9-10 and Acts 12:1-12). The latter leads to death and an eternity in hell. Sometimes, God mockers and scoffers are struck dead instantly, at other times within hours or weeks, often suffering in a most miserable way and under demonic torment. Some, like Judas who betrayed Jesus will kill themselves.
- There are always those who were mockers of the things of God (especially those who spoke badly of the revival and publicly maligned the leaders); upon conversion or under the light of the Holy Spirit will apologise and / or retract previous statements.
- In all revivals there will be elements of flesh involved, but this swings on a pendulum from the over-the-top emotionalism to the traditional stale and stagnant, no emotion. We can be just as much in the flesh jumping up and down with our mind not on the Lord in worship, as singing from a hymn or chorus book with disdain and hardness in our heart. The flesh can be one who tries to 'work up' the blessing, one who imitates certain manifestations or those under the influence of the evil one or who have been completely taken captive by the enemy to do his will. On the other side, it could be one who resists, quenches or grieves the Holy Spirit, often by not

allowing Him to work in their lives. Their opposition to change could be their comfort zones have been infringed upon, a dislike of: the freedom of worship, protracted meetings, physical phenomena or because the Holy Spirit is moving in a way that they are not happy with, as it goes against their preconceived theology of what happens, should happen and should not happen in revival. 'Those who are in the flesh cannot please God' (Romans 8:8).

- Sometimes the leaders of certain denominations will not embrace a revival but those within their churches will. Roman Catholics have frequently disdained revivals often believing them to be "Protestant and not Catholic." Some openly mock the Protestant 'excitement' yet still some get converted. During the Argentine Revival (1982-1997), God gave Omar Cabrera a real heart for nominal Catholics. His purpose was not for them to abandon the Catholic Church, but rather they should enter into the Kingdom of God through their faith in Jesus Christ.
- Denominations that hold communion weekends (generally they are traditionally held from Thursday to Monday in Scotland), have on more than a handful of occasions witnessed revival or if they were already seeing revival it was intensified. I put this down to the fact that prior to partaking of communion; we examine ourselves, (get right with God, confess our sins and ask forgiveness) so as not to partake in an unworthy manner as 1 Corinthians eleven states. The Shotts Revival (1630) and the Cambuslang Revival (1742), both in Scotland are good examples of this.
- Many of those who have been in revival or converted in times of revival will be led or called into Christian ministry and some will become missionaries in a foreign field. I would go so far and state that if nobody was called into full-time Christian ministry during a period of revival then I would have to question whether or not a revival really took place. Heaven-sent revival has positive knock-on effects.
- Ladies and young women have been used in revivals, as revivalists, evangelists, singers, helpers, or intercessors who accompany a revivalist as part of a team. Only around two percent of revivalists are female, though many more partake in the work of revival alongside their husbands such as Catherine Booth of the Salvation Army.
- In many revivals, there have been instances of heavenly music, as if the angels themselves are singing in the

heavens above and can be heard on earth. These events have happened inside and outside of the church, even in the open fields. This has happened as recently as the Shillong Revival (2006-2007) in Shillong, India.
- Fishermen or sailors who have been aboard their trawlers, boats or ships upon coming near port where there is a revival, have been struck by the Spirit of God, whilst others have been converted on the open seas, having had no contact with the revival! This happened amongst the fishermen during the East Anglia Revival (1921-1922) in England, which led into the Fishermen's Revival (1922) when it reached Scotland, and amongst the U.S. Navy at New York, during the American Great Awakening (1857-1859).

Revival and Time
- In the presence of the Lord time does not exist, five hours in the presence of the Lord can seem like ten minutes. During the Indonesian Revival (1964-1974) a five hour sermon was common, but could be as long as fifteen hours! This is why revival meetings are so protracted and frequently go through the night, until sunrise. If a revival persists for some time, the leader will usually try to end a meeting in the early hours, or earlier so as to allow those present to get some rest, ready for the next day's work. Worship as well as preaching (if there is any) can go on for hours and hours, without people getting restless.
- During the first two or three days of a major revival when the Holy Spirit descends in awesome power, some people will not be able to sleep for two or three days or for a week, or will be satisfied with a minimal amount of sleep, say 2-4 hours a night. Some are driven by what I term 'spiritual adrenaline' or 'spiritual hyperactivity.' This was noted during the Congo Revival (1953-1957) at several mission stations. When the Holy Spirit descended at the Bible College of Wales, South Wales, UK, at Easter 1937, under the leadership of Rees Howells, the early hours of the morning seemed as midday to staff and students alike!
- There are times when a revival begins and continues day and night without cessation in one continuous meeting, with people coming and going. This was evident in Mount Hawke Revival (1852) in Cornwall, England, under Rev. William Haslam when a meeting lasted for eight days and

during the Asbury Revival (1970) in Wilmore, Kentucky, America, which continued for 185 hours, a little over seven and a half days. I know of no continuing meeting lasting longer than eight days, but after the Moravian Revival (1727) in Herrnhut, Moravia, a twenty-four hour prayer meeting begun which continued unbroken for one hundred years! The Azusa Street Revival (1906-1909) in Los Angeles, America, had three meetings a day for three years. During that time the doors to the church / mission hall were never locked, and people were continually coming and going, often to pray and worship.

Revival and Work

- In past revivals down the centuries there have been many cases where businesses (shops and factories) have had to close for a period of time. The workers being dismissed for a few days because of God's Spirit falling on the workforce. Firstly, the saving of the workers' souls is more important than profit, see Luke 9:25. Secondly, it can be unsafe to work amongst heavy machinery, some under such deep conviction of sin can barely think straight, let alone stand up! Thirdly, the workers' minds are occupied with something of a far greater importance (eternal issues) than manual work. Self employed persons have also had to take time out.
- Whilst work productivity increases amongst the saved it decreases amongst those under conviction of sin. Though on occasions, within rural districts, production of all sorts will just cease, even harvests of grain have been left uncut as seen at Lurgan, county Armagh, Ireland, during the 1859 revival.
- Workers (who are not under conviction of sin), who are soundly saved will have a greater capacity for productivity. A happy labourer is a productive worker and a converted worker will want to put in an honest days work. This was very evident during the Congo Revival (1953-1957) when natives in several mission stations who had procrastinated in construction work for months, completed buildings in a matter of days! During the Kilsyth Revival (1742) in Scotland, Rev. James Robe stated that the hay harvest was brought in 'a third part of time sooner over the ordinary.'

Chapter 11

The Church and Revival

'To everything there is a season, a time for every purpose under heaven' (Ecclesiastes 3:1).

God can sometimes appear disruptive and He will disturb us out of our religious rituals and comfort zones – but the "disruption" of God in times of revival produces abiding fruit and what is considered 'decently and in order' today, is a far cry from the first century Church! Peter preached at Cornelius' house and in the midst of the sermon the Holy Spirit fell upon them and they spoke in tongues, thus disturbing the meeting (Acts 10:23-48). It was similar to what happened on the Day of Pentecost (Acts 2), when the people began to cry out and three thousand were saved!

Common Characteristics within the Church
- Praise and worship to exalt and honour God will become more real, regardless of our preferred style of worship. In every national revival, (Reformation or renewal) new songs or hymns have been written, composed and sung to the praise and glory of God.
- Some revivalists aim their sermons at stale, dying and dead Christians, before they begin to preach the gospel to sinners (though in most audiences both are present). There is no point in trying to win the lost if they will only be suffocated by dead religion.
- Denominational and sectarian barriers are often broken down as God's people thirst after righteousness and aim at unity. For example, Pentecostals and Baptists, Methodists and Presbyterians, and Congregationalists and Anglicans come together. Those with opposing views, Calvinistic and Arminian theology will also rejoice and work together in the harvest to promote the work of God. Sometimes the clergy of certain denominations will not embrace the move of God, but those within their churches will. Brethren will not be focusing on the minor issues of doctrine. They will realise that we are united by our faith in Jesus Christ and not our doctrinal preference. They will focus on the more

important task of glorifying Jesus, reaping the harvest and aiding discipleship.
- A greater compassion for the lost, hurting and needy will be manifest in practical social concern and action. It will be love in action and / or social reform.
- Members of the body of Christ will feel that it is their duty, even their obligation to question (in humility) how another's walk with the Lord is. 'Let the righteous strike me, it shall be a kindness and let him reprove me, it shall be as excellent oil; let not my head refuse it' (Psalm 141:5), c.f. Proverbs 27:6a, 17. This *should* be done gently in love, with a concerned humble attitude, with the other person's best interest at heart. Giving and receiving a challenge is part of assisting in building up the body of Christ; being concerned for each other's spiritual well-being.
- Many revivals have been so life changing in a community, town or city that many of the body of Christ have genuinely believed that they were living in the millennial reign of Christ! Also, some of the leaders or Christians of these large revivals have believed that the revival they were experiencing would be the last revival before the return of Christ, such as the Brownsville Revival (1995-2000), Shillong Revival (2006-2007) and numerous other large revivals from previous centuries.

Church Services
- Poor weather will not affect people attending meetings when a revival is in progress. This feature was more noticeable in times past when there was little to no public transport or when people had to walk over hills and through valleys in driving rain or sleet, or through thick snow, or over some distance on foot. It was an effort to get there.
- The attendance at prayer meetings greatly increases, resulting in a much higher percentage of committed members per congregation.
- If churches or chapels are kept unlocked, people will gather to meet without a service even being announced. If a meeting is announced people will be there hours before its commencement. If the doors are locked, they will be waiting outside and a meeting may begin in the courtyard.
- Church services will increase. For the first fifteen months of the Rusitu Revival (1915-1920) under Rees Howells in Africa, they had two services every day! The Brownsville

Revival (1995-2000) had five services per week (four evening services {Wednesday-Saturday} and one Sunday morning service, with a Tuesday evening prayer meeting and afternoon teaching session for church leaders and Christian workers.
- During revival, a leader who is taking a meeting will find it difficult to dismiss the people. Often he (or she) will try several times to bid the people to depart. In the first few days of a revival it is common for an evening meeting to go through until sunrise!
- Most of the older style church buildings during times of revival in the last century were unable to accommodate the masses that attended the services. William Romaine (1714-1795) was dismissed from his parish at St. George, Hanover Square, England, because the parishioners were annoyed at continually finding their pews (which families rented per annum) occupied with strangers! Prior to Health and Safety regulations it was common for churches to be so filled, that people would be standing in the aisles, sitting on the window ledges and even on the pulpit steps! Many church buildings become so thronged with those unable to get in (100s or 1000s of people) that meetings were often held in the churchyard amongst the graves.

Preachers in Graveyards and at Funerals
- During revivals there may appear irreverent acts, such as the preaching from a tombstone, as did John Wesley from his father's grave in Epworth, England, when he was not permitted to preach inside the church. If preaching is taking place within the grounds of a cemetery or churchyard then the people assembled will be standing on the graves! Some who are spiritually dead in trespasses and sins will be prostrated on the graves of the physically dead, crying out for mercy while others are praising the Lord. As an example, this was seen in Dunrod during the 1859 revival in Ireland and at Limavady, where 2,000 people assembled in the graveyard of Drumachose, Presbyterian Church.
- Clear cut, uncompromising gospel messages will be preached at funerals and if the person concerned had led an evil life, the preacher will tell the congregation so, without trying to appease the family – the truth sometimes hurts, but godly sorrow leads to repentance. Steve Hill, from the Brownsville Revival (1995-2000) stated, that when

a family asked him to take the funeral of their drug-taking, wild reprobate son, he informed them that he could take the service but would not lie and tell those present that, "Johnny was a good boy." Also, Steve will not take a funeral service unless he is permitted to give an altar call.

Notes for Leaders and Church Workers
- Unless the leader is wise and delegates responsibility to others he will soon become worn out, or encounter burnout and have a breakdown. Some have died prematurely for neglect of the human body (deprivation of food and sleep); this has been recorded by many ministers during the 1859 revival in Ireland. Evan Roberts had several breakdowns during the Welsh Revival (1904-1905) and after 18 months.
- The leaders within a localised revival, especially ministers, elders, deacons and other committed members of the congregation will find that their lives will change dramatically, as there will be extra responsibilities and duties which will need to be dealt with, especially enquirers (those burdened by sin) and interviews with the press and media etc. Social media will have a role to play.
- Leaders will have to lovingly rebuke Christians (Proverbs 27:5) who act in the flesh (trying to imitate the things of God) and on occasions those who oppose the things of God (Proverbs 28:23). But we can also be in the flesh by resisting what the Holy Spirit is doing; rebellion is as the sin of witchcraft (1 Samuel 15:23). Do not quench, resist or grieve the Holy Spirit; openly, or in your heart.
- Revival is a revolt from low spirituality. New converts or revived Christians are prone to question the reality of the conversion or commitment of others, but especially those in positions of authority when they see no life or joy. This can cause offence, but one has to wonder why they are asking such a question in the first place! It is a flippant remark to say that they are full of pride when the leader or elder may be too proud to accept a rebuke!
- Leaders can hinder revivals in many ways, but especially by their opposition (including silent, non-commitment, non-embracing opposition) and rejection of the Holy Spirit and His ways. They can also advance and promote revivals by preaching and teaching on revivals / Divine visitations, coupled with their prayers and the congregation's prayers for God to 'rend the heavens' and to 'pour out His Spirit.'

Chapter 12

The Community in Times of Revival

'Surely His salvation is near those who fear Him, that glory may dwell in the land' (Psalm 85:9).

Revival is essential for the life and well-being of the Church. Revival glorifies God, vindicates His name, exalts Jesus, gives the Holy Spirit His rightful place in the Church, raises the high and holy standard of the body of Christ and saves sinners who become part of the Church. Revival is a church saturated with God, spilling out into the community and transforming lives. Revival is a deep work of the Holy Spirit touching the lives of saints (Christians) and sinners (non-Christians), sometimes simultaneously to bring about the quickening and reviving of the saints followed by the saving of sinners with the potential to transform a community, society or even a nation into a habitable praise of God.

Revival and the Community

- During revivals (unless it is only a localised revival in a church) crime will drop; the police and local magistrates will notice the effect, though not all in authority will acknowledge the decrease of crime as a work of God. During the Welsh Revival (1904-1905), many magistrates were given white gloves, a rare British tradition, as there were no cases to try in their area of jurisdiction!
- Wrongs will be righted; restitution and reparation, where applicable will be commenced and followed through.
- It is not uncommon to find whole families turning to God in times of revival, but like a conversion at any time it can also split a family, as some stubbornly refuse to surrender their lives to Jesus Christ. See Luke 12:51-53.
- There will be a greater freedom to worship in public. Before the popular advent of motor cars and private travel, it was common to hear passengers on trains or buses singing hymns, as well as pedestrians, as they were going to and from revival meetings. Sometimes Christians would walk through the streets worshipping the Lord, before and after the meetings, even in the early hours of the morning!

- There is always a social impact (ministry of helps), where those converted want to do more to reach and help their fellow man, e.g. temperance societies, missionary organisations, orphanages; change or implementation of laws etc. Sometimes this impact is immediate, at other times these ministries are birthed during or after a revival from those who were converted, transformed or influenced by it. This was very notable during and after the Evangelical Revival (1739-1791) in Britain, where godly men and women (including MPs, Lords and Ladies) and ministries were raised up to elevate society.
- The sales of Bibles and other Christian literature, merchandise and resources always increase, as Christians are revived and the young converts (as well as older ones), hunger for more biblical truth. See Appendix A and B.
- Many young converts will frequently advance from milk to meat in a short space of time, as if being fast-tracked by God in a greenhouse environment of accelerated growth, see Joel 2:25a. The biblical principles that have taken us years or decades to learn, they may learn in as little as a few weeks or months.

God's Compassion and Mercy
- God's compassion and mercy is frequently demonstrated to those who appear least deserving such as murderers, God mockers, drunkards, wife beaters, habitual adulterers and blasphemers, as they come under dreadful conviction and get saved. None of us deserves God's mercy; it's His grace – all are guilty sinners before a holy and just God.
- God's judgment (and mercy) is sometimes demonstrated towards mockers, scoffers and blasphemers who are in the midst of their rants. They are struck down whilst under the sound of the preacher. Instant death or conversion is not unknown! Some are so tormented that they take their own lives. Some of these deaths are not instantaneous (see Ezekiel 11:1-2, 13), but within hours, days or weeks and some die most horribly and painfully. George Whitefield was in Yorkshire, England, standing next to a pair of gallows (which were used in public executions) and was about to preach on Hebrews 9:27, 'It is appointed for man to die once and after this the judgment,' when a shriek was heard and a person dropped down dead. A few seconds later, another person within the crowd made a shriek and

dropped down dead – apparently the open-air audience were very attentive after that!

Revival, Alcohol, Smoking and Sinful Habits

- During revival, the consumption of alcohol always drops and thus trade declines. Pubs, drinking houses and bars in small communities or even larger towns may go out of business as the consumption of alcohol decreases rapidly. Landlords and brewery owners will be furious. Charles H. Spurgeon in July 1859, speaking in London about the Ulster Revival (1859-1860) said, "In the small town of Ballymena, [in Ireland], on market day, the publicans have always taken one hundred pounds for whisky and now they cannot take a sovereign all day long in the public houses." A few years after the North Uist Revival (1957-1958) in the Outer Hebrides, Scotland, the local press reported 'that the drinking trade in North Uist has been ruined!'
- Inevitably those who were former drunkards or social drinkers upon conversion will find themselves on a better financial footing. This was more evident during the revivals in the eighteenth to early twentieth centuries in Britain. People were a lot poorer, they did not get a fair wage, wives and children were often shamefully neglected and ill treated; and there was no welfare system to fall back on.
- When the owner of a drinking establishment gets converted, they will always stop selling alcohol and close the establishment down. They prefer to lose money and change their profession rather than prop up an institution which leads to unrighteousness and assists in a number of vices. During the Congo Revival (1953-1957), those who grew palm trees from which palm wine was obtained, cut them down at a great financial loss to themselves.
- During the Indonesian Revival (1964-1974), Christians refused to partake of communion as wine was used. On the Island of Timor there were no grapes grown so the church used tea and sugar. After some time they felt they should use what Jesus used. One church at Soe, saw water turning into non-alcoholic communion wine on sixty occasions since October 1967! One other church saw the same miracle happen on ten occasions.
- Often in revival, the Holy Spirit will instantly set a person free from alcoholism, smoking and other addictions if they have been bound by demonic forces, whilst at other times

He does not instantly deliver them – for whatever reason. Billy Bray from Cornwall, England, was a drunkard for seven years, but was set free from his alcohol addiction immediately when he was converted. However, for some time, he still smoked a pipe which was part of Cornish culture in the 1820-50s. He came under conviction and gave up his pipe but compromised – he began chewing tobacco! Under conviction, he struggled with his tobacco craving, but by the grace of God was able to give it up. Conversion and forgiveness of sins do not put away bad habits – that is the choice of the believer who wants to declare that Jesus Christ is Lord of their life. Because either He is Lord of all, or He is not Lord at all. The flesh must be crucified daily. Billy Bray saw at least eight revivals from 1824-1867 and built three chapels by hand!

In the early 1930s, Nikodemo Gatozi, a government herdsman from Ruanda (now spelt Rwanda) went to Gahini where he accepted the Christian faith, but he did not know the meaning of the cross and death to sin. One night while taking family prayers he read Luke 21:34, 'Take heed…lest at any time your hearts be overcharged with surfeiting and drunkenness…and so that day come upon you unawares.' A. C. Stanley Smith wrote: 'God's arrows of conviction pierced his heart;' he could read no further. 'At that moment he saw himself as a sinner and in danger of the judgment. He arose, poured out the beer that was hidden in his house and smashed his pipe to pieces. From that moment he was truly born again and became on fire for God.' Months afterwards, in 1932, he offered to work for God at Kigeme for the Church Missionary Society Ruanda Mission.[1]

In one district in Ruanda, sometime between 1941 and 1946, though probably nearer the latter, 'the move against all intoxicating drink was so effective that the Government in one district assessed its estimate for the beer tax receipts at twenty percent lower than the preceding year.'[2]

Bill Butler, one of the team at the heart of the East Africa Revival (1930s-1950s) wrote about a chief in Ruanda, a nominal Christian who had been baptised and confirmed, yet he was 'notoriously evil' and 'a heavy drinker, with many concubines' who was 'suspected of dabbling in witchcraft.' During a mission, sometime after 1947, the chief got converted. He went home and returned the concubines to their respective homes and made financial provision for each of them; reinstated his 'ring wife' as he described her and also poured away the 'calabashes of drink' and burned his witchcraft charms.³

Rev. William Haslam of the Baldhu Church Revival (1851-1854) in Cornwall, England, wrote: 'Conversion and forgiveness of sins do not put away present bad habits. Such a master habit as this [referring to drinking alcohol] requires a direct dealing with. 'Zacchaeus was a man who had been led astray by the love of money; when he was saved, he put his idol away from him at a stroke. This is the first thing to be done and if it is done in the power of one's first love, it is a more easy task than afterwards. But it must be done with a firm and whole heart; not, "Lord, *shall I give* the half of my goods to feed the poor?" but, "Lord, behold the half of my goods *I do give.*" [Luke 19:1-10] ... "I do here and now give up drink [smoking, greed, lust etc.] and will totally abstain from it henceforth." This is the first step, and the next...is to carry out the determination in the Lord's power and not in our own. The resolution and determination once made must be given over to the Lord to be kept by Him; not by our own effort and energy, but with perfect distrust of self and in dependence upon Him to enable us to keep it. Without this there is no security whatever for anything more than temporary success, too often succeeded by a sorrowful fall. The flesh is too strong for us, and even if it were not so, the devil is; these two together, beside the lax examples of the world, are sure to overpower the weak one. Young Christians need to put away at *once* the sin, whatever it is, that 'so easily besets' them, or they will be entangled by it. There is no real and thorough deliverance except by renouncing sin and self too, giving up and yielding to the Lord.'⁴

Revival, Business and Finances
- There is also a decline in attending theatres, dancing halls, the cinema and other places of amusement. During Charles Finney's campaign in Rochester, New York, America, in 1830, the only theatre in town was converted into a livery stable. 100,000 people were reported to have joined a local church and there were 150,000 professions of faith! These establishments of entertainment may not be sinful in themselves, but believers often have better and more important things to do with their time (like spending time in God's presence at home or by attending other meetings) and often see the amusement of entertainment as wasted time or money that could be put to better use. Spiritual growth is of prime importance.

- In smaller villages and even towns, revival Church history records that more visitors than inhabitants can swamp a location. As one example, during the Cambuslang Revival (1742), there were 900 inhabitants of this town near Glasgow, Scotland, but when George Whitefield along with twelve other preachers came for the communion weekend in August, 30,000 people turned up; a little more than thirty-three times the population and some even came from afar away as Ireland and England! Those who did not bring enough provisions (e.g. food) had to either share others or purchase them.
- When news of a revival becomes known, Christians will travel vast distances to go to where God is moving. With the advent of trains, cars and planes and with disposable income this has made travel much easier than in previous centuries. Some go to get revived or blessed, others to check the reports out for themselves, whilst for many they know that it will probably be the only time that they will ever be in a revival and take the opportunity while they can.
- These visitors will naturally spend their money on hotels, B&Bs, food, petrol / gas, spiritual resources etc., and the community benefits with new jobs being created. During the Brownsville Revival (1995-2000), which the author visited in the summer of 1997, the local pizza takeaway, just across from the church could not keep up with demand! One outlet of a restaurant chain gave ten percent of its profits to the Brownsville Church after the evangelist, whilst preaching, said that they ought to for all the trade that was going their way!
- During revival, Christians always become more generous and liberal in their giving. The finances will in some shape and form frequently filter into the community and church. In many revivals this has included: employing new staff, social aid, paying off the church mortgage, being able to afford essential repairs to the church building, purchasing new(er) church vehicles (the old ones cost too much to repair and are a false economy) and supporting budding evangelists and new missionaries etc. Beginning in September 1907, when the Holy Spirit came to All Saints parish hall, Monkwearmouth, in Sunderland, England, genuine revival (and the beginning of Pentecostalism in Britain) – 'it burned up the debt' as the plaque on the outside of this (formerly Anglican) hall declares.

Chapter 13

Educational Establishments in Revival

"Not by might nor by power, but by My Spirit," says the Lord of hosts (Zechariah 4:6).

Some educational institutions have been founded in revival, others witnessed localised revival, whilst still others are caught up in revival. Sometimes, revival in an educational institution is like a ripple effect, moving from one classroom or floor to another. On occasions, revival has travelled outside of the gates of the educational establishment and into the community and even further afield.

Localised revivals in an educational institution such as a school, college, Bible College / Seminary / Institute, missionary training centre or university have been more prevalent in the eighteenth to nineteenth centuries, but during the mid 1930s, early 1950s, early 1970s and during 1992-1995, there was an explosion of Bible College / Seminary revivals across America.

Revival and Educational Establishments

- When revival comes to a Bible College / Seminary or school then classes will be suspended for a period of time, from the morning or afternoon off, up to a week. The school of the Holy Spirit in times of revival is better than the most educated and anointed of professors or lecturers. The Bible Institute for women and girls at Tsingtao, China, saw revival in 1934. Miss M. Clara Sullivan, a faculty member wrote: '…The work of the school continued, but class work, Mr. Scholz definitely reminded all, was not then, nor at any time, of prime importance, the most important of all being a right relationship with God and with one another. And more were led to repentance. We believe all have benefited.'
- When revival comes to a Bible College / Seminary or Institute; cases of discipline will greatly diminish; much to the pleasure of staff. Students and staff are also revived.
- When revival comes to a Christian school, the worst of pupils under the chastening of the Holy Spirit can be transformed into true saints within days! However, for

some, it may take a little longer to transform their mind to the mind of Christ (1 Corinthians 2:16). See Rom. 12:1-2.

On the sixth day of the Asbury College Revival (1970) in Wilmore, Kentucky, America, (a continuation of a service that had lasted 120 hours), more than one hundred adults, faculty and locals alike got right with God and each other during the Sunday service. Professor of Bible at Asbury College, Howard A. Hanke, in the book, *One Divine Moment – The Asbury Revival* wrote: 'The spiritual and social healing which occurred on that Sunday morning has solved more problems than any other event in the town for many years.'[1]

In 1904, Principal Philips of Newcastle Emlyn College, Wales, UK, (of which Evan Roberts was a student) gave his students a week's leave to attend daily meetings held by the renowned Welsh evangelist, Seth Joshua at Newquay, North Wales, where the Holy Spirit was moving. Philips said to his students, "You'll learn more in one week of revival than a year of theological study."

In a house meeting, some university students were probing a travelling preacher over *their* various views of activities that *they believed he* considered sinful. After an open discussion on various questionable activities, the preacher turned to the students and said, "Did you ever feel constrained of the Spirit to go to – ? Just you try and say grace [or God's blessing] before – the same as if you say grace before meat." [See John 8:29b, does it please God?]. The students trying to justify their position responded, "Is it a sin to go once a week?" "With your own words I condemn you!" replied the preacher. "You spend three and a half hours at – each week. Do you spend three and a half hours on you knees per week?" The students admitted their prayerlessness. "Well, if you did pray half an hour each day these questions would never arise. The main point is to remember that the sins of worldliness are surface products of deeper sins, the spiritual sins. Get right with God, and you will get a passion for souls filling you to overflowing and crowding out any desires for questionable things. Tell me, how many souls did you win for the Lord last year? *None*. And yet you dare argue about what is proper for Christian living – why you are not living on the Christian plane yet."[2]

Revival at Schools and Colleges
- It is possible to see the entire atmosphere of a school or college changed during a time of visitation of the Holy Spirit. Briercrest College in Canada, would vouch for that when the Holy Spirit came in late 2006 and the students in

2007 began praying for a deeper work, a true revival – the campus was transformed.
- Some student are too full of joy to come back to earth and others are too burdened to pay attention to schooling!
- Mission schools were very popular in Africa and China, especially in the nineteenth and twentieth centuries. On a few occasions, some school pupils (notably teenagers) ran away and left the school during revival at a mission station, because they did not want to confess their sins before God. (Often these sins were publicly confessed).
- At other times, school children on mission stations have gone back to their villages during holiday / vacation time and brought blessing to their pagan villages! Some have also, brought back with them new students for the mission school. At Imabi Mission Station during the first year of the Congo Revival (1953-1957), two hundred and twenty boys left for a month's school holiday and returned with thirty new students!
- When the Holy Spirit turns up at a state school, pupils may be suspended for 'mucking around' or playing the fool. The Holy Spirit would come upon them (or their non-Christian friends) in the classroom or the hallway and some would jerk and shake, others would fall over and it could not be humanly stopped.

On Wednesday, 6 September 2006, dnaindia.com had an article, which was titled: 'Meghalaya school students exhibit 'unusual' behaviour.' Meghalaya is a province in northeast India with Shillong as its capital and these events happened during the Shillong Revival (2006-2007). The report states: 'The Meghalaya government is looking into reports that a number of students from Christian schools in the state were exhibiting "unusual behaviour" like uncontrolled weeping and convulsions. There have been reports during the past few weeks that students of 15 schools in Shillong and other institutions in the Khasi and Jaintia hills region were fainting, weeping, chanting hymns and having convulsions.... Deputy Chief Minister, Donkupar Roy, who is in charge of education, said the government was watching the situation but wanted the heads of institutions to handle the matter.'

Before the Brownsville Revival (1995-2000) only three out of the thirty-two junior high schools in the area had Christian Unions, within two years, they all had them, some of which were 250 strong! Students in class would be touched by the Holy Spirit and collapse on the floor and many of the schools had separate rooms where these pupils could be placed. Countless testimonies of people poured in over the years and the healing power of God was very evident.

Richard Crisco, the youth pastor of the Brownsville Church, had for many years tried to get to meet many of the principals, but to no avail. Prior to the revival, the Brownsville Church had one hundred youth and within two years they had five hundred attending. After a process of discipleship they found that after two years, ninety percent of the youth converts were still going on with the Lord.

Soon, school principals started to phone up Richard Crisco and invite him out for lunch. After the third time, a principal explained that the administrators and the principals of the different schools had come together and informally decided that they needed to seize the opportunity. Richard Crisco was asked to hold Youth Rallies on a Tuesday night, every month in a different public school. The principals told him that they would announce that the Brownsville youth team would be in on a certain date and the rest was left up to him.

At one Youth Rally, seventy people were converted. The sports coach had a list of the ten worst sinners; promiscuous girls, heavy drug users and prideful sports stars and all ten had been converted! Dr. Michael Brown retelling the story said, "He [the coach] was in a state of shock."

At one school, some students decided to have a prayer and praise time during break and the Holy Spirit came and prostrated one of the fourteen-year-old boys. His mates carried him to his typing class and the teacher was not amused. She asked two boys (non-Christians) to carry their classmate to the principal's office. As they were doing this the power of God hit them! Dr. Brown went on to say that different principals phoned up Brownsville Church asking them what to do. Whilst some Christians phoned up Brownsville and were "flipping out" because they heard that people were shaking and falling over at school, wanting to know if it was true. But as Dr. Brown stated, when these same kids were going into school carrying guns, dressing like prostitutes, guys with multi-coloured hair, cussing at the teachers, getting kicked out of school, séances in the hallways, pornography in kids lockers, gangs etc.; these concerned Christians were not getting worked up about it, some of whom were their own children. "You know what's nice," said Dr. Brown, "God knows how to make Himself real to a young person."[3]

Chapter 14

Evangelism and Missions During Revival

God said, "Ask of Me, and I will give You the nations for Your inheritance" (Psalm 2:8).

Revival is not evangelism yet 'the most prominent idea generally associated with the word revival is the regeneration of many souls' as Henry C. Fish wrote in 1873. 'Multiplied conversions are the great outstanding characteristic of a time of revival. Multitudes lying dead in the valley of vision, find that it becomes the valley of decision.' Albert Barnes noted that if you 'take the case of a single true conversion to God, and extend it to the community – to *many* individuals passing through that change, and you have all the theory of revival of religion.' Fish concluded: 'It is bringing together many conversions; arresting simultaneously many minds; perhaps condensing into a single place, and into a few weeks, the ordinary work of many places and many years.' In revival, Christians are revived and awakened to be more earnest in their endeavours to promote the cause of Jesus Christ and the Kingdom of God.[1]

Evangelism and Mission Work

- During revival, evangelism always takes on a new and important responsibility, for every layman and woman, and children are no exception! New converts are also the best evangelists, as they give their testimony and talk about their salvation by God's grace and their faith in the atoning work of the Lord Jesus Christ. Their lives are living testimonies to all they meet and to all who know them.
- New converts become the newest evangelists and desire their friends, family and work colleagues to come and meet God for themselves (Num. 10:29b, Jn. 4:29 and Acts 4:20). There is also a new boldness for seasoned Christians, realising that life is short and the Lord will come at anytime and if He did, their unsaved friends, associates and neighbours would be weighed in the balance and found wanting, damned for all eternity in the fires of hell.
- There will be places where no preacher or missionary has travelled to, yet there could still be a fledgling Christian

community or church. Often it is by people 'gossiping the gospel.' One of the community has got saved and gone home and shared the little of what they know and others follow. This has also been known to happen on the mission field outside of revival. In spring 1829, some lumbermen from Pennsylvania, America, visited Philadelphia, where Charles Finney was holding evangelistic meetings and they got converted. They returned home to an area known as the lumber region and five thousand in that district were converted along an area of eighty miles and there was not a single minister of the gospel there!

- At other places, heathen will come under the influence of the Holy Spirit and will decide to follow the One true God. During the Gold Coast Revival (1875-1878), Thomas Freeman's wife wrote to him from Anamabu, (also spelt Anomabo, approximately ten miles from Cape Coast along the Gold Coast in modern-day Ghana), asking him to return as the chapel congregation was overflowing into the streets. She wrote: 'One of our sisters, reports that, as she was passing along the street, she met a group of about twelve heathen people, men and women, from the fishermen's quarter of the town, who were saying, "We will go to chapel to be Christians; we will go and give ourselves to God omnipotent." '
- Greater numbers than normal are obedient to the call to Christian ministry during times of revival and this leads to more labourers being trained and then thrust forth into the harvest field, at home or abroad. See Matthew 9:35-38.

Revival by Extension – Evangelism, Fire-Carriers

- During revival, people love to give their testimony and tell others what God has done for them, as a trophy of God's grace. Often visitors from another town who have tasted of the heavenly fire, upon giving their testimony in a place where revival has not yet started, will become a fire-starter in that church or community. If they are asked to pray for believers (the laying on of hands) they will soon realise that they have received a level of anointing which has been transferred to them which can bless others.
- In many of the revivals from Church history, groups of evangelists, lay workers or prayer bands, travel from one 'hot spot' to a spiritually dead location to help ignite the flames of revival, to stir the Christians to pray (or to

encourage those who already are) and to hold meetings or campaigns. During the Welsh Revival (1904-1905) there were a number of teams ranging in size from three to eight people, often with a male leader (Evan Roberts, Dan Roberts or Sidney Evans) with teenage or young women singing evangelists / preachers. However, the first team consisted of only five young women and no men!
- When people hear of what God is doing in another town or country, this acts as an encouraging stimulus to pray for God's Spirit to come to their location.
- Often, teams of people (or individuals) who have been revived will travel to another location as evangelists, singers or to give their testimony and revival often breaks out. This was seen during the Asbury College Revival (1970) which led to Anderson College Revival (1970) which in turn led to about fifty other localised revivals as individuals or teams of students were asked to go and speak in other colleges and churches across America and beyond! At other times, the revivalist cannot be in two places at once, having received numerous invites and those closest to him (or her) are frequently sent to fill the pulpits and invitations of others.
- In many Asian revivals of the twentieth century, revival bands (laypeople evangelistic teams) are designated and grouped together by the leadership of a church to evangelise. The Indonesian Revival (1964-1974) had at least seventy-six evangelistic bands in operation by 1966, which also included some children's teams whom themselves decided to evangelise. The Shantung Revival (1930-1932) in China, also saw children's bands. These bands have been most prominent in China, Japan and Indonesia. The reason why these 'designated and grouped together bands' of laypersons were almost exclusively confined to Asian countries was because many of the people lived off the land and are used to submitting to their elders as part of their culture. They were not tied to any nine till five job which would have prevented them from going away from home for a few days to weeks at a time, and because of their communal culture and tight-knit family bonds, other kinsfolk would take up the slack in the fields or farms. In 1925, Paget Wilkes, founder of the Japan Evangelistic Band was preaching at a conference during the Shanghai Revival (1925) in China, when Andrew Gih

heard the call to form the Bethel Worldwide Evangelistic Band, who went across Asia preaching and saw revival.

Revival and Infant Churches
- On occasions, revival has come to an 'infant' Church when the missionaries have either been expelled from the nation, as in the Nagaland Revivals (1949-1952) which brought about the Nagaland Awakening (1950s), or when the missionaries had handed over the administration control of the Church to the indigenous believers, as in the Pyongyang Great Revival (1907-1910) in Korea. In both these instances the young Churches threw themselves upon the Lord for strengthening and guidance.
- Similar to above, the Imbai Revival (1936) in North East Belgian Congo, came just before the missionaries were told to close the Imbai Mission Station because the Belgian Government would not allow the Worldwide Evangelisation Crusade (WEC) to have more than twelve European-run stations. The missionaries prayed for revival so the Imbai Church would not crumble, but stand because their dependence was more on the missionaries and their tribal leader, rather than on Jesus Christ.
- The China Awakening (1927-1937) did wonders for the Church in north China. The Japanese invaded in 1937, and during the revival God raised up Chinese men and women and prepared the indigenous Church to be self supporting; independent of its Western founders. God knew what He was doing as many Western missionaries were interred under the Japanese invasion / occupation and died during World War II. Later, all missionaries were expelled from the country which was under Communist rule.
- During the Ruanda Revival (1937-1950s), the Ruanda Mission Church (founded by the Church Missionary Society), '...transformed the spiritual life of the Church, [and] could not fail to affect its organic life too. Perhaps the first sign of this practical outcome of deep religious experience was seen in the love towards self-support,' so wrote a senior missionary to Ruanda. The Ruanda Mission had begun in 1921 at Kabale on the Uganda / Ruanda border. 'By 1941 the church work at Kabale was fully self-supporting and they began to bear the [financial] burden of the Evangelists' Training School.'

Chapter 15

Physical Phenomena

'My heart within me is broken because of the prophets; all my bones shake. I am like a drunken man, and like a man whom wine has overcome, because of the Lord, and because of His holy Words' (Jeremiah 23:9).

Physical Phenomena
Physical Phenomena, bodily manifestations, are always present during any move of the Holy Spirit because we are emotional beings. During revival they affect people to a lesser or greater degree, but should not be sought. The more extreme the phenomena, the deeper the work of the Holy Spirit, whether in conviction of sin (amongst unbelievers), or in inner healings, a work of grace (amongst Christians). Jonathan Edwards noted that there was a vast difference in *degree* and *manner* of experience at, and after conversion. Physical phenomena can be varied from weeping to dancing; unrestrained worship to repentance and like Israel during the completion of the foundations of the rebuilding of the temple, it can be difficult to 'discern the noise of the shout of joy from noise of the weeping' (Ezra 3:13). It is what is known as 'Divine disorder' or 'a solemn commotion.' We are commanded to 'let all things be done decently and in order' (1 Corinthians 14:40), but what is *now* considered as 'decently and in order;' propriety, is not the same as what we read in the New Testament! In times of revival, the Holy Spirit is in charge and He does things His way, which to the traditional and ritually observant will appear disorderly.
Puritan revivalist, Richard Baxter of Kidderminster, England, in *Five Disputations* wrote: 'It is better that men should be disorderly saved than orderly damned; and that the Church be disorderly preserved than orderly destroyed.'
Not everything you see in revival is from God. The enemy will always be looking to take advantage and there are always attention-seekers. But there can be a danger in hastily reacting to physical phenomena in another and deciding that it is either fleshly or of demonic origin. If it is of demonic origin then the demons ought to be cast out, if they are not already fleeing! On the other hand, if the person's bodily movements are a reaction to God's

presence then the danger lies in if we try to suppress him or her and thus hinder the work of God in the person's life and thereby quench the Spirit. There is a difference between genuine emotion felt as the *result* of an experience and attempting to work up an emotion in an attempt to *produce* the experience.

Charles H. Spurgeon who saw revival in London in the 1850-60s said, "He [God] *can* bless us as He wills and He *will* bless us as He wills. Let us not dictate to God. Many a blessing has been lost by Christians not believing it to be a blessing, because it did not come in the particular shape which they had conceived to be proper and right."

At the beginning of March 1860, Rev. T. H. Baxter, a United Presbyterian minister from Banff, UK, was in Buckie and Portordon. In his church the following Sunday he gave his opinion of the revival in Scotland from personal observation. 'He did not deny there were improprieties, but if they waited for a revival of religion without improprieties, they never would have one at all. The means, instruments, manifestations and results connected with the revival, so far as he could discern, were similar to those connected with every genuine revival since the Day of Pentecost.'[1]

During the 1930s, revival was sweeping China. Rev. Richard S. Bjorkdahl describes a series of meetings held at Wuchang, during 7-21 October 1934. He wrote: 'Rev. Wu Djen Ming of the Lutheran church in Honan had promised to help us out…. After Rev. Wu, we had four days help from the so called Bethel Band, from the institution planted by Dr. Mary Stone in Shanghai. It was composed of two pastors, Chi and Lin, and a singer by the name of Sun. Their aim was mostly to win outsiders. They were very lively and somewhat noisy. They would make sketches on the blackboard illustrating their sermons, they sang and played, and sold their books with a good deal of flourish. Some of our members, who had not fully come through during Rev. Wu's meetings, were awakened and helped. People differ much as to nature and disposition, and God has many means at His disposal. *What seemed distracting to me, sometimes even repelling, proved liberating to others.* A very good result of the meetings of the Bethel Band was the formation of voluntary preaching bands, which have started to go out witnessing about the salvation in Jesus.'[2]

Dr. Martyn Lloyd-Jones in reference to physical phenomena in revival said, "These phenomena [from Acts 2:14-18] are indicative of the fact that some very powerful stimulus is in operation. Something is happening which is so powerful that the very physical frame is involved...the phenomena are not of importance in and of themselves. The phenomena therefore should not be sought, they should not be encouraged, they should not be boasted of.... The body is weak, some bodies are weaker than other bodies, and so when this mighty spiritual power comes there are certain bodies that break down and they should be helped and dealt with in a semi-medical manner, they should be prayed for, they should be pacified, and that is how these great leaders of revival have always dealt with them.... Anybody who tries to work up phenomena is a tool of the devil...."[3]

Dave Roberts in *The 'Toronto' Blessing* wrote: 'To suggest that all our physical reactions to a Divine encounter must correspond exactly to a proof-text criteria is to turn the Bible from the story of salvation and grace into the rule book of salvation.'[4]

Roberts also wrote: 'Allowances must be made for congregation members learning to respond appropriately to the Spirit, and for leaders learning to discern between the Spirit, the flesh and the devil. Judgments about a church's conduct on the basis of one meeting do a disservice to those involved.'[5]

Common Characteristics of Physical Phenomena
- Inside and outside of the church building, people, sometimes only a few, whilst at other times it can be hundreds or thousands will be shouting out praises to the Lord, such as "Glory," (Psalm 29:9), "Hallelujah / Praise the Lord" (Psalm 106:48). It is as if the person will explode and so is compelled to shout aloud to the glory of God! (Psalm 5:11). Billy Bray from Cornwall, UK, of the Twelveheads Revival (c.1824), Cross Lanes Revival (c.1830), the Crantock Revival (c.1867) and at least five other revivals; all in Cornwall was always full of the joy of the Lord. He abounded in shouts and praise and leaped and danced not only at church, but in the street, at the market, even when he was hundreds of feet down the mineshaft at work!
- Holy laughter (and holy joy) is an interesting phenomenon which practically outworks itself through an individual's vocal cords and is expressed on the face of the recipient. It is often uncontrollable and unrestrained and comes from deep down inside a person. '...Whom having not seen [Jesus] you love. Though now you do not see Him, yet believing, you rejoice with joy inexpressible and full of glory' (1 Peter 1:8). Evan Roberts from the Welsh Revival (1904-1905) would often be in the pulpit, laughing and

smiling and some thought that this was irreverent. A missionary during the Hwanghsien Revival (1932) in China told the Lord that she did not want any manifestations but only Him. In a few minutes she was on her feet and giving her testimony. She wrote: 'I began, "Who can lay anything to the charge of God's elect?" (Romans 8:33), and burst out so in praise to God that I knew that the Power in me was from above and my heart was filled with holy laughter and praise (Psalm 32:11 and Psalm 126:2). Many others have received this blessing, some not in full, some more fully...' Also, Mr Kiang Fang Nan surrendered his all to the Lord and received the fullness of the Holy Spirit. Great joy and floods of laughter came over him and he praised the Lord for two hours!

- There are always sceptics because of physical phenomena, bodily reactions during revivals. Physical phenomena can be emotional reactions which are transmitted via the body due to the convicting and illuminating power of the Holy Spirit, while some can be of human origin (imitation) or of demonic origin (infiltration and demonic manifestation).
- Physical phenomena can be: screaming, shrieking, falling down (prostrations, strikings, swooning, fainting etc.), turning pale, looking fearful or petrified (visions of Calvary, hell or the coming judgment etc.), perspiring, heaving of the chest, sighing heavily, incapacitated, immobilised, unable to walk, jerking (spasmodic contraction of muscles), trembling, shaking, shivering, convulsions, rolling on the ground, flaying arms, crying, laughing, praising, shouting, weeping, sobbing, moaning, or groaning etc. When revival came to the Gahini Mission Station in north-east Rwanda in late June 1936, people in many different circumstances would begin to shiver, which led the missionaries, at first to believe that they had some sort of African fever. They soon realised that they were under conviction of sin and in fear of a holy God. I have only read about shivering on two occasions, whereas shaking or trembling is common. Convulsions are generally not that common.
- On rare occasions, those under conviction can lose their speech (being unable to communicate in any way, shape or form), sometimes being in a trance-type state and can be physically, as stiff and rigid as a board. This happened to the ringleader of a four-man group who intended to

disrupt a meeting during the Golant Revival (1854) in Cornwall, England; he was converted the following day. In the Hwanghsien Revival (1932) in northern China, a Communist schoolboy was so convicted of his sins that his body became rigid. He fell against one of his teachers and cried aloud for mercy, being terribly afraid. He was told to pray to God and felt that his very life was being crushed out of him. Teachers and friends prayed for him and urged him to pray. After one hour he did and then for a further hour he confessed his sins and asked forgiveness towards his fellow pupils and found the peace of salvation.
- In a similar incident, during the Shantung Revival (1930-1932) in northern China, a healthy young man, a so-called 'Christian' worker deceived himself and others by insisting he was saved. One night in the courtyard he was suddenly struck down and had to be carried inside, stiff, blue and cold! Missionaries called into his ears, "Confess your sins quickly!" As soon as he could open his mouth he poured out his black sins and stood on his feet again, a forgiven sinner. Several others had God's hand on them in similar ways. Note: Some intercessors have out of body experiences (2 Corinthians 12:2) and they can appear dead, being physically cold like Mary MacLean who had been used in the 1939 Lewis Revival, Scotland.[6]

Physical Phenomena and Inner Healing
- Jerking, jolting, shaking or trembling can be a process that the Holy Spirit uses to literally shake things out of people, bringing inner healing to old wounds and scars. It has been known for people to shake so vigorously that their cowboy boots have come off! The outward is merely a bodily reaction to an inward working and should not be alarming. Some who are overcome by the Holy Spirit are motionless.
- The Holy Spirit during times of revival (and outside of revival) can come in so much power that frail human bodies are unable to cope – it is like electricity flowing through one's body, tingling all the nerve ends, though without any pain. One missionary from the Congo Revival (1953-1957) described it in similar terms when the Holy Spirit came upon her. Sometimes in intercession the body will shake, tremble or jerk as the person is burdened for souls (or other situations) under the anointing and leading of the Holy Spirit – this was testified and recorded by a

number of people in both the Brownsville and Congo Revival. One night, Alison Ward testified for around fifteen minutes at Brownsville Church and immediately at the end, an altar call was given, (with no preaching that night) and hundreds came to the front. This unnatural repetitive movement can cause the body to ache (though not painful), as muscles are moved in ways that is not normal for everyday life. See Jeremiah 23:9 and Habakkuk 3:16a.
- It is common during revival to see people crying. Crying for joy, crying under conviction of sin or because they are repentant. In times past, when a revival was in the vicinity of a mining community, it was common for miners to come straight out of the pit and attend a service. At other times the preacher ministered in the open-air near the pit, and tears would be streaming down the miners blackened faces making white gutter lines down their cheeks. This was noted under Billy Bray and other revivalists in the 1820-50s in Cornwall, England, and in the mining valleys during the Welsh Revival (1904-1905).

In 1956, David Du Plessis, the former General Secretary of the Apostolic Faith Mission, was invited to attend the World Council of Churches as a member of staff. On one occasion, in a rebuttal concerning the criticism of emotionalism in meetings he said, "I would rather see people, any time, weep for sheer joy in the Holy Ghost, than to see them weeping in a theatre because of some 'make-believe' show. I fear we are so afraid of emotionalism that we have caused people to give expression to their feelings in amusements centres."[7]

J. Edwin Orr was in a meeting in Norway, when the Holy Spirit swept in. People wept, confessed sin, others praised the Lord, whilst some knelt or stood and a few trembled. In a rebuttal to claims of emotionalism he wrote: 'Sorrow is an emotion, and if Christians are overwhelmingly sorry for their disobedience, may they not weep? Joy is an emotion, and if someone suddenly realises that his awful sins are forgiven, may he not shout, "Hallelujah?" I have never yet heard of a revival which was *not* accompanied by emotional phenomena. Emotion is not revival, for revival is a deep and abiding work of grace in the innermost core of our beings. But we are only human. I have seen brothers reconciled, and falling into each others arms, weeping. The change of heart was the work of God's Spirit, but I and all others rejoiced to see the outward manifestation of the work of grace.'[8]

Chapter 16

Conviction and Confession of Sin

'And it shall be, when he is guilty in any of these matters, that he shall confess that he has sinned in that thing' (Leviticus 5:5).

Conviction of Sin

- It is common during revival to see people crying under conviction of sin, because they are repentant, or crying for joy of sins forgiven, conversion of friends etc. If a godly Christian begins to weep, cry and moan, it is often a form of identification (Matt. 28:18 and Rom. 8:26-27), how God feels, or compassion for the lost – being burdened, whilst at other times people can moan and groan being weighed down under conviction of sin (Ps. 32:3-4 & Ps. 38:3-4, 8).
- People can be under conviction of sin for days, weeks or months as they are in the 'Valley of Decision.' Revival Church history records that people have been under conviction of sin for years prior to a revival, which is greatly intensified during revival. Metaphorically speaking they will either be broken or ground to powder. See Matthew 21:44. Broken by submission or crushed by their rebellion.
- In revival there will be conviction of sin to a lesser or greater degree. Some will be in great anxiety and deep distress (or even tormented) and a small portion of these will be unable to sleep or eat. In China during the revivals of the 1930s, they called it sin-sickness!
- Many non-Christians will writhe in agony of soul and be in deep torment until they bow the knee to Jesus Christ, or if they are already a Christian, until they get specific sins out of their life. When George Whitefield preached his first sermon in the last week of June 1735, in England, complaints were laid at the bishop that he had driven fifteen people mad! During the early Salvation Army meetings, the small hymn books would be torn to shreds by those under conviction! Leonard Ravenhill stated that in 1926, at a W. P. Nicholson's meeting he also saw song books torn to shreds by those under conviction! (Many evangelism campaigns had their own worship books).

- In extreme cases, those under conviction of sin will beat the floor (or whatever inanimate object is around them); depending on if they are on the floor or sat down etc. Their thumps will be so hard and prolonged that those present will fear that the person will do themselves an injury! I have never read of an instance where injury has occurred.
- Those who are under conviction of sin will be encouraged and urged by believers to repent of their sin (sometimes to confess) and to turn to Jesus. See 2 Samuel 12:1-23 and Psalm 51, when King David was confronted with his sin.
- Some who cry out under conviction will often drown out the preacher's voice; sometimes they need to be removed outside or to another room, and at other times, the cry of the repentant brings conviction to those who are hardened and they too become convicted of their sins. Some scream so loud and so terrifyingly, it is as if they have been shot, stabbed or attacked by an assailant!
- Some people will fall out of the pew or off their seat, or fall over if they were standing up as the arrows of the Lord fly forth, bringing conviction which can lead to prostrations. Some Christians will be prostrated but are not necessarily under conviction of sin.
- Some under conviction will wring their hands, heave their chests with emotion, sigh, perspire, shake, tremble, roll on the floor, cry out loud, or jerk, while others who have been struck by the arrows of the Lord appear to be in a coma or even dead – motionless. Some will be in such a weakened condition that they will be laid up in bed for days or weeks.
- Not all who are under conviction of sin (those who have been awakened to their sinfulness) will come through to conversion and there are numerous reasons for this.
- There is false repentance, when a convicted person simulates repentance, or even appears remorseful, sometimes shedding tears but they are just going through a simulated process with no regeneration and are not "born again" as Jesus said (John 3:3,7). It could just be crocodile tears. Malachi 2:13 reveals that the people were weeping because they gave their offerings with a reluctant heart and were upset because of their loss! Sometimes people are repentant or remorseful because they were caught or found out. Outwardly, they appear changed, but they have not come to God and asked His forgiveness. They are talented actors, self-deceived or double-minded.

- Some Christians will manifest similar if not identical physical phenomena as those already mentioned in this chapter (e.g. jerking, shaking, weeping, perspiring etc.) and or bow (a sign of humility and respect) yet are not necessarily under conviction of sin. The Holy Spirit may be doing a work inside of them, often an inner healing of the emotions from the scars of the past or Divine deliverance from demons (e.g. rolling about or screaming). Generally, the wringing of the hands or perspiring in revival is associated with conviction; unless it's hot!

Christians under Conviction of Sin
- During revival, Christians will have a sharper conscience and will feel quick conviction for seemingly minor offences, (though in God's eyes, sin is sin). I remember reading about one person who wrote a letter during a revival and decided not to dot the i's and cross the t's. This person came under conviction and remedied the letter. For some, this will appear extreme, but God is always looking at the heart and motives, and diligence is very important.
- Christians will be more spiritually sensitive, not wanting to grieve the Holy Spirit and will mourn over their sin, realising that they have injured Jesus.
- Christians will be broken and humbled before God, as they see Him afresh in all His holiness, majesty and splendour. In such a spiritual state, they will also be broken that their sin nailed Jesus to the cross of Calvary – their sin, our sin, put Him there.
- Christians will come under conviction for sins of commission – what they know is wrong and still do.
- They will also come under conviction for their sins of omission – what they know is right or should be done and did not do. Neglect of prayer, Bible reading, careless in word or action or neglecting widows and orphans etc. During the Shantung Revival (1930-1932) in China, the sin of robbing God in tithes and offerings (Malachi 3:8-10) appeared to be quite common and was even paid in arrears because they saw it as an outstanding debt.
- Some people after conversion come under conviction of sin as the Holy Spirit shows them their past; things that have been left undone and need to be remedied. It may be a sin that needs to be confessed by name (Leviticus 5:5). There may also need to be restitution (Luke 19:5-10), but more

commonly, reparation, dealing with the past and making a wrong (if possible) right (Matt. 5:23-24), or acknowledging a wrong and asking a person for their forgiveness. See Dealing with the Past in the following chapter. Please note that once sin has been confessed (1 John 1:9) and restitution made (if need be and if and where possible), there is no condemnation for those who are in Christ who walk not in the flesh, but in the Spirit (Romans 8:1).

Confession of Sin
- There will always be confession of sin (Proverbs 28:13 and James 5:16), often in public meetings. These confessions are prompted by the Holy Spirit and aid the joyous release of forgiveness. However, some confess whilst in the flesh.
- There is a danger in public meetings in getting caught up in the atmosphere and openly confessing sexual sins without the prompting of the Holy Spirit. People can be unknowingly used by the enemy to cause harm or shock sensitive people or introduce ideas not already there. Wisdom is needed; but especially when members of the opposite sex are present.
- Public confession of sin is a humbling process and a way of accountability. In oriental countries, such as Korea, China and Japan, it would appear that confession of sin is a lot harder because, culturally, the person will 'lose face.' However, it is better to lose face before man and fear God (Prov. 29:1, 25), than to resist the Holy Spirit (Acts 7:51).
- During the Pyongyang Revival (1907-1910) in Korea and the Shantung Revival (1930-1932) in China, incidences occurred where indigenous Christians had to confess their sins of being prejudiced against the foreign missionaries. This type of prejudice does seem more common in oriental countries. Sometimes it is also the Western missionaries who have had to confess their incorrect attitude of superiority, especially in Oriental, Asian and African countries. After confession, a greater level of unity is achieved and a true blessing can flow (Psalm 133).
- Confession of wrongs to an unbeliever (especially if coupled with restitution where an item has been stolen or something has been withheld) can greatly affect their outlook. It may have been the wrong committed by a Christian, that made them reject Christianity and thus the confession can soften their hearts to Jesus Christ.

Chapter 17

Conversion and Dealing with The Past

At his conversion, Jesus said to Saul (later renamed Paul), "...The Gentiles to whom I now send you, to open their eyes and to turn them from darkness to light, and from the power of Satan to God, that they may receive forgiveness of sins and an inheritance among those who are sanctified" (Acts 26:17b-18).

The Bible states that we are saved by grace through faith because of Jesus Christ's atoning work on the cross of Calvary. He paid the price and shed His blood so that we can be redeemed and reconciled back to God. There is no other name under heaven given to men by which we must be saved. He died and rose again that we too might live; live for Him and with Him through all eternity. The conversion of each person is special as it is unique; however during times of revival, conversions are often a more deeper work of grace and more refining in their outworking.

Conversion
- The conversion of friends and work colleagues (especially during times of revival) can promote 'hope,' because they knew the person's former character and lifestyle and see that the change is real. If God has forgiven them, He can forgive me.
- Nominal Christians who get converted will see the Bible in a new light. The truths of Scripture will come alive, and be easier to understand and apply.
- Some new Christians will be unable to tell you *exactly* when they were converted (though most can); when the Divine transaction took place and they were born again and the Spirit of God entered them at regeneration. However, they will often be able to pinpoint that it was between certain dates, period or events. This is often because revelation of their sin, the cross, and Christ's all sufficiency, has come in waves.
- For some people these waves of conviction (and then revelation) are a means to protect their minds, as if it came all at once, they could have a breakdown.

- Jonathan Edwards in the Northampton Revival (1734-1735) in America, spoke of people who were on the "borders of despair." Some were quickly converted, whilst for others it took longer for them to come through to saving faith and saving grace through Jesus Christ.
- Jonathan Edwards also noted that those of a melancholy disposition (deep thoughts of sadness, often depressed) frequently had "mixed emotions" which the enemy used to his full advantage.
- Jonathan Edwards recorded that some who had been under conviction of sin had resigned themselves to their fate, knowing the sovereignty and justice of God. That they were due and deserving of condemnation and were able to glory in God's justice. These came through to saving faith. I believe that this type of understanding, revelation or mental state is more common upon churchgoers who sit under Calvinistic preaching (because they are predestined). Read Edwards' 'Sinners in the Hands of an Angry God' that he first preached in Enfield, New England, in June 1741.
- Many people will go to bed under conviction of sin (for those who can sleep), and a minority can wake up converted! Winkie Pratney calls it: 'Divine regeneration without explanation!'
- Jonathan Edwards recorded that in Northampton Revival (1734-1735) amongst his own parishioners, people were converted but did not yet know it! They exhibited changed lives and godly fruit. Some were still dealing with "legal issues" as Edwards called them; that we are all sinners, deserving of damnation, until "free grace" has been shed abroad in our hearts. God's work upon the soul is mysterious. It is better that a person be *truly* born again and to pass from death to life, than to fall again. It is better that a Christian shows a saving experience by their changed and redeemed lifestyle than just by words, "I'm saved" without a changed nature, the marks of true grace.

Dealing with the Past

If we want to see revival, then each of us needs to be revived. But before we can be revived we need to repent of all known sin and deal with the past, because 'he who covers his sin will not prosper, but whoever confesses and forsakes them will find mercy' (Proverbs 28:13). There is a world of difference between saying "sorry," which is often meaningless and without heart and asking someone's forgiveness for a wrong that has been done against them which is humbling. If we do not deal with our sin in private, when revival comes we will have to deal with it in public! Deal with it now, rather than blush in public.

It is the job of the Holy Spirit to bring conviction of sin to our lives, but our confession is our response to it. Once we have repented of specific sins, then we can express outwardly what has been revealed inwardly – the forgiveness and cleansing in Christ Jesus (Isaiah 1:18 and 1 John 1:9).

We have all sinned against God by breaking His laws, and sinned against each other by personal sin or failure by our wrong actions, reactions, attitudes or decisions that we have made. We may have also sinned against our own body by being sexually immoral, see 1 Corinthians 6:18. Specific sins need to be specifically repented of and confessed by name, 'when he is guilty in any of these matters, that he shall confess that he has sinned *in that thing*' (Leviticus 5:5). We must repent of specific sins and pray, "Lord please forgive me for being lustful, for stealing, for lying, for being bitter, for being critical or angry, for prayerlessness or unbelief etc." If we are not sure about certain situations (or habits) whether we have sinned or not, then we can pray the prayer of the psalmist, "Search me, O God, and know my heart: try me, and know my thoughts: and see if there be any wicked way in me" (Psalm 139:23-24), AV.

Within the Christian Church there is a place for private confession to another brother or sister whom we have wronged (Matthew 5:23-24 and 1 John 1:8-10) and at times, a place for public confession so that our brothers or sisters can pray for us to be healed and delivered (Mark 1:4-5 and James 5:16). If we have sincerely confessed our sin before God then we have received His forgiveness; therefore there is no reason to keep the confession alive because God has forgiven and forgotten (Psalm 103:12 and Micah 7:19).

J. Edwin Orr in his book, *This Is The Victory* (1936) wrote: 'If you sin secretly, confess secretly, admitting publicly that you need the victory, but keeping the details to yourself. If you sin openly, confess openly to remove stumbling-blocks from those whom you have hindered. If you have sinned spiritually (prayerlessness, lovelessness, and unbelief as well as their offspring, criticism, etc.) then confess to the church that you have been a hindrance. The devil is ever ready to take advantage of distress of heart, but the Holy Spirit can give the last word in wisdom.'

Rev. D. R. Wahlquist of the Swedish Missionary Society, described a series of meetings at Macheng, Hupeh, China, about fifty miles north of Hankow. The meetings were held from 22 September to 5 October 1934, under the leadership of Pastor Liu Dao Sheng and meetings were afterwards held at the various outstations under the leadership of the missionaries and local workers. Rev. Wahlquist wrote: 'The winds of revival which have been blowing over wide areas of China have also come to our field, the martyr district, where the blood of the martyrs now bears its richest harvest. No wonder our heart rejoices with an unspeakable joy.

'Sins as black as night have been confessed, such as child murder, fornication, etc. One woman had killed six girls during the course of her wedded life. Another had killed four, etc.... The latter was the widow of a church member. As long as the husband lived, she cared nothing for God, but now she was gloriously saved. Some tried in the beginning to confess their sins in a lump. "Forgive me all of my sins." Or they tried to mention only the 'small' sins. But peace did not come in that way. Only when each individual sin was mentioned by name, whether 'small' or 'great,' and when no sin was purposely hidden, could assurance of forgiveness come, and the heart be filled with peace and joy. Many sought us privately for confession and prayer. We sang frequently a little stanza: "The sins of the heart pour out, pour out; *your* sin's account make clear, make clear!" '[1]

Dr. William Newton Blair, missionary to Korea, witnessed the beginning of the Pyongyang Great Revival (1907-1910). In his book, *The Korean Pentecost* he wrote: 'Then began a meeting the like of which I had never seen before, nor wish to see again unless in God's sight it is absolutely necessary. Every sin a human being can commit was publicly confessed that night. Pale and trembling with emotion, in agony of mind and body, guilty souls, standing in the white light of that judgment, saw themselves as God saw them. Their sins rose up in all their vileness, till shame and grief and self-loathing took complete possession; pride was driven out, the face of men forgotten. Looking up to heaven, to Jesus whom they had betrayed, they smote themselves and cried out with bitter wailing, "Lord, Lord, cast us not away for ever!" Everything else was forgotten, nothing else mattered. The scorn of men, the penalty of the law, even death itself seemed of small consequence if only God forgave. We may have our theories of the desirability or undesirability of public confession of sin. I have had mine; but I know that when the Spirit of God falls upon guilty souls, there will be confession, and no power on earth can stop it.'[2]

Chapter 18

The Supernatural of Revival

'So the Spirit lifted me up and took me away, and I went in bitterness, in the heat of my spirit; but the hand of the Lord was strong upon me' (Ezekiel 3:14).

Secrets in Revival
There are experiences that happen during times of revival, which for many reasons are not talked about or published. The apostle Paul was caught up to the third heaven and was not permitted to utter certain things (2 Corinthians 12:1-4). John was not permitted to write about the utterance of the seven thunders (Revelation 10:4). After the Mukti Revival (1905-1906) in India, Helen Dyer in her book *Pandita Ramabai* wrote: 'Some few saw visions and experienced the power of God and things too deep to be described.' Beware of improper worship! (Colossians 2:18-19).

Rev. Gordon I. Thomas, in the foreword to *The Lewis Awakening* by Duncan Campbell wrote: 'Story after story could be told of incidents that are in the realm of the miraculous and which indeed are positively breath-taking to hear. Practically none of these has been mentioned in this booklet....'

Eva Stuart Watts, in her book *Floods On Dry Ground,* writing about the Imbai Revivals of 1935 and 1936 in the Belgian Congo, wrote: 'When the natives were out in the forest in the morning for communion with the Saviour, things happened about which they could scarcely speak afterwards – experiences of the utterable joy of His blessed presence.' But she was able to write about the experience of Lily Roberts, a missionary who saw revival. In an open vision, the heavens were opened and she saw Jesus.

Charles Finney wrote: 'If anything is to be said about revivals [writing about it during the lifetime of the revival], give only the plain and naked facts, just as they are, and let them pass for what they are worth.'

We should not seek supernatural experiences, nor glory in them (Col. 2:18-19) or physical phenomena but also, we should never deny them or try to dust them under the carpet. In times of revival, supernatural events orchestrated by the Holy Spirit are largely manifested. We are encouraged to 'desire the best gifts' and 'desire spiritual gifts' (1 Cor. 12:31 and 1 Cor. 14:1) though we should not be seeking signs or the miraculous in themselves, but seeking God and giving Him the honour that is due unto His name. All the glory must go to God, for whatever He is doing in a person's life, which often reacts with a physical response as soul and body are interlinked. Humans have five distinct functions, we are: physical beings, thinking beings, longing beings, choosing beings, and feeling beings (physical, rational, personal, volitional and emotional), which can be placed into three categories: the mind, the will and the emotions, which connect to the body, the spirit and the soul. The different capacities are not designed to work isolated from each other but as part of the whole. The body and mind are so inextricably connected that what affects the mind affects the body and vice versa. Jesus Christ came to heal the whole man, physically, mentally and emotionally (Isa. 61:1-2 & Luke 4:18-19).[1]

Let us not be confused over God's dynamics and the demonic. In any meeting where God is moving, a person's face may be contorting, but let us not be hasty in our judgment, are the demons manifesting or fleeing?

In revival or whenever the Holy Spirit moves, demons are frightened and may cry out and depart from a person. It is a clash of two worlds, the Kingdom of Light and the kingdom of darkness. Whilst at other times they will publicly manifest and it is the Church's responsibility to bind the strong man and to cast them out in the mighty name of Jesus Christ (Mark 3:24, 27).

Supernatural Events of Revival

Everything to do with revival is supernatural, as it is a move of the Holy Spirit. Some things are a testament to the world so that they take notice, shock factor, even a sign that is spoken against, but the knowledge of the work spreads. Others are drawn to Christ because of these events, whilst some are repelled. The following items are just a glimpse of what God has done and can do in revival, though some of these supernatural events should be the norm, as revealed in the book of Acts and so do the Church Fathers and beyond in their respective writings of Church history.

- Certain persons, (Christians and non-Christians) men, women and even children will have dreams and visions. Some people have visions of hell, the lost, of heaven or of the Saviour / Calvary etc. Generally speaking, during revival, Christians have often had visions to give extra impetus to the work of evangelism, whereas non-Christians have had visions to either show them where they were

going (hell, the judgment of God) or visions of the Saviour / Calvary (the mercy of God).
- Unusual visions: During the Shillong Revival (2006-2007), Iba Warjri, an eight year old girl came out of a church building, looked up at the moon, which looked like a close cloud and saw a vision of Jesus in the cloud. Outside of revival, I know a man whom whilst in Wales, UK, was looking out of a window up at the sky. He saw the face of Evan Roberts (the Welsh revivalist) with a big grin on his face in the shape of a cloud. This vision lasted for several minutes until it faded away. The man was so taken back by what he had seen that it never occurred to him that it was a vision, as he initially believed it was a sign in the heavens that could be seen by all.
- There will be prophecy. Often speaking about the nearness of the Second Coming (very prevalent in the last two hundred years) and the call to get right with God, to be ready for Jesus Christ's return, as in the Shillong Revival (2006-2007) in India. In connection with this there have been those who have prayed, "Oh, Lord, wait a year or two before coming to give these people time to repent." This was what a lady prayed during the Hwanghsien Revival (1932) which was part of the Shantung Revival (1930-1932) in China. Prior to the Welsh Revival (1904-1905), Evan Roberts after receiving a vision of hell; a fiery bottomless pit surrounded by impenetrable walls with countless numbers of people surging towards it, pleaded that hell's door be closed for one year so that they might have opportunity to repent. George Fox had a vision of an 'ingathering of people' and William Booth had a vision 'of the perishing lost,' both were impetuses for their future revival ministries.
- To a lesser or greater degree, the supernatural hand of God will move. Anything from instant healings, instant deliverance from demonic powers, to angels appearing or hearing angels singing or supernatural lights, such as orbs appearing. On occasions, Jesus Himself has appeared or a special fragrance wafts through the room or building as God's presence can be smelt. During the Shillong Revival (2006-2007) one man filmed angels flashing across the sky on his camera phone and I've seen the clip.
- It is not uncommon for non-Christians to fall, drop or sink to the ground under agonising conviction of sin (though some

do appear peaceful), being stricken by God. Some shake, tremble or jerk; others appear to be unconscious, in a coma or even dead, lifeless. They can stay in that state for hours or days, and have to be carried from the meeting or the field, depending on where God struck them.
- Some Christians will agonise in prayer for the lost, being burdened by the Holy Spirit. Their prayers will be of great intensity. Those under such burdens may fall to the ground and groan in the Spirit. Others will perspire (even when it is cool) and be as in great agony of soul. David Brainerd who saw revival amongst the North American Indians (1745-1746), knelt in the snow to pray. He prayed with such intensity and passion that the heat he generated melted the snow as he sunk lower into the ground! It was also said of the apostle James that his knees were like camels' knees, calloused because he spent so much time praying.
- Some of the physical phenomena during revival can be that non-Christians lose their sight, hearing, ability to speak or the ability to walk for a period of time. Some Christians can become drunk in the Spirit and have to be carried from meetings; others are incoherent for a time – intoxicated by the Spirit of God. We do not need to be alarmed at these things.

Rare Supernatural Events
- Buildings have been shaken in past revivals as the Holy Spirit comes down, as in Acts 4:31. This was witnessed during the Lewis Revival (1949-1952) when a granite house shook like a leaf as Duncan Campbell and others were inside praying. At the village of Phiro, Wokha District, Nagaland, during the 1960s, a building was physically shaken by the power of God. Others have felt the wind of the Spirit as He blows through a meeting, sometimes as a hurricane, as in the Congo Revival (1953-1957).
- On rare occasions, when the Holy Spirit has descended, people have seen flames as like on the Day of Pentecost. Prior to the Azusa Street Revival (1906-1909), in late February 1906, a house church was started at William Seymour's lodgings in North Bonnie Brae Street. When the Holy Spirit descended, many witnesses believed the house itself was literally on fire and the fire brigade was called out! At the Mukti Mission, India, in June 1905, immediately before the Mukti Revival (1905-1906), one of the senior

girls woke her teacher and informed her that one of the girls had received the Holy Spirit. The senior girl said, "I saw fire, ran across the room for a pail of water, and was about to pour it over her when I discovered she was not on fire!" Tongues of fire were also seen on 22 September 1957, in the town of Wokha, Nagaland, flickering above the roof of a church as the congregation were inside praying.

- On very rare occasions, the 'fire of the Lord' can appear. In 1959 in Nagaland, pastor Kegwahi Kent of the Sendenyu Baptist Church was at his home praying for the nations when the fire of God descended and illuminated his entire house. In the Ulster Revival (1859-1860) at county Antrim, Ireland, an old Roman Catholic woman was in her garden in the afternoon when 'a perfect flood of light as she imagined bathed her dwelling.' She rushed inside, cried out in mercy and 'fainted away.' She woke up saved! In Nagaland during a worship service, a member prophesied that God would send a pillar of fire as a sign and that all must confess and repent of their sins, but also that it would burn down an unbeliever's home. That night, between 8-9pm a pillar of fire shone above the church with pure light, yet it cast no shadow or reflection. The pillar soon vanished, but the thatched home of an unbeliever called Tesinlo Khing was in flames!

- On very rare occasions, during times of intense worship amidst revival, people or buildings can hover or lift off the ground! In 1954, during the Nagaland Awakening of the 1950s, in a village called Phiro; the church lifted off the ground about two to three feet as the believers were inside praying. Unbelievers saw this and the majority repented of their sins and turned to the Lord whilst some hardened their hearts! In a public meeting, Michael Howard, who has seen at least five revivals in Africa during the 1980s and 1990s, told those present that he was in a church worship service and some of the members, including himself were literally hovering in the air, levitating about a foot off the ground whilst worshiping the Lord!

- Also, the Holy Spirit has been recorded as lifting people over the heads (or backs if they are kneeling) in a church meeting and placing them at the front of the church – the place generally designated for sinners to come to public repentance and confession of Jesus Christ as their Lord and Saviour. I have only found this in print twice out of nearly three hundred revival related books that I have read. At one service at the Ibambi Mission Station in the North East Belgian Congo, in 1953, the entire congregation were prostrated before the Lord, 'screaming out their sins' when 'the head printer seemed to fly through the air over the backs of the people, landing on the floor, where he began crying out his sin.'

In a video interview which can be viewed online, Leonard Ravenhill, who was in his eighty-fourth year was recalling how in 1932, whilst in South Wales, UK, as a Christian worker in his mid twenties, he was introduced to Major Russell of the Salvation Army, who was in his eighties. Major Russell had shared an office with General Booth and told Ravenhill that in the early Salvation meetings, altar calls were never given. The old Major hesitantly told the following incident to young Ravenhill who told him that as he was a link to the past, so he would be a link to a future generation. After the preaching, General Booth would look at the workers and in a gruff voice, tell them to pray. Major Russell stated that at one meeting on a Sunday evening in a theatre on the Strand in London, after the General had told them to pray three times, people were literally transported, "bodily over their heads" by the Spirit and landed down at the front at the penitent form!

Carol Arnott speaking on *The 700 Club* to Pat Robinson, retold the incident that in a conference in north Australia, "When the Holy Spirit fell" the wife of a Pentecostal superintendent who was sat down was "taken up, did a double backflip and landed two rows back!"[2]

Revival and the Human Intellect
- On very rare occasions, and only during the duration of the revival, God may give a person the supernatural ability to be able to remember / recall everything they have heard or have ever read, so as to be able to teach more ably – supernatural intellect. This ability, which is instantaneous, is removed just as quickly as it has come. I have only read of this experience twice and two years is the longest duration I have come across. Dafydd (David) Morgan the Welsh revivalist, just prior to the outbreak of the Welsh Revival (1859-1860) awoke at 4am and realised that the Holy Spirit had illuminated his faculties so that he could remember everything of a religious nature that he had ever learnt or heard! This lasted for about two years.

- God can give remarkable stimulus to a person's mental powers and spiritual graces, which can last longer than the duration of a revival. Whilst this is not a rare feature, as it is similar to the previous one, I have included it here. The Holy Spirit gives them boldness to pray publicly or to evangelise whereas before they were afraid to. In the Ulster Revival (1859-1860) in Ireland, there are several recorded instances of this. In a sense it is like Jesus on the road to Emmaus with the two disciples when He opened their understanding and expounded the Scriptures to them (Luke 24:25). During the Imbai Revival (1936) in the Belgian Congo, after a sermon on Isaiah 58, even old women, who could not read and were not given to such consecutive thoughts, were able to use and pray every clause from Isaiah 58 in order.
- It has been known that during times of revival, the Holy Spirit has changed illiterate people into literates, without study and sometimes angels have assisted! This was prominent in China during the revival of the 1950s. There is at least one recorded instance of this in Nagaland, India, during the same period for a man called Jihlo Bukh.
- At other times, illiterate people will learn to read. During revival in the Sudan, which was part of the East African Revival (1930s-1950s), Bishop Oliver Allison of the Sudan asked one native pastor at a crowded congregation, "How is it that those elderly people seem to be able to read their Bible so well? How did they learn?" The pastor stated that they were some of the Praising Ones (the name given for the converts during the revival – because they praised the Lord so much!) and that the pastor and the people thought that they would never be able to learn to read. "But since they were 'revived' they have been so keen to read their Bible that they have learned to read in their special classes. It is the work of the Holy Spirit."
- On occasions, missionaries under the anointing of the Holy Spirit can preach fluently in a foreign tongue, but in normal day-to-day communication their ability is poor. Iba Warjri, an eight year old girl, from Nogrim Sadew, (17 miles from Shillong, in India), could not speak the Khasi language well and therefore usually used her own dialect. But during the Shillong Revival (2006-2007) when she had a revelation from God, she could speak it fluently! This has also happened outside times of revival during evangelistic

preaching or when a missionary is sharing the good news of the gospel one-on-one.
- In 1994 at a conference in Hamilton, Canada, a 'little girl' prophesied over John Arnot in perfect rhyme!

Revival Miracles

There are not many miracles in the Bible that have not been repeated and recorded in revival Church history – I am unaware of waters dividing, axe heads (or similar) floating or the dead being raised through a dead man (Elisha's bones, 2 Kings 13:21). Outside of Scripture I have never read about a shadow healing the sick. Raising the dead is more common! The Indonesian Revival (1964-1974) is perhaps the most supernatural revival the world has ever seen, with many personalities involved, followed by the Nagaland Revival of the 1950s and 1960s amongst tribal people.

In Indonesia, Muslims were affected as were nominal Christians and the animists or heathen. During the Indonesian Revival (1964-1974) under the Indonesian 'umbrella,' multitudes were converted and set free from demonic oppression, curses and sorcery were defeated. The blind saw, the deaf heard, the lame walked, the lepers were healed, the dead were raised, the waters were calmed, the rain was commanded to stop; all in the name of Jesus. Others were protected from the rain as it fell ten feet all around them and they continued to walk for miles in this state, whilst one team crossed a 300 yard wide river in flood, which was from 20-30 feet deep, the water did not go above their knees and their feet touched the bottom! People received visions and dreams, words of knowledge, prophecy and extraordinary discernment – knowing the secrets of men's hearts; whilst others received songs from God, a few were taught by angels (being illiterate) and Jesus even appeared to others. Some of the missionary teams ate supernatural food (manna from heaven). Another team had flames of fire over the churches where they preached at. When revival first came to Soe, on the island of Timor, the whole village saw flames above a church. Others saw supernatural light, which guided their footsteps by night, one mission team was transported by the Spirit (Ezekiel 3:12-15 and Acts 8:39), others witnessed food multiplying, and food not going-over in the tropical heat. In one place the house shook as they prayed (Acts 4:31). In addition, at least two churches saw water turning into non-alcoholic communion wine – this happened at two churches on at least ten and sixty occasions.

Chapter 19

Persecution – Verbally and Physically

'...What persecutions I endured...yes, and all who desire to live godly in Christ Jesus will suffer persecution' (2 Timothy 3:11-12).

Jesus was sinless, perfect and went about doing good yet He was hated and despised by many, and there were at least ten attempts on His life prior to His crucifixion! See Luke 4:24-29, Luke 19:47, Luke 20:19, John 7:19, 30, 44, John 8:37, 59, John 10:31, 39 and John 11:53. Jesus said, "If they persecute Me they *will also* persecute you" (John 15:20). Therefore all disciples of Jesus Christ will suffer persecution in some form because of their allegiance to the King of kings and Lord of lords.

Leaders of revival will suffer persecution and several have encountered attempted assassinations! Thankfully, most attempts have only been in the hearts and minds of the perpetrators who have turned up at a meeting with a sword, knife or gun etc., but have been struck by the mercy of the Spirit of Grace and Supplication and repented of their vile intentions.

On one occasion, a gun was pointed at Daniel Rowland, the eighteenth century Welsh revivalist; the trigger was pulled but it failed to fire, on another occasion they tried to blow him and his congregation up with gunpowder!

George Whitefield was attacked in his lodgings by a gentleman who said he was seeking Christ. He pulled out his sword to kill Whitefield who cried, "Murder, murder!" People came to his rescue!

The Methodists of the early eighteenth century were a despised sect and were accused of being Deists, Jesuits and Puritans; being in collusion with the Pope and even workers of the devil because they preached salvation by faith and not of works! As the decades passed and especially towards the last two to three decades of John Wesley's life (died in 1791), it became easier for those who were known as Methodists. In some towns and villages, John Wesley was escorted into the district as if he were royalty, with people lining the streets. It was a far cry from when he was shouted at, spat at, pelted with mud, stones and even dead pieces of cat! On one occasion, a bull was let loose in the crowd when he was field-preaching! At other times, drunken horsemen would ride through the crowd and it was not unknown for the parson (the Church of England vicar), to employ mobs, ply them with drink, and encourage them to bang drums, to drown out the preacher's voice, tell them to get up to other mischief and encourage them to riot! In Barnsley, Yorkshire, 'bating the Methodist' as one author wrote 'was a favourite pastime with those of the rougher sort.'

On many occasions, the houses in which John Wesley or other Methodist preachers were lodging at or preaching in were damaged. They and the buildings were pelted with stones and rocks, once, a firebomb was thrown through the window! On a few occasions, walls or even the house itself were torn down by the violence of the mobs! John Wesley could hold his own, though he was just five feet tall and weighed less than 126lbs. He would try to find the ringleader and confront him. On most occasions, they would be subdued and sometimes converted! One such person was a pugilist (boxer) who became Wesley's bodyguard for a time and as a new Christian, he threatened "to lump" (to punch) anyone who tried to disturb the peace when Wesley was in town!

John Wesley had no qualms in speaking to the local magistrates in seeking for justice and financial compensation for damages caused to his hosts. If the magistrate was in collusion with the rioters he would go higher up the chain of authority and get his justice. If the offenders were repentant over their actions then he would not press charges, but compensation for damaged property was always expected.

Rhodesian born, Michael Howard, has seen at least five revivals across Africa during the 1980s and 90s. He has had stones thrown at him. At one "checkpoint" in Moçambique (Mozambique), a rebel soldier put a gun through the open window of his vehicle and threatened to kill him. Howard thrust it away and declared to the soldier that he could not kill him! He got out his vehicle and preached the gospel to the soldiers. I believe there were about twenty soldiers present and they all got down on their knees and surrendered to Jesus Christ.

Christian Bodyguards and Preventive Measures

'All who desire to live godly in Christ Jesus will suffer persecution' (2 Timothy 3:12). Even Jesus for a time did not walk in Judea, but moved to Galilee because He knew the Jews would try to kill Him (John 7:1). Christians are martyred for their faith, 'the souls of those who have been slain for the Word of God and for the testimony they held' (Revelation 6:9). Someone once said that you cannot have a true [open-air] revival without a riot! The apostle

Paul can confirm that statement – read the Acts of the Apostles. Within some churches and chapels, they have a space in front of the pulpit called the "Big Seat" where the elders sit and face the congregation. This was birthed from the occasions where people would try to mount the pulpit and assault the preacher!

John Knox who became the Scottish Reformer, used to carry a two-handled sword to defend his master, George Wishart who was a fiery preacher and prayer warrior. Wishart ordered Knox to leave him in January of 1546 knowing his fate, saying "...One is sufficient for sacrifice" and Wishart was martyred.

Young Canadian evangelist, Oswald J. Smith, in the summer of 1913 was on his way to preach at Hog's Hollow, Kentucky, when conspirators set an ambush, pulled out their guns and fired, thankfully nobody was hurt. He went on to see revival in the Russian Mission Fields of Europe in 1929 and beyond and became the famed pastor of Toronto People's Church, Canada, a church which supported more missionaries than any other in the world.

In 1949, Billy Graham, an evangelist for Youth For Christ was preaching in downtown Los Angeles when a man shot at him with a pistol. Graham has preached to more than 215 million people in person and in November 2016, celebrated his 98th birthday.

Carlos Annacondia from the Argentine Revival (1982-1997) after a meeting in La Boca, in 1985, was celebrating his birthday with his ministry team when some hoodlums approached and threatened them. One of them pulled a knife and ran towards him. Pablo Bottari shouted, "I bind you in the name of Jesus" and the young man fell to the ground subdued.

Prior to 1998, on one Saturday night at Brownsville Church, during the Brownsville Revival (1995-2000) in Pensacola, America, a toxic gas bomb was ignited within the church. The back of the church had to be evacuated and the air conditioning shut down. At the same time a bomb of the same type was released in a nearby grocery store and those within the store became very ill, though those at the church suffered no ill affect.

On one Saturday, after a Ladies Meeting, a man verbally harassed Brenda Kilpatrick, wife of John Kilpatrick of Brownsville Assembly Of God. This was during the Brownsville Revival (1995-2000). She boldly proclaimed the name of Jesus and claimed the victory (then the man was subdued).

In March 2003, Bill Wilson of Metro Ministries, in America, was mugged on the streets not far from the ministries headquarters. A gun was put in his mouth and in the struggle that ensued he was shot and the bullet went out through his cheek.

Todd Bentley of the controversial Lakeland Outpouring (2008) also known as the Lakeland Revival or Healing Revival which was beamed live to 215 nations of the world via God TV and webcasts, openly stated on air about the death threats and hate mail he had received. He said, "I can't go out or be in the park with my children without at least ten people coming up to me; *most* of them friendly." His wife (whom he later divorced) also needed security when she went out.[1] See the last section of chapter 27 for more information regarding the Lakeland Outpouring.

Some present day high profile ministers do have bodyguards whilst others live in high security monitored homes. During the Brownsville Revival (1995-2000), Steve Hill had a bodyguard who kept close to him when off the platform praying for people during the services. I would not be surprised if some ministers wear an executive stab / bulletproof vest that are very discreet and can be worn under a suit.

High profile churches and especially mega churches have security guards. On Sunday, 10 December 2007, Matthew Murray, entered the east entrance of the New Life's Church in Colorado Springs, America, firing his rifle. In the car park (parking lot), he had killed two teenagers, injuring their father and others. Murray was carrying two handguns, an assault rifle and over 1,000 rounds of ammunition. About 7,000 people were on the church campus at the time of the shooting.

Jeanne Assam, a member of the church and a security guard who is licensed to carry a weapon, identified herself and shot the gunman dead. When asked by a reporter if she felt like a hero, Assam said, "I wasn't just going to wait for him to do further damage." New Life's Senior Pastor Brady Boyd called Assam a real hero because Murray had enough ammunition on him to cause a lot of damage and she saved the lives of fifty to one hundred people.

Revival and Persecution
- Revival sometimes precedes a time of judgment or persecution. This is to prepare the Church for the hardships to come; this was clearly seen ten to fifteen years after the revival in the Belgian Congo of 1953 when civil war coupled with the Simba Uprising / Rebellion tore the country apart.
- At other times, amidst persecution, revival can breakout; this was most clearly seen in the Indonesian Revival (1964-1974), the Nagaland Awakenings (1950s and 1960s)

and the revival in China from the twentieth century onwards, where the Church has seen phenomenal growth during great tribulation.
- Also, revival can cause persecution; this is what happened during the Eggon Revival (1930s) in Northern Nigeria, when former spirit worshipers, including spirit priests came and burned their fetishes and followed Christ. But this persecution purged the Church and the opposition came from the senior tribe leader who was financially hit in pocket by the lack of offerings to the spirits, which became his property.
- Sometimes persecution comes from the Church, as the leadership or the denomination with its traditions, rituals and rote, coupled with empty form and ceremony fail to understand the move of God. Four to five hundred years ago it was a crime across parts of Europe to have a Bible in your own language! Services were held in Latin, a language that the common people could not understand! The Reformation beginning in Germany in 1517 under Martin Luther changed this, and Protestantism was at the fore. When revival broke out in the church in 1960 during the Nagaland Awakening in North East India; some Christians who had an assurance of salvation returned to their village in the northern Sumi territory and were stoned, beaten, tortured and their Bibles were taken from them. One day, in the same location, the villages joined together with three others and stripped fifteen women revivalists to the flesh and paraded them naked before all the people – these shameful acts were carried out by the so-called Church, by people who professed to be Christians! But, by the patient witness and love of these Christians, some of whom had the gift of healing; within a few years the whole village was touched by the fire of revival!

Some dislike the work of revival because they are not the instruments of it. Others have been misinformed of the nature of the work. Others have been offended because they have never experienced anything like it, and if they did, they would have to begin again in their theology and build on a new foundation of Scriptural truths. Others dislike the work because it confirms and supports that which they have not embraced because of their prejudice, which they cannot easily shake off – William Cooper of Boston, America, November 1741.[2]

Chapter 20

The Old and New Wine

Jesus said, "No one puts a piece of unshrunk cloth on an old garment; for the patch pulls away from the garment, and the tear is made worse. Nor do people put new wine into old wineskins, or else the wineskins break, the wine is spilled, and the wineskins are ruined. But they put new wine into new wineskins, and both are preserved" (Matthew 9:16-17).

Opposition from the Old and the New

There is a danger that some of those who witnessed the last move of God may oppose a new move of God. This is because it looks different than the previous one, but Jesus stated that new wine must have new wineskins and that those who have tasted the old *do not immediately* desire the new, because they believe the old is better (Luke 5:38-39). In genuine revival, there are diversities of operation by the Holy Spirit, but the essential features are the same. The Holy Spirit may come as a dove or as a refiner's fire, like falling dew or an earthquake amid thunder and lightning! On the other hand, much of what is called or claimed to be revival is not heaven-sent revival but man-made delusions of emotional excitement and soulish pleasures. It is often human propaganda and profit to promote and stimulate human desires, and these 'works of the flesh' are to be avoided and shunned.

- There will always be opposition to revivals and new moves of God. There are always a minority of Christians who resist change.
- Some Christians who have faithfully and persistently prayed for revival have rejected it when the Holy Spirit came, as it did not line up with their preconceived ideas.
- Revival can come so unexpectedly and in a guise which may be different than what is expected or perceived that it is initially rejected and / or not believed to be from God. In 1860, Andrew Murray was the new minister of a Dutch Reformed church in Worcestor, Southern Africa. He had been praying for revival. A prayer meeting of sixty young people led by his assistant was being held in the hall when Divine thunder rolled in and shook the building – revival broke out! Murray was summoned and amidst all the

unusual manifestations of loud and also murmured intercession, he told the congregation to be silent – he was ignored. Thrice he tried to calm and stop the congregation, not realising it was the answer, he and many others had been praying for. Bewildered, Murray walked out of the hall and exclaimed, "God is the God of order and here everything is in confusion!" It took some time before he was convinced that this was the nature of the Divine visitation. A heavenly disorder and a solemn commotion!

- Others will stand aloof when revival comes, not being sure whether it is from God or the devil. This aloofness, even among leaders or missionaries may only last for a day or two, as what happened at a few of the WEC mission stations during the Congo Revival (1953-1957). But when revival came to the Union Seminary in Shekow, China in 1933, the students embraced it, heart and soul yet the teachers stood aloof. Rev. Erling Gilje from Denmark noted: 'There was so much in the revival methods and manifestations that they did not understand.'

- Revival within a denomination, network of churches or a mission organisation can make people impatient of the organisation that seems so powerless, because it is not fully embraced or endorsed and / or certain key leaders stand at a distance with a critical, sometimes even scoffing attitude. During the Ruanda Revival (1937-1950s) which flowed into the East Africa Revival (1930s-1950s), the Balokole (saved ones) and Abaka (those on fire!) caused tension in the early 1940s amongst the Church Mission Society (CMS) Ruanda Mission which was Anglican. It nearly split the CMS Mission in East Africa because the Balokole and the Abaka continually questioned the reality of those who professed Christ when they saw no life. For senior leaders to be told that they were not born again or that they had not the Holy Spirit was deeply resented by many, whilst for others it was a God-sent rebuke and a wake-up call. A missionary noted that 'it sometimes arose out of confusion between the truths of justification [conversion] and sanctification [a deeper work of the Holy Spirit giving victory over sin (holiness) and fullness of joy].'

In 1945, A. C. Stanley Smith, in his book, *Road to Revival – The Story of the Ruanda Mission* wrote about the revival at Mukono Theological College (1936) in Uganda. Thirty-two years later, Bill

Butler in *Hill Ablaze* wrote about prayer for revival beginning in 1939, by some twenty-five students at the Bishop Tucker Theological College at Mukono – they are the one and the same College. In 1936, the Diamond Jubilee of the Uganda Church (Anglican) was approaching and the Bishop knew that the greatest need for the Church was revival and planned that missions should be held throughout the diocese.

Bill Butler stated that most of the students of the Mukono Theological College in 1936 had no assurance or clear understanding of salvation, and 'most reflected the attitude widely prevailing in the Church of Uganda at that time; that provided they were baptised and confirmed and not *discovered* in any particular wrong doing, they were Christians. Stealing in the College was rife and to some extent, were drinking and immorality.'

A. C. Stanley Smith wrote: 'The key to the whole situation in Uganda was the Theological College at Mukono, where the Christian leaders of the Church were trained. Here was the place where revival needed to start' and it did!

In 1941, the Warden of Bishop Tucker Theological College, Uganda, who had himself been blessed through the aftermath of the Welsh Revival (1904-1905) had little sympathy which he deemed a 'subversive movement,' the Balokole (saved ones) of the East Africa Revival (1930s-1950s). He had embraced the aftermath of one move of God, yet rejected the present one.

The Warden implemented three new rules: No student was to leave his dormitory before 6am; they were forbidden to meet together in groups of three or more, and no student was permitted to preach inside the College without the Warden's permission. Most of the students were married men with years of Christian service behind them and not accustomed to flouting authority. They pleaded with the College authorities to rescind the rule. Though after prayer and fasting, in the half term holiday, they knew it was better to obey God than man, and met once again at 4am to pray for revival and worship the Lord.

After their expulsions in late 1941, their licenses to preach in the Church of Uganda were withdrawn. They were branded as 'rebels,' but this event proved to be God's means of scattering them across Uganda, for revival was to breakout in the late 1940s, and these former students, amongst others, would be the revivalists across East Africa.

A. C. Stanley Smith wrote: 'Every movement of the Spirit sweeping through a lifeless church makes some people impatient of the organisation which seems so powerless. It would be so simple to break away and start afresh. We are convinced that there are far too many denominations as it is.'[1]

'The Church in Ruanda is clear that God's will for us is to live out the new life within the Church of which we are already members. Our Mission is a Church of England Mission. We believe that communion with the Church not only ensures for the African Church a share in the rich heritage of the past, but supplies a basis which can be both broad and flexible enough to allow the indigenous Church free scope for development under the guidance of the Holy Spirit…. We do not transport the whole Church of England system into Africa. The main essentials of its organised life and its doctrine ensure that the African Church shall have the heritage of the past; but we plead for simplicity that there may be room for truly African expression in the worship and form of the Church.'[2]

The Incompatibility of the Old and New School
- Jesus said that new wine, must be poured into new wineskins, thus preserving both, otherwise the skin will burst and the wine will be spoilt (Matthew 9:17 and Mark 2:22). In revival, views of what God can do, cannot do, will do or will not do may have to change. Otherwise the Holy Spirit will do a work and could pass us by and that would be a tragedy.
- There is a danger that those who embrace the revival, the new school, reject the traditionalists, the old school. By not seeing eye-to-eye, the new school may unwittingly break the spirit of unity by not having the bond of peace. The Evangelical Revival (1739-1791) had lots of different personalities and views; see Appendix C. As Christians it is wrong to reject brethren who are unable to embrace a move of God. If they are born again, then they are part of the family of God. Some people have all their lives been taught a certain doctrine or been loyal to their denomination, or a member of *their* church for decades and are simply unable to accept certain things, or are bound, or hold dear to *their* traditions. If we denounce them (or vice versa) then surely we are only hindering the fulfilment of Jesus' prayer in John 17 – "That they may be one" (v22). If we do not "love one another" as brethren, then how will the world know that we are Jesus' disciples? (John 13:34-35).
- Even during revival when the Holy Spirit begins to move, there are those who reject His gifts – simply believing that

the gifts of the Holy Spirit ceased at the death of the apostles. There are no Scriptures to back this up; quite the contrary, and nearly two thousand years of Church history disprove it.
- Some denominations will embrace the fruits of revival such as: renewed or revived Christians, new converts and transformed lives, yet still vehemently hold to *their* doctrine – though it does differ from member to member. They may still reject the Reviver – the Holy Spirit, or when the revival has ceased will go back to the way things were prior to the revival. This is especially true in regard to women who were raised up in revival with powerful ministries and afterwards were no longer permitted to speak in church.

Leaders who Disapproved of Elements of Revival

President of the Norwegian Lutheran Mission in south western Honan and north Hupeh, Rev. Olav Espegren, writing from Nanyang, in January 1934, noted: 'That the revival is still going forward at all of the stations in that field.... In a couple of places there have appeared signs of an ecstatic movement resembling heathen "spirit-possession." In this condition, they will claim to speak on God's behalf, dispense forgiveness of sins, etc. Also, he mentions signs of the Pentecostal movement which had taken firmer hold to the east. He voices surprise that the Chinese, who are so practically minded in the affairs of the world, can be swept off their feet so easily when it comes to religious things. A very subtle temptation comes in the form of a desire for holiness; and the fullness of the Spirit and holiness seem so easily achieved through this one ecstatic experience. He emphasizes the need for responsible shepherds who...exercise authority.'[3]

In 1934, Miss Erva Moody, of the American Lutheran Mission, in Tsingtao, China, wrote from personal observation in connection with the revival. She mentioned 'among desirable manifestations the following: Ability to lift the voice in public in prayer to Almighty God; eagerness to witness, whereas formerly there was no desire to witness; deeper appreciation of the meaning of stewardship; enthusiasm for reading and studying the Bible. On the other hand there are the undesirable manifestations such as: babbling, which is called "tongues," and believed by some to be an indication of the fullness of the Holy Spirit; Pharisee-ism, a pious attitude eliciting men's praise; cases of people possessed by evil spirits instead of the Holy Spirit; a feeling of superiority over a person who does not see eye-to-eye in the revival movement.'[4]

Chapter 21

Divine or Demonic – True and False

'Beloved, while I was very diligent to write to you concerning our common salvation, I found it necessary to write to you exhorting you to contend earnestly for the faith which was once for all delivered to the saints. For certain men have crept in unnoticed, who long ago were marked out for this condemnation, ungodly men, who turn the grace of God into licentiousness and deny the only Lord God and our Lord Jesus Christ' (Jude 3-4).

Divine or Demonic

A "revival" may be part of the River of God where blessing flows or it may be a stagnant pond because not everything that is called "revival" is. Is the water muddy, murky, polluted and dirty or holy, heavenly, glorifying and God-exalting? The Bible tells us to 'test the spirits' (1 John 4:1) because there is much which is false and of satanic origin, coupled with deceiving spirits and their lies which are doctrines of demons! (1 Timothy 4:1-3).

On the other hand, we should not write off a "move of God" or discount the leader(s) as not being a brother or sister in the Lord because of questionable or dubious practices (within reason) without finding out the facts for ourselves. The person(s) may be a bit off beam in some areas, but still hold to orthodox teaching of Christianity. They may think we are off beam also!

It is also one thing to say, "I'm not sure" – but quite another to denounce a work as counterfeit or demonic! Dave Roberts, editor of *Alpha* magazine wrote: 'Open-minded doubt is biblical. Closed-minded unbelief is what God abhors.' The fountain of revival can be open but some still stay parched because they will not come and drink of the refreshing life-giving waters.

Jesus stated that John the Baptist, who preached repentance (Mark 1:4) did not come eating bread nor drinking wine yet the Pharisees and lawyers rejected the counsel of God and said He had a demon! (Luke 7:28-35). They also said that Jesus was a glutton who drunk to excess and then derided Him for being a friend of tax collectors and sinners. Jesus' response was, "Wisdom is justified by her children" (Luke 7:35) because fruit, changed lives and transformed people (Luke 3:8) speak for themselves.

During the 1859 revival in Ireland, there were many people claiming the work to be from the evil one. One country boy who had been affected by the revival stood on a stone and addressed the people in a street in Coleraine, saying, "Some people call it the work of the devil. All I can say to this is, that up to last week I have been serving the devil as well as I could, and I am sure he was well pleased with my service; but if he is employing me now, he is so far changed that I would not know him to be the same man!"[1]

Neither Jesus nor the apostles ever said or wrote that we judge a work (as whether being from God or not) by its phenomena (physical manifestations), but by its fruit, or by the lack of it. A good tree bears good fruit, a bad tree bears bad fruit. "You shall know them by their fruit," said Jesus (Matthew 7:15-20). Is it good fruit or bad fruit, from God or the devil, Divine origin or demonic, is it the Holy Spirit or a hellish spirit, from above or from below?

Revival is 'a sign that is spoken against' for 'the fall and rising of many' because God's presence will reveal the true state of people's hearts (Luke 2:35). When Jesus healed the woman with a spirit of infirmity on the Sabbath, who was bent over (Luke 13:10-17), and healed the bedridden man (John 5:1-16), the religious people (Synagogue ruler and the Jews) were not happy! Some people are jealous and prejudiced against it! Revival is a reproach to formality, hypocrisy and lukewarmness.

A. C. Stanley Smith noted that among the Ruanda missionaries during 1941-1946, 'there was a great deal of distressing division' and at one time, there were three parties. 'Those who threw themselves right into the Revival Movement confident that the Holy Spirit would deal with the difficulties. A central group, who while rejoicing in the movement as of God, were critical and apprehensive of some of its features and so felt excluded from real fellowship. Thirdly, those who were so troubled at what they thought were dangerous and evil tendencies in practice and in doctrine as to feel they must take strong measures of control.'[2]

At one mission station during the Congo Revival (1953-1957), the missionaries thought a hurricane was coming as the wind of the Spirit blew through the building and came upon many. During the revival, numerous shy native women shouted, "Hallelujah!" at the top of their voices. Others shook all over and collapsed on the floor in groans and travail as intercession for souls was birthed in them, whilst others groaned and writhed under conviction of sin. Some people in different mission stations saw holy light or a bright light as part of a vision. People were slain in the meetings and would tremble and jerk uncontrollably or perspire and fall off their seats and roll in the mud in agony of soul. At first some of the missionaries were naturally hesitant about these manifestations were they from God or not? However, as people came through to victory and testified of their sin in front of all, knowing that they had been pardoned by God through the shed blood of Jesus Christ, the wavering and hesitant missionaries knew it to be a genuine heaven-sent revival. Also, mentally disturbed people were set free from demons, by the power of God, in the name of Jesus Christ.

A senior missionary of the Congo Revival wrote: 'Grieve not the Spirit. Criticism, or attributing to the flesh that which is of the Spirit, can hinder revival tremendously; let us not be guilty of either.'[3]

Some in the meetings in the Congo would try to imitate the manifestations of the Spirit as seen upon other people, whether by shaking, jerking or just getting over-excited in the flesh, trying to 'work up' the blessing. Those in charge of the meetings who had spiritual oversight rebuked those who were in the flesh and instructed accordingly as there is a difference between hindering the Spirit and working with the Spirit. Those with positions of authority who negate their responsibility to exhort and to correct in the spirit of meekness and humility, sin and grieve the Holy Spirit when they fail to do their duty.

A. C. Stanley Smith wrote: 'The years 1940-45 were times of much conflict arising out of the [Ruanda] Revival [1937-1950s]. The Muyebe Convention [of 1942] opened with a scene of wild tumultuous welcome of the Africans coming from the CMS stations. It took place in full view of the European delegates and many of them were shocked at what seemed to them hysteria or worse.' An African leader said, "What is the matter with you Europeans? Down below [where the majority of the delegates were] there are souls blessed and saved; but up here [on the platform] you are all anxious and worried."

A. C. Stanley Smith wrote: 'They felt rebuked and yet they were passing through a conflict which if won would mean much to the whole cause of Christ. The African joy was a bit too exuberant; but the Europeans had to learn to leave the African to express his joy in an African way and to sing to his own rhythm.'[4]

Jonathan Edwards noted that you can be astonished at a move of God but not convinced (that it is from God). He noted that many ministers are guilty because of their silence and are in secret opposition – are you for Christ or against Him? (Mark 9:40). They do not give God the glory. For those who are quiet, does the principle of prudence justify a *long* refraining? Prudence can be the greatest imprudence! Those who are silent and inactive, like

Meroz, may be cursed because they did not come to the help of the Lord (Judges 5:23). Are you for or against the Holy Spirit?

Warnings and Wisdom

In November 1885, missionaries to China, Stanley Smith and C.T. Studd wrote to a friend in Cambridge, England: 'Let Christian men wait on the Lord to know his mind and will as to where He would have them to go.... There are some of whom God says, "I sent them not, yet they ran and prophesied [Jeremiah 23:21, 32]." God will guide those who wait on Him.

'Let them beware of thinking, "Now that I have made up my mind to this 'great sacrifice' in going out to the heathen, I shall grow in grace very easily, temptations will be almost gone, and worldliness will have no power over me." As a matter of fact, temptations are far stronger and more subtle.

'Unless in the foreign field they are prepared to find their joy and satisfaction in the Living God, and not in circumstances (neither being discouraged by failure, nor puffed up by success), they will not have with them the weapon which is "their strength," namely, "the joy of the Lord [Nehemiah 8:10]."

'Let them beware of riding one side of truth to death; take the whole Word. Beware of the devil who is strong here; and beware of fanaticism – by "fanaticism" we mean unbalanced truths. Let them beware of being carried away with everything new.

'Lastly, let them seek to be led of God and not of man. Blessed be God, *all* these dangers are avoided by being in communion with God – abiding in Christ.'[5]

Principal John D. Drysdale of Emmanuel Bible School, Birkenhead, UK, wrote: 'The early Church was forceful and fearless in her language. She did not hesitate to call men liars who denied the Incarnation; who walked in darkness (sin) and yet professed to have fellowship with God, or who professed to love God and yet hated their brothers [1 John 1:1-10]. She boldly declared that 'Whosoever sins has not seen Him, or known Him' [1 John 3:6]. She declared that a man was deceived who professed to be righteous if he did not live righteously. She declared that if a man abided in Christ he would 'Walk as He walked' [1 John 2:6]. He would be righteous – 'Even as He is righteous,' [1 John 3:7] and that every man who hoped to see Him as He is – 'Purifies himself even as He is pure' [1 John 3:3]. Yes, the Holy Spirit cannot lie! And we would do well to treat with suspicion all contrary teaching, and treat it as 'man's traditions' rather than sound doctrine.'[6]

Chapter 22

Enemies of the Cross

'For many walk, of whom I have told you often, and now tell you even weeping, that they are enemies of the cross of Christ, whose end is their destruction...' (Philippians 3:18-19a).

Enemies of God, haters of the cross of Christ are scattered throughout the Bible and engraved on the pages of Church history, therefore should we expect it to be any different today or any less during times of revival? The devil, knowing that his time is short will rage as we are nearing the end of the age (Revelation 20:1-3, 8).

Old Testament Enemies
- Various kings of Egypt (Exodus 1:12-14 and Exodus 5:14).
- Korah, Dathan, Abiram and On, Israelites, rebelled against Moses' leadership, and they died (Numbers 16:1-35).
- Tobiah and Sanballat tried to lure Nehemiah into a trap and even sent letters to try to frighten him (Nehemiah 2:19 and Nehemiah 6:1-19).
- Geshem the Arab despised the Jews, laughed them to scorn and tried to do mischief against Nehemiah (Nehemiah 2:19 and Nehemiah 6:2).
- Haman tried to annihilate the Jews (Esther chapters 3-9).
- Jannes and Jambres resisted Moses (2 Timothy 3:8).
- Jesus spoke about the Jews' forefathers who shed the blood of the prophets (Matthew 23:29-33).

New Testament Enemies, Strays and Deceivers
- King Herod tried to kill the promised King, the Messiah and ordered the death of all the males in Bethlehem who were aged two or under (Matthew 2:16).
- Judas, one of the twelve disciples, the son of perdition betrayed Jesus for money (Matthew 26:14-16, 47-49).
- Simon the sorcerer was converted and baptised during a time of revival! He thought he could buy the ability to impart the Holy Spirit. Peter declared, "Your heart is not right in the sight of God...you are poisoned by bitterness and bound by iniquity" (Acts 8:9-23).

- Hymenaeus and Alexander 'suffered shipwreck' after rejecting the faith (1 Timothy 1:19-20).
- Hymenaeus (as above) and Philetus strayed concerning the truth and spread malicious lies, thus overthrowing the faith of some (2 Timothy 2:16-18).
- Demas 'having loved this present world' forsook the apostle Paul (2 Timothy 4:10).
- Alexander the coppersmith did the apostle Paul much harm and resisted his words (2 Timothy 4:14-15).
- Some professing believers are insubordinate, they are deceivers who profess to know God 'but by their works deny Him' (Titus 1:10-11, 18).
- Diotrephes, a self promoting leader of the church told his congregation lies and expelled those who followed elder John (3 John 9-19).

Enemies and Tares

An enemy is not necessarily one who is on the outside, but can be on the inside and they may set up camp very near you. Tobiah hated the Jews yet wormed his way into the temple of the Lord and even set up his home! (Nehemiah 13:4-9). An enemy can be a secret informer (Nehemiah 6:10) or false brethren who have come to spy (Galatians 2:4-5). 'For certain men have crept in unnoticed, who long ago were marked out for this condemnation, ungodly men who turn the grace of our God into licentiousness and deny the only Lord God and our Lord Jesus Christ' (Jude 4).

An enemy can also be a tare, a plant from the devil who has infiltrated your church, Bible College / Seminary or ministry. Some tares having been taken captive to do the devil's will (2 Timothy 2:26 and 2 Timothy 3:6) can be set free (delivered from demons) whilst others can only be distinguished and separated at the end of the age (Matthew 13:26-40). A tare can be so deceived and deluded that they really believe that God is with them, yet they are fighting against Him, by opposing His servants. 'But evil men and impostors will grow worse and worse, deceiving and be deceived' (2 Timothy 3:13). They can be wolves in sheep's clothing (Matthew 7:15). See *Tares and Weeds in Your Church* by R. B. Watchman.

An enemy can also be one who sits in silent opposition with a smile on their face but with anger and bitterness in their heart. The silent opposition, by not jumping into the River of God can reveal their lack of commitment to the things of God. (However they may be undecided and have honest doubts and questions). Jesus stated that we are 'either for Him or against Him,' there is no place in between, that is the sin of indifference. If we are for Jesus then we are for the things of God, the Father, the Son *and* the Holy Spirit. Let us not reject the Spirit, as Jesus came to destroy the works of the evil one so that we could have abundant life (John 10:10, Hebrews 2:14 and 1 John 3:8). Jesus promised the Holy Spirit to those who believe in Him and that they would do "greater works" (John 14:12-17 and John 16:7-14), but if we reject Him, we insult the Spirit of Grace and trample the Son of God underfoot (Hebrews 10:28-29).

Demons (evil spirits) cannot hide before the manifest presence of God and they will frequently rise to the surface and expose themselves, often to the dismay of the person who is manifesting under these demonic influences or those present. Jesus at the beginning of His ministry cast out 'an unclean spirit' from a man who was crying out. The man convulsed and the demon cried out with a loud voice (via the man's voice box) before it was expelled (Mark 1:21-26). Demons should be cast out or off a person by the brethren in the mighty name of Jesus Christ of Nazareth. During times of revival, under the Holy Spirit's dealings or when God's presence descends some will writhe on the floor (or other physical manifestation) and sometimes the demons will flee by themselves and thus look for a new home. At other times, these open manifestations, e.g. shrieks or slithering etc. reveal to the body of Christ that a person has demons and needs to be delivered in Jesus' mighty name.[1]

Rejecters of Revival

There will be those who pray earnestly and persistently for revival who will reject it when revival comes, because it did not come how they had anticipated it. Religious rulers had been praying for the Messiah to come for over one thousand years and when He came (Jesus), many rejected Him, because He did not fit in with their preconceived ideas, regardless of the fact He fulfilled the prophecies and signs concerning Himself as stated in the Scriptures, which they proclaimed to follow and ritually observed.

Dr. Kurt Koch in a rebuttal that his book *The Revival In Indonesia* contained falsified reports, in a small folder wrote: 'In all revivals there are people, indeed even pious people, who stand beside the revival and are not caught up by it. God performs mighty deeds and pious pastors and Pharisees stand alongside cursing or criticising. At all of God's special acts there were those who stood alongside. The disciples of Jesus testified that the Lord had arisen. He had appeared among them. The Pharisees said that the disciples had stolen His body and now they were spreading these lies. Whomever has not himself been seized by the spirit of revival and by the Holy Spirit will not understand a revival (1 Corinthians 2:14). What we declare and write often reflects the condition of our own heart. One can possess a good deal of orthodox theology and yet stand alongside.'

Sadly, there are Christians, who have an unteachable spirit; they have a know-all attitude and a pre-programmed mindset and will not listen to truth, reason or even Scripture. When Jesus was resurrected, some 'worshipped Him,' whilst 'some doubted' (Matthew 28:17).

Some people are only happy in promoting *their* denomination, or pet doctrine to the exclusion of everything else and as the Proverbs declare, 'A fool has no delight in understanding, but in expressing his own heart' (Proverbs 18:2). It is like casting pearls before swine (Matthew 7:6), and fools despise the wisdom of words (Proverbs 23:9). If you have been on a Christian forum, you would have undoubtedly come across these people. They do not ask questions because they are unsure, they ask so that they can give their own opinion or distorted view regardless of any other point of view, without Scriptural backup, and they are adamant that they are right and everyone else is wrong. Let us also remember that 'any fool can start a quarrel' (Proverbs 20:3) and we are to 'avoid foolish and ignorant disputes, knowing that they generate strife and a servant of the Lord must not quarrel but be gentle' (2 Timothy 2:23-24).

The Devil Instigates Riots

The Bible is full of instances where the enemy is aroused at the things of God and pours out his vengeance through men and women against God's servants. The prophet Micaiah was punched on the cheek for telling the prophets via the Lord that they had a lying spirit and were therefore deceived. Jezebel killed hundreds of the Lord's prophets and followers; Jeremiah was put in the stocks and also placed in a dried up well, whilst his messages from the Lord were ignored for twenty-three years as he spoke the Word of God. Jesus was whipped, beaten and then crucified and Stephen became the first Christian martyr. The apostle Paul was stoned, whipped, beaten and imprisoned on numerous occasions.

Saul (later renamed Paul) believed he was doing the work of God, persecuting the followers of Christ; with a flash of light he fell to the ground and whilst on the floor, Jesus asked him, "Why are you persecuting Me?" 'Trembling and astonished' Saul asked what he should do and when he opened his eyes he was unable to see! (Acts 10:1-9). Saul was blinded by the Lord for three days.

Whenever you do the work of God you can expect opposition even when the work is going well and bearing fruit. The apostle Paul and Barnabas were on their first missionary journey when they encountered opposition, in most of the places that they went, from Jews and Gentiles, the religious and the non-religious.

The apostle Paul preached in the synagogue in Antioch, in Pisidia, with great success, 'many of the Jews and devout proselytes' heeded their message (Acts 13:14-43). On the following Sabbath, 'almost the whole city came together to hear the Word of God' but the Jews seeing the multitudes, 'were filled with envy; and contradicting and blaspheming, they opposed the things spoken by Paul.' Both Paul and Barnabas 'grew bold' and stated that as the Jews rejected the truth they would 'turn to the Gentiles' and more people were won to the Lord. 'But the Jews stirred up the devout and prominent women and the chief men of the city, raised up persecution against Paul and Barnabas and expelled them from their region' (Acts 13:44-52).

In Iconium, Paul and Barnabas entered the synagogue and preached the Word of the Lord and 'a great number of multitudes of Jews and Greeks believed. But the unbelieving Jews stirred up the Gentiles and poisoned their minds against the brethren.' They stayed there a long time preaching with signs and wonders following. But 'the multitude of the city was divided; part sided with the Jews, and part with the apostles.' But when both Jews and Gentiles violently attempted 'to abuse and stone them' they fled to the cities of Lycaonia (Acts 14:1-6).

Paul and Silas went into the synagogue in Thessalonica and preached. A great multitude of devout Greeks and many of the leading women followed them, which led to a riot. The people said, "These who have turned the world upside down have come here too" (Acts 17:1-9).

Paul and Silas were sent to Berea and they preached in the synagogue. Many believed, both Greeks and prominent women of the city, but Jews from Thessalonica stirred up the crowd and another riot began! (Acts 17:10-15).

Paul preached on Mars Hill, in the midst of the Areopagus in Athens, to the pagans, 'some mocked' but 'some men joined him and believed' (Acts 17:22-34). Paul also taught in the school at Tyrannus for two years and all who dwelt in Asia (Minor) heard the Word of the Lord, both Jews and Greeks, but *some were hardened* and 'spoke evil of the Way' (Acts 19:8-9).

Chapter 23

False and Counterfeit Revival

Jesus said, "...I will build My Church, and the gates of Hades shall not prevail against it" (Matthew 16:18).

Not Everything that Glitters is Gold
There is a saying which became popular in the days of the gold rush, 'Not everything that glitters is gold.' (Its origins go back to the twelfth century). There is real gold and there is fools gold. Fools gold is counterfeit; it still comes from the ground and looks like the real thing, but after testing or examination by a well-trained eye, it can be seen for what it is, fake and worthless – a disappointment to those who were searching for the real thing.

In March 2006, there was a well-known Christian leader on Christian television claiming that his church was experiencing revival and had been for many months. At first, I wondered whether it would be an evangelistic campaign as since the 1860s, but especially after the 1920s, many North Americans refer to revival as such. As J. Edwin Orr replied to a man about a 'failed revival' (which was in reality an evangelistic campaign where no-one got converted) said, "For many it is the only place where a meeting can be a non-starter." Edwin Orr then went on to explain to the man how he did not have heaven-sent revival.

I watched the thirty minute broadcast, which in reality was more of a 'show' and came away disappointed. It was not an evangelistic campaign so there were no misperceptions of the word in that context. However, what I saw shocked and grieved me, I saw a lot of hype and people being worked up in the flesh. There was no mention of God being glorified (or Jesus being lifted up, praised and worshipped), no mention of repentance, the cross, the blood, sin, of people getting right with God or souls being saved. But within this thirty minute broadcast there were five appeals for money (that's one every six minutes which by anybody's calculation has to be excessive), one of which stated, 'if you want a part of this revival then the *only* way is to partner with us.' This really disturbed me, linking a "promise" of blessing from God to the giving of finances as the pastor said who was presenting the show. This was not revival. This was fleshly manipulation, hype and a mentality of I-want-to-build-my-own-kingdom. To state that by giving to that ministry was the *only* way to receive was unscriptural, unjustifiable and was playing on the hopes, dreams and emotions of weaker brethren.

It is wrong to pass judgment on just one hearing so I tuned in again a week later. Once again, there were talks about this revival, more talks from the pastor and more appeals for finances. By now I was feeling quite an aversion to this choreographed charismatic hype and appeals to fleece God's people of their hard-earned cash all in the name of revival, in the name of God Himself!

Another week passed, the pastor came on air and claimed that the revival had started eighteen months earlier to what he had stated previously – when he gave a 'prophecy.' This prophecy was shown, but he was prophesying from his own imagination (or under the influence of evil spirits), parts of which were not even Scriptural; it was as if this was 'another gospel' of which the apostle Paul warned of. I visited this ministry's website to confirm what had been spoken on TV the night before and watched their thirty-minute web broadcast. There were eight appeals for finances, one of which was approximately two minutes long; 'sow your very best seed' was a constant theme. Some of these appeals were linking anointing with finances, whereas anointing is linked to sacrifice, taking up one's cross daily, denying self and abiding in the Vine, see John 15:1-11, Romans 12:1-2, Galatians 2:20, 2 Corinthians 5:15 and 1 John chapter 2.

When the ministry website was advertising their pastor's conference, the commentator said, "…We will be anointing this revival into your life." But this is not Scriptural. Revival cannot be given away, bought, sold or imparted (for thirty shekels of silver!); though an anointing to some degree can be imparted, as can a gift (see 2 Timothy 1:6). God gives His gifts freely and in measure to the level of our obedience to Him. God does not fill dirty vessels or anoint or empower us to entertain others, but to do the works of the Father. Revival is a sovereign work of God, coupled with man's obedience – the Divine-human partnership and is seen in the fullness of time.

On the final part of the broadcast, there was an advertisement to visit the church (an opportunity to sow your very best seed) and the commentator said, "…Miraculous move of God in every service, the atmosphere is charged with signs and wonders…" He continued, "As revival continues at —— church…join us at —— for revival as God shines the spotlight of His favour on you." Two weeks later, I tuned in again, but the entire thirty-minute show was about money and you were still encouraged to 'sow your very best seed.' The pastor repeatedly said, "Try an experiment and send your best gift, a month's wage, or a week; however you get paid…if you do sow into my ministry a spirit of revival will be released into your life, into your church!"

This is not revival. It was pure lies, hype and manipulation, which is witchcraft. You cannot buy God's favour or blessing. More than ten years have elapsed since the proclamation of this 'revival,' yet no ministry or Christian (or secular) media outlet ever mentioned or posted an article about this alleged revival. Within the ministry itself, the claims of revival were quietly forgotten and the weekly broadcasts moved on to other subjects, though they still want your money!

Real Gold or Fools Gold?

Whilst in every revival there will inevitably be mistakes made, but the basic fundamental truths of any revival have to remain and where they are not present then it cannot be revival. God will not share His glory with another. He will not be mocked, because what a man sows, he shall reap and if we sow to the wind, we shall reap the whirlwind of His wrath. But in His wrath He can still show mercy because He does not treat us as our sins deserve.

I was disturbed by what I had seen and heard but had to base my conclusions not on my emotions, but on the Word of God. We must all beware of having preconceived prejudices, (nationalistic, racial, personal, theological or denominational) which can distort biblical doctrine and sound unbiased judgment. I also compared the counterfeit revival from accounts from revival Church history. God does not contradict Himself and throughout Church history, there are always common characteristics and features in every revival which reappear regardless of time, country and culture. But what was present in this false revival?

Genuine and Counterfeit Revival – What was Missing?

1. God was not being glorified, given honour, worshipped, praised or adored for the alleged revival, which was claimed to be taking place. It was about a personality, a church and a ministry.
2. There was no mention of Jesus, the cross / Calvary or the blood of the Lamb that was slain. There was no mention about Jesus' life, His work or His sacrifice for fallen mankind.
3. There was no mention of the Holy Spirit / Holy Ghost / God's Spirit or the Spirit of God. He comes to convict the world of sin, righteousness and judgment; to guide believers into all truth (John

16:8, 13), who manifests His presence (which brings about revival) to glorify God, to revive those who are spiritually stale, to give life to the spiritually dead and to draw the wandering sheep back into the fold of God. The Holy Spirit also guides and directs,
4. There was no mention of sin, of people getting right with God, forsaking sin, confession of sins, living holy or taking up one's cross and daily following Jesus.
5. There was no mention of Christians having being revived (getting right with God and each other, humbling themselves), backsliders being restored or souls being saved.
6. The Word of God, the Holy Bible was not being honoured, that is, it was not being used to give, to build up, to challenge or to convict, but used only to get financial support.
7. There was no mention of any ethical or social results, such as restitution and reparation; marriages and relationships having been restored, sinful habits having been abandoned / forsaken, bad debts being repaid or helping the poor, orphans or widows.

The Counterfeit / False Revival – What was There?
1. There was great emphasis about the pastor, the church and the ministry involved. There was no humility displayed by the leadership team and it was a showmanship performance.
2. There was repeated talk about money, and that it should be sent to those involved. Some of these financial appeals were linking anointing with finances. It was also stated that the revival could happen in our church or imparted into our lives if we gave financially and this was the only way! This is not Scriptural and is the sin of simony, see Acts 8:18-24.
3. There was a contradiction on the start date of the revival by eighteen months. If the basic facts (which had been changed) are incorrect then there is little hope for the deeper things. Those who are double-minded are unstable in all their ways (James 1:8).
4. There was a self-appointed (or demonically inspired) prophecy which was not of the Spirit of God.
5. There was a lot of hype, Scriptural manipulation and false promises because they were not based on the Word of God – you cannot buy God's favour, blessing or anointing.[1]

Changed Lives or Not
The previous work explained and showed what a counterfeit revival was, based on the lack of evidence, of things ignored or omitted, coupled with what they said and did not say. The following is comparing true revival (and genuine Christian discipleship) with

that which is false, based on the *majority* of the lifestyles of those present, 'as the truth is in Jesus' (Eph. 4:21-23). Are those present:
- Giving glory to God or to a person?
- Drawn to Christ or away from Him?
- Do they allow the Holy Spirit to have His way in their lives?
- Drawn to the cross or to the things of the world?
- Are they drawn to the light (holiness) or to the darkness (evil deeds)?
- Are they more Christ-like or devil-like?
- Are their lives transformed for better or for worse?
- Do they promote the Kingdom of God or the kingdom of the devil by their words and deeds?
- Do they bear fruit (a changed life) or froth (lovers of fads and phenomena)?
- Are they attention-seekers or Christ-seekers?
- Do they honour or dishonour the Word of God (the Bible), obey or disobey that which is written in the Word of God?
- Do they now spend more time in Bible reading, and in prayer (fellowship with God, in their quiet times) or less?
- Are they eager to fast and pray or to feast and play?
- Do they have an attitude and spirit of repentance and reconciliation or pride and rebellion?
- Have they been brought to a place of humility and contrition (brokenness) or do they have a "bless me," "give me," self-seeking attitude?
- Do they try and bring glory to God or are they looking for glory for themselves?
- Is there open fellowship with other Christians or a disassociation from others?
- Are they building up the body of Christ (the Church) or trying to tear it apart?
- Are they more eager to share the good news of Jesus Christ or ashamed of Him?
- Do they attend Christian meetings (e.g. prayer and Bible study) or prefer to go shopping, to the gym or cinema etc.
- Are they more eager to support world missions without any recognition out of love or do they try and buy God's favour?

Sparks of the Flesh or Heavenly Fire

A man-made spark (Isaiah 50:10-11) that sets alight wood shavings on a floor of concrete in an attempt to 'work up' excitement and emotions will soon go out as human adrenalin drops. The flesh does not transform lives but the Spirit does. We need the fire of God to fall from heaven (1 Kings 18:38-39 and Isaiah 32:15), the Divine conflagration of revival fire will burn up the dross (rubbish / trash) from our lives and refine, and purify us so that we can walk in the newness of the Spirit. 'If indeed you have heard Him and have been taught by Him, as *the truth is in Jesus*; that you put off, concerning your former conduct, the old man which grows corrupt according to the deceitful lusts, and be renewed in the spirit of your mind' (Ephesians 4:21-23).

Henry. C. Fish in *Handbook of Revivals* (1874) quoting Ephesians 4:21b, wrote: '*The truth as it is in Jesus* accompanies a real work of grace…. Suppose there were to be a powerful excitement on the subject of religion produced by means which are at war with the spirit of the gospel. Suppose doctrines were to be preached which the gospel does not recognise, and doctrines omitted which the gospel regards fundamental. Suppose that for the simple, and honest, and faithful use of the sword of the Spirit [the Word of God, the Bible], there should be substituted a mass of machinery designed to produce its effect on the animal passions; suppose the substance of religion instead of being made to consist in repentance, and faith, and holiness, should consists of fallings, and groanings, and shoutings. We should say unhesitatingly that that could not be a genuine work of Divine grace; or if there were some pure wheat, there must be a vast amount of chaff and stubble.

'On the other hand, where there is an attention to religion excited by the plain and faithful preaching of God's truth in all its length and breadth, and by the use of simple and honest means which God's Word either directly prescribes or fairly sanctions, we cannot reasonably doubt that there is a genuine work of the Holy Spirit.

'Again, there will not be simple *excitement or feeling* in a true work of grace, but *knowledge and reflection* as well. Truth enters the heart through the understanding, and if the feeling manifested, whether of peace or distress, be the effect of an enlightened apprehension, and intelligent conviction there is reason to hope that God's Spirit is really at work. But when the mind is in great degree blind and passive while yet the sensibilities are wrought to a high pitch, there is reason to doubt the genuineness of the supposed conversion, and that which claims to be a revival is pretty surely not a genuine but a spurious one.

'Again the genuineness of a work is to be suspected unless the *holiness, zeal and devotedness of Christians* are increased…. Where the work is genuine there will be *abiding results*.'[2]

Chapter 24

The Dangers of Revival

'For such are false apostles, deceitful workers, transforming themselves into apostles of Christ. And no wonder! For Satan himself transforms himself into an angel of light' (2 Cor. 11:13-14).

Judging and Discerning – Is it from God or the Devil?
The enemy tries to undermine all that God is doing and has done, and during times of revival, there are inevitable elements of the demonic and the flesh as he infiltrates and imitates.

Many Christians are too hasty to judge and say a work is of the devil (or his demons) whereas it could well be the finger of God. Often all we see is what John Arnott of the Toronto Airport Christian Fellowship calls a 'snapshot,' where a person is being touched and affected bodily, but the snapshot is just a moment of time and the fruit will show forth later. We need to learn to distinguish between the holy and the unholy, the clean and the unclean and separate the precious from the vile before we start denouncing people or a work as counterfeit. We have a preconceived mindset, a bias towards thinking the worst ("Who sinned, this man or his parents?" – "Neither" – John 9:1-3) which is the opposite of 1 Corinthians 13:4-7, 'love…thinks no evil.' Alarm bells start ringing and all too often we jump to the wrong conclusion and miss the best. 'It is the Spirit' that 'searches all things, yes the deep things of God' (1 Corinthians 2:10b). So we have to be spiritually in tune with God to appreciate what He is doing. God is too complex to understand. Most of us cannot even understand the opposite sex, let alone God!

Zecharias was in the temple serving the Lord and came out mute. Was the devil attacking him because of his devotion and service towards the Lord? No, it was because he disbelieved the Word from the angel of the Lord that his wife Elizabeth, who was past the age of child-bearing was to have a son. He was mute for at least nine months until his son, John (the Baptist) was born (Luke 1:5-25, 57-64).

Saul the persecutor of the Church who had endorsed the stoning of Stephen was sometime afterwards struck to the ground and blinded – was it the devil or God's judgment? Neither, it was how

God revealed Himself to the persecutor of the Church so that Saul, later renamed Paul, could be converted. He was blind for three days and went on to become the Church's best promoter (Acts 9:1-19). When the Lord appeared to Saul, his companions all saw the light and were afraid, but none except Saul heard Him speak (Acts 22:16-19) – an encounter can be seen or interpreted differently.

We should be cautious, but not hasty in our judgments, childlike, but not childish. We are to 'test all things' not reject all things and 'hold fast what is good' (1 Thessalonians 5:21). We should not 'throw out the baby with the bath water' to use a contemporary phrase, but to take the best and leave the rest. We should be 'swift to hear' but 'slow to speak' (passing judgment) and not angry or full of wrath because of what we see (James 1:19). God is more than capable of looking after His work, but 'every move of the Spirit needs to be pastored in a responsible way,' so wrote John Arnott. Just like in the book of Acts, the book of revivals and riots! Church leaders were present or summoned to supervise, watch over, correct and rebuke where necessary as did Peter during the Samaria Revival; he denounced Simon, the former sorcerer for his sin of simony (Acts 8:18-24).

If God comes and meets with you then it is very probable that what has happened on the inside (an inner healing or sifting and shaking) will express itself on the outside to a larger or lesser degree, be it mildly or wildly! However, 'if God is in control can we really be out of control?' so wrote John Arnott. Sometimes God may touch you in such a way that you have little choice in how you respond. But ever remember and do not forget that holiness is better than the miraculous because we are called to bear fruit.

In late 1995, during the Toronto Blessing in Canada, Christian sociologist, Margeret Poloma interviewed a cross-section of people who had fallen under the power of the Holy Spirit. About one thousand people were surveyed, each of whom had time to reflect on their experience. It transpired that 92% stated that they were now more in love with Jesus. The second highest statistic revealed that 82% were more motivated and excited to share the good news. John Arnott went on to say how people had attributed so much in the church meetings as demonic, 'but loving Jesus more and wanting to tell others about Him doesn't sound like the devil's doing, does it?'[1]

John Wimber said, "In my experience all who have been overcome by the Holy Spirit – whether they fell over, started shaking, became very quiet and still, or spoke in tongues – thought the experience was wonderful and that it drew them closer to God.

They found that prayer, Scripture reading, caring for others and the love of God all increased."[2]

Has God lost His power? Cessation Theology

It is unfortunate that some Christians reject all things spiritual but notably the gifts of the Holy Spirit, believing that either the gifts are not for today (cessation theology), that God's power has diminished or that the gifts ceased at the death of the last apostle.

Equally unfortunate is that all too often some Christians give the devil too much credit – something supernatural happens and they attribute it as from the evil one! Whilst the devil can counterfeit (e.g. a healing or a miracle, Matthew 13:22-23 and Matthew 24:24), yet these same people say that God cannot or will not heal! How shameful and unbiblical. The healing Scriptures of: Isaiah 53:5, Matthew 8:17, James 5:16 and 1 Peter 2:24 still apply because 'the Scripture cannot be broken' as Jesus reiterated (John 10:35b) & 'the Word of the Lord endures forever' (1 Peter 1:24-25).

God is the originator of the supernatural whilst the enemy is the infiltrator and imitator. Has the devil more power to deceive us than God has to heal us? Who has the greater power? Let us not be confused over God's dynamics and the demonic – the Kingdom of Light is stronger than the kingdom and works of darkness. 1 Corinthians 12:7 informs us that 'the manifestation of the Spirit is given to each one for the profit of all' – that is for the corporate benefit of the body of Christ. God has not ceased His concern for the Church, His Bride and still wants to benefit her.

We believe all of the Bible or nothing – 'a double-minded man, [is] unstable in all his ways' (James 1:8). If one part is false or no longer applicable then all of it is no longer applicable, and let us not be confused over the Old and New Covenants or the Scripture's spiritual principles. If one portion of the New Testament has been abrogated then who is to say that other parts have not also? The first formal recognition of a fixed list, or canon, of New Testament writings can be dated to about the middle of the second century, though it took longer for both East and West to agree on the 27 books of the New Testament. These books (or letters) were inspired by God and are just as applicable then, as when they were written and therefore are still valid for today.

If we disregard, say prophecy, as "not for today," one of the nine gifts of the Holy Spirit as recorded in 1 Corinthians 12, then it is only fair that we disregard prophets as "not for today." Prophets are part of the five-fold ministry of Ephesians 4, so it is only right, fitting and proper, if we hold to this view to also exclude teachers, evangelists, pastors and apostles! Dare we say that? But if we do, should we not go all the way and disregard all of the Pastoral Epistles as they were also written by the apostle Paul.

If the gifts ceased at the death of the apostles then why not the responsibility towards the Great Commission and our command to 'love' as revealed in 1 Corinthians chapter 13; how can we disregard portions of one chapter (1 Corinthians 12) and not the subsequent one? Rather inconsistent isn't it? Or what about the preceding chapter (1 Corinthians 11) on propriety of worship and the Lord's Supper? Do we also say it has been abrogated and sweep it under the carpet as not for today? Dare we tell the Holy Spirit what He can and cannot do and how He is to go about it, just to keep us happy? Is Jesus Christ no longer the same yesterday, today, and forever? (Hebrews 13:8). Our 'faith should not be in the wisdom of men, [self imposed doctrines and opinions] but in the power of God' (1 Corinthians 2:5).

Jesus speaking to Nicodemus (a Pharisee), about being "born again" told him plainly, "We speak what We know and testify of what We have seen and you *do not receive* Our witness. If I have told you earthly things and you do not believe, how will you believe if I tell you heavenly things?" (John 3:11-12). Nicodemus did eventually believe and assisted Joseph of Arimathea in taking Jesus down off the cross (John 7:50 and John 19:39).

Jesus spoke on the parable of the rich man and Lazarus, when each had his own reward in the afterlife, the rich man in hell and Lazarus at Abraham's bosom. The rich man was in terrible torment and asked Abraham to permit Lazarus to dip his finger in water and to cool his tongue, but as there was a gulf fixed between the two it was impossible. The rich man then asked for Lazarus to be sent to his father and five brothers so that they would not end up in hell. Abraham told him that they have Moses and the prophets, let them hear them (the Scriptures – in the Old Testament), but the rich man wanted Lazarus to be raised and *then* they would believe. Abraham said, "If they do not hear Moses and the prophets, *neither will they be persuaded* though one rise from the dead" (Luke 16:19-31).

In John 5, Jesus healed a paralytic at the Pool of Bethesda on the Sabbath day and told him to take up his bed and walk. The Jews persecuted Jesus and 'sought all the more to kill Him because He not only broke the Sabbath, but also said that God was His Father, making Himself equal with God' (v18). Jesus plainly told those gathered, "You search the Scriptures, for in them you think you have eternal life and these are they which testify of

Me. But you are *unwilling* to come to Me that you may have eternal life" (John 5:39-40).

Sometimes it is impossible to get through to people who are unable to hear or see the truth. Some believe what they want to believe, whose hearts have been hardened, whilst some have an unteachable spirit and a know-all attitude. We are told not to give what is holy to the dogs; to try to convince some people of biblical truths is like casting pearls before swine (Matthew 7:6) and we should not speak in the hearing of a fool who will only despise the wisdom of our words (Proverbs 23:9).

'The natural man does not receive the things of the Spirit of God, for they are foolish to him; nor can he know them because they are spiritually discerned, but He [God] who is spiritual judges all things…' (1 Corinthians 2:14-15). If we presume to judge another, then with the measure we use, it will be measured back to us (Matthew 7:1-2). It is also advisable to remove the plank of our preconceived ideas from our own eye before we speak to a brother or sister about his or her speck of sawdust (Matthew 7:3-6).

Let us be like the Bereans who 'searched the Scriptures daily' to see if what had been said was true (Acts 17:11). Apollos was an 'eloquent man and mighty in Scripture' and was humble enough to receive correction (he only knew the baptism of John, a baptism of repentance) and was taught the 'way of God more accurately' by Aquila and Pricilla (Acts 18:24-28).

'…Faith comes by hearing and hearing the Word of God' (Romans 10:17). William Cooper of Boston, America, in Nov. 1741 wrote: 'Some cannot see the signature of the Divine hand.'

The Devil and Revival

- When God moves, the devil likes to rear his head and cause opposition. Christians who may be unspotted from the world, can still come under the influence of the evil one. If those who have received God's grace can cause problems, how much more the graceless! The opposition from the conservative Baptists during the Nagaland Awakenings (1950s and 1960s) in India, were most cruel indeed, from those who thought they were doing God a favour, because what they saw did not line up with their theology.
- Opposition towards a revival comes from all quarters, though revival Church history records that during revivals in India in the nineteenth and twentieth centuries the opposition generally came from Hindus.

During China's phenomenal Christian growth over the past one hundred plus years, opposition came from the Boxers (a secret society) and then the Communists. During the Indonesian Revival (1964-1974) the opposition came from the predominant Muslim population. In the Koran (Qu'ran), leaving the faith is punishable by death. Whilst most Hindu families have no qualms with their relatives putting their faith in Jesus Christ, but being baptised in water (into the Christian faith) can cause them to be outcasts! During the 1859 Irish Revival (Ulster Awakening) in many localised towns and communities where Roman Catholicism was strong, it was the Catholics who opposed the 'Protestant' move of God. The Established Church: Roman Catholic, Church of England, Egyptian Orthodox and Ethiopian Copts have also persecuted those who have been "born again" within their denominations; the latter two in the past one hundred years, often because of unconverted clergy.

Demonic Dangers with Revivals

- The devil is a liar, a deceiver and a great antagonist of the Son of God, who despises all things from God and of God. He will try to deceive and beguile us so we must put on the full armour of God (Eph. 6:10-18), stay close to Jesus Christ and have a deep understanding of the Word of God. There is also the two-pronged danger of either being too proud of the revival, "Look at *us*, what *we* have achieved," or too worldly within the revival, committing sin (or being too lax, too familiar and taking it for granted). Beware of self-exaltation, self-glory, self-promotion and slipping or sliding into sin – keep to the narrow road, close to Jesus.
- The devil is an imitator and an infiltrator though he cannot produce good fruit in a person's life. John Wesley discussing enthusiasm (physical phenomena) at Rev. John Berridge's church in Everton, wrote: 'In some, nature mixed with grace,' and that 'Satan mimicked this work of God.' George Whitefield, talking generally about young people in revival wrote: '…others were guilty of great imprudences.'
- Even within a revival there will be those who prophesy, but not of the Spirit of God, it could be demonic or of the flesh (Job 26:4, Jeremiah 14:14-15 and 23:21). It is the leader's responsibility to address the situation and the person concerned, to rebuke the devil and to protect the flock.
- Depending on the country and area, during revival there could be witches, warlocks, satanists, witchdoctors or shamans turning up at the meetings to do spiritual battle. It

may be chanting, incantations, casting spells, cursing or placing accursed objects etc., in and around the church building – even cursed money on the offering plate. They should be challenged in the name of the Lord. Intercessors remember, 'we do not fight against flesh and blood, but against principalities and powers…' (Ephesians 6:12). See also Ephesians 3:10. Some of these children of the devil will get converted, and some will not.

We have just read about the dangers from others who are not what they appear, or those who have been taken captive by the evil one, but we also need to be careful of ourselves! An author from the nineteenth century writing about the Evangelical Awakening (1739-1791) in Britain, wrote: 'When men's feelings are roused to a high pitch of excitement, it is not always easy to keep them within the bounds of prudence and reason.' Beware of allowing your emotions to run away with you. There are natural dangers due to the human makeup. We cannot go persistently breaking natural laws, which are there for our benefit and expect our bodies to stay strong even when we neglect ourselves.

Physical Dangers with Revivals
- Extensive and prolonged revivals, those that go on for months or years (and the longer the better) are exhausting. Evening meetings can continue until the sun rises, but it is unwise to rise up early and to go to bed late. There is a big danger in being so excited about the things of God, 'spiritual hyperactivity' that people neglect to rest, sleep and eat at sensible times. This can lead to burnout or a physical breakdown which is what happened to Evan Roberts during (and after) the Welsh Revival (1904-1905). Duncan Campbell during the Lewis Revival (1949-1952) once took eight meetings in twenty-four hours!
- Daily life still goes on, children have to go to school and most adults have a job to hold down. Do not neglect the necessities of life and sleep is essential. We dishonour God by doing shoddy workmanship when we have the ability to do better. Work *and* rest is part of God's plan.
- Sometimes a well-meaning leader may begin to interfere with the revival, having good intentions and pure motives, but interference and not allowing God to do what He wants to do, resisting can quench or grieve the Holy Spirit and thus the revival can cease.

- A leader must have great discernment during revival and be sensitive as to when to address an issue and when to keep quiet and allow the Holy Spirit to point out the error; otherwise, a young convert could be crushed, rejected and lost forever. If you want to see fruit, don't damage the blossom. As an example, speaking about women dressing inappropriately (modesty and decency, especially in warmer climates where less is worn and more is revealed), has frequently been addressed from the pulpit in general terms. But at the Brownsville Revival (1995-2000), after stating, "Some of you dress like prostitutes," the leaders would state that they were talking to those who were older in the faith, not new converts, as the older ones should know better. Also, a new convert who has been rejected and down-trodden all their life, upon radical conversion will be very emotional and will have uncontrollable joy – 'joy inexpressible and full of glory' (1 Peter 1:8). They should not be restrained with their joy in the Lord and shouts of, "Hallelujah / Praise the Lord" (Psalm 106:48), "Glory" (Psalm 29:9), "Jesus is Lord" (Acts 10:36 and 1 Corinthians 1:9) etc. It is the only way they know how to express it. Jesus is looking down from heaven smiling on them and shame on us if we frown on them. See Psalm 5:11, Psalm 47:1, Isaiah 44:23 and Romans 15:11.
- A church or small village could be overrun with visitors, seeking to have an encounter with God – this is a good thing, but your church could get swamped with people, having protracted meetings, day in, day out and this will take its toll on the church buildings, furnishings, and workers. You may also have car parking problems. People will be queuing to get inside church but the neighbours may not appreciate it. In recent revivals, security guards and nursery carers have been employed to assist.

Jesus learned obedience through His suffering, as did Paul and all the other apostles. Many today repel discipline and suffering yet willingly embrace denominational denial of biblical truth. Even Barnabas was led astray for a time in his day. The enthusiasm of the flesh knows no bounds, encouraged as it is by the sinful self-nature of the flesh. That which is not crucified under the direction of the Holy Spirit will lead many into self-deception and delusion, believing that they can take or win whole towns, cities and nations without the leading or direction of the Holy Spirit.[3]

Chapter 25

Nurturing Revival

'To everything there is a season, a time for every purpose under the sun.... A time to gain and a time to lose; a time to keep, and a time to throw away' (Ecclesiastes 3:1, 6).

A Time for Everything

Ecclesiastes chapter three reveals that 'to everything there is a season, a time for every purpose under heaven.' Just like the tide that ebbs and flows in relation to the moon's position, so too revival has its seasons. This is not to say that at regular intervals revival will appear, but merely that it has its season to end, just as there is 'a time to be born and a time to die, a time to plant and a time to pluck what is planted' (Ecclesiastes 3:2). There is a time for revival and a time when each individual revival wanes or ceases. The Church is either how it should be (for a period of time) or sin has grieved the Holy Spirit and He departs.

We do not want to grieve the Holy Spirit, or to see the fires of revival to wane and die out, so revivals have to be nurtured and guarded. The best way to nurture and guard revival is stay in the Word of God, close to Jesus Christ and obey the Holy Spirit. Also, learn from past revivals, what went wrong and why did they cease?

Why do Revivals Cease?

Why do revivals cease? Hundreds of reasons could be given but they can be listed under three categories:

1. Sin – Members of the Church, but especially leaders committing sins of commission or sins of omission. Doing things which should not be done: lying, stealing, cheating, boasting, committing adultery, coveting etc. and neglecting things which ought to be done: Bible reading, prayer, evangelism, missions, loving one another, tithing, assisting the poor, orphans and widows etc.

2. Breaking physical laws – Neglecting the needs of the body, especially the leadership or those on the frontline who have additional responsibilities or pressures and are under constant spiritual attack. A lack of rest, sleep deprivation, not eating a balanced diet (or eating at irregular hours), lack of exercise and fresh air can lead to a physical breakdown, a heart attack, illness

or burnout. Nobody is invincible and spiritual adrenaline or spiritual hyperactivity will only last so long before something gives.
3. A revival has run its course – The Church is now revived and the subnormal Church is now the normal Church.

Common Causes for Revival to Cease

The most probable reason why any revival will cease is when those involved become complacent and prideful in action and attitude and thus take the revival for granted. Never be foolish enough to boast and brag about the sparks that you have kindled, and walk in the light of your own fire (Isaiah 50:11). If you neglect the One who is a Consuming Fire (Hebrews 12:29) then the work of God will soon fizzle out, because the Spirit will be grieved. Never trust in your own works rather than the Spirit of Grace and Supplication, the Baptiser in fire! (Matthew 3:11).

To keep a revival burning and blazing hot it must be continually fed and stoked by prayer, humility, abiding fellowship and the observance of the commandments of God. It is possible to be so caught up in the things of God that apathy sets in, and the wrong mindset comes over us, "No need to pray, God is here to stay." He won't stay where He is taken for granted, neglected or not wanted.

There is also a big danger in being led of our emotions rather than of the Spirit of God. Revival and any move of the Holy Spirit are time-consuming events – time just flies, but there is a danger in neglecting essential aspects of the human body, such as food and rest. Though man can not live on bread alone, but by every Word of God (Luke 4:4), without nourishment, he will surely deteriorate.

Most people even in the midst of revival will have family to care for and a job to hold down. Let us not become so spiritual that we become of no earthly good. A tired man is an unhappy man and it is difficult to be a light in the world if we stay up all night. We must learn to pace ourselves, whilst running the race so that we can obtain the prize and enjoy it!

Diluting the precious Word of God will also stop a revival; sin needs to be called sin and truth needs to be thundered from the pulpit, with a heart of love and compassion, as well as the streets. Revival rocks the boat and often upsets it, but vain is the lifeboat which is filled with the seas of worldliness. Any unworthy boat or ship that is unable to contain the precious holy cargo will sink.

There will be opposition and bad press, levelled not only at revival, but especially the revivalist or leaders at the fore. If they begin to move in the flesh, revival can stop. If you're part of 'a great work' like Nehemiah; don't waste your time with opponents.

'Why should the work cease...?' (Nehemiah 6:3-4) and reply graciously (if at all) like George Whitefield did to one of his accusers: 'I thank you heartily for your letter. As for what you and my other enemies are saying against me, I know worse things about myself than you will ever say about me. With love in Christ, George Whitefield.'

Why a Revival Would Cease by Charles Finney
- When the church thinks revival will cease, it will. It does not matter what enemies say or believe, but if the church loses its faith, it will lose the revival.
- When Christians consent that it will cease, it will. But if they see the danger, which drives them to their knees in agony and concern, it can be avoided.
- When the church stops to speculate and argue about abstract doctrines that have no bearing upon practice.
- When anything distracts the attention of the church, even the appearance of an angel.
- The church taking wrong ground on some great moral question such as slavery [homosexuality, abortion etc.].
- Ecclesiastical difficulties, the revivalist is called away from the work [or not permitted to return] to answer charges before his [or her] superiors regarding the use of new methods etc.
- When Christians become proud of their 'great revival' in what they have done!
- When Christians begin to proselytise to their denomination, stirring up sectarian difficulties, promoting this or that denomination.
- The Spirit may be grieved by boasting of the revival, to puff up the church; the pastor foolishly writing to the local newspapers [or emailing everyone/social media, having impure motives].
- Some, under pretence of publishing things to the glory of God, have (often unknowingly) exalted themselves or their denomination.
- When Christians lack brotherly and sisterly love, one for another.
- Christians of all denominations should lay aside all prejudices. Prejudices hinder the person so that they cannot come to a correct understanding on the subject and are unable to correctly pray in this state of mind.

- A protracted meeting should be conducted throughout by the same minister (or evangelist) if possible. Sometimes through courtesy, visiting ministers are invited to speak and there has been no blessing as they did not come in a state of mind, which was right for such a work. [This was evident on some nights in the Lakeland Outpouring (2008) in Florida, America].
- When Christians become mechanical in their attempts to promote revival and prayer begins to wane, praying without emotion as before.
- When the minister does not pour out fire (arousing passionate preaching) upon the hearers, when he is behind the pulpit.
- When the church becomes exhausted by the labour, neglect to eat and sleep at the proper hours and let the excitement runaway with them so that they become exhausted and their bodies or mind give way and breakdown. [This is what happened to Evan Roberts of the Welsh Revival (1904-1905) in Wales, UK].
- When Christians do not feel their dependence on the Holy Spirit, believing they can do the work in their own strength, or promoting themselves or their ministry instead of the Lord.
- A revival will decline and cease, unless Christians are frequently revived – frequently convicted and humbled and broken down before God.
- Revivals can be put down by the continued opposition of the old school, combined with a bad spirit in the new school. When those who are for or against a revival battle it out, with a bad spirit, printing articles and rebuttals in the papers for public viewing. Those who are engaged in revival should keep to the work [Nehemiah 6:3] and mind their own business when they or the work are slandered, as it is God who vindicates.

Joel Hawes of the nineteenth century wrote: 'Let your heart be much set on revivals of religion. Never forget that the churches have hitherto existed and prospered by revivals; and that if they are to exist and prosper in time to come, it must be by the same cause which has from the first been their glory and defence.'

Chapter 26

Wisdom and Discernment

Jesus said, "If a kingdom is divided against itself, that kingdom cannot stand.... No one can enter a strong man's house and plunder his goods, unless he first binds the strong man, and then he will plunder his house" (Mark 3:24, 27).

The Two Kingdom's Clash
When the Holy Spirit comes into a meeting there will be a clash between the Kingdom of God and the kingdom of darkness. Physical phenomena can be from God, the devil or of the flesh when over excited humans work it up. They may be attention seeking or trying to be part of the crowd, not wanting to be the odd one out, as some believe that if they imitate phenomena (what they see around them), then they too will receive a touch from God, not realising that the phenomena is a result of God touching people and not the other way around. Bishop Thomas Birch Freeman during the Gold Coast Revival (1875-1878) in Ghana (and beyond) held 'conventions with his leaders advising them how to act during the various phases of the revival in progress. Lest the people should come to view that loud cries and tremblings as a necessary part, or as adjuncts to conversion, he exhorted them to guard against all unnecessary excitement.'[1]

Demonic Influences
There is also a combination of the flesh and the devil which can be hard to distinguish. A manifestation may be demonic in its origin but flow into the flesh, whereas at other times it begins in the flesh and then becomes demonic. If a person is under the influence of demons / evil spirits then he or she needs deliverance. If a person is trying to 'work up' a blessing then he or she should be taken to one side and gently spoken to out of a pastor's heart of love and compassion, "Brother / sister, that is not the Spirit" with a smile.

God's presence affects people differently and if they have demons or are under the influence of the evil one then the demons will manifest. This is true not only in times of revival, but in a church meeting or a Christian conference, demons may play up, cause a scene, or will try to get out of God's presence as fast as they can – with or without their human host! In any move of God there will be a minority who willingly or unwillingly attempt to bring the work of God into contempt. More often than not it is because these people are under the influence of the evil one and have been taken captive by him to do his will.

Christians cannot be possessed, that is completely taken over like Legion from Gadarenes (Mark 5:1-20), yet many Christians still need deliverance, because at the point of conversion we are not always automatically delivered. Many Christians have weak spots, areas which they have never allowed God to touch or have chosen not to fully surrender to Him. Even Spirit-filled Christians may still have demons / evil spirits. These demons may have come in prior to conversion or after conversion, through an entry point of habitual sin, an open doorway which gave the enemy a legal entry point into their life or during a time of fear or trauma. See *Discipleship For Everyday Living* by the author, chapters 40 and 48.

The Audience and Mystical Experiences

In any Christian meeting there can be too much emphasis on some things and not on others. Naturally if we attend a conference on healing, then the focus will be on healing. But within revival, the focus must always be on Christ, the cross, repentance, getting the sin out of our lives, holiness unto the Lord, praise and worship, evangelism, and everything else should be subservient to that.

In any Christian meeting there will be a wide variety of people and it is unwise to constantly share one's deep spiritual or mystical experiences. Some present are just babes in Christ, probably the majority, who have not grasped or applied the basic biblical truths. By constantly sharing these experiences these young Christians may think that the central emphasis of Christianity is on experiences and encounters, but from Scripture we know that it is becoming Christ-like; hence why the focus must always come back to Christ and the cross and not a person and their experiences. Would we teach at PhD level to those who are still in school? The apostle Paul in a letter to the Corinthian Church made reference to one who was caught up to the third heaven – a vision of paradise (2 Corinthians 12:1-5), but he didn't dwell on his experience or elaborate, but moved on.

Bible teacher, John Piper very aptly wrote: 'Oh, Lord, forbid that we should lose our biblical bearings; forbid that we become trendy or faddish and begin to substitute the sand of experience for the rock of revealed truth. Show us the fullness of the power of the gospel, Lord, and keep us from preoccupation with secondary things, no matter how spectacular.'[2]

An Experience, Personalities and Spiritual Gifts

There is a difference between those who come to seek an experience at a meeting and those who come to seek the Lord and it is to the latter category that we should belong. We are to bring our sacrifices of praise and our very lives as an offering to God – we should not go to a meeting as receivers, but givers – givers of ourselves (Romans 12:1-2 and 2 Cor. 5:15). We should all prepare ourselves before we come to the house of the Lord, but especially before we partake of the Lord's Supper, lest we be found unworthy and bring judgment on ourselves (1 Corinthians 11:23-34).

There are some Christians who come to a meeting or conference only to seek a personality or for an impartation or anointing; rather than looking for Christ and the benefits of the teaching. An anointing can only come by personal sacrifice and paying the cost, spiritually speaking. God does not fill dirty vessels and an impure impartation can be transferred through the laying on of hands if the imparter has evil spirits, because areas of his or her life have not been dealt with. A speaker may have the gift of knowledge but can also be influenced or moved by a spirit of divination or a familiar spirit; the latter two can be just as accurate as the first, though the source is demonic and not of the Spirit of God.

God cannot be bought and we cannot purchase His blessing, a healing, a prophetic word or an anointing – this is simony, the sin which Simon the former sorcerer fell into and he had been converted and baptised in the revival at Samaria, see Acts 8. There are personalities who prostitute their gifts whilst some specialise in fortune telling and divination under the guise of words of knowledge, words of wisdom or prophetic utterances. Some false preachers, teachers and apostles bring in just enough truth so as not to arouse suspicion, whilst some genuine Christian workers have a mixture in their gifting which are contaminated and polluted by the enemy. This makes it more difficult to discern the wheat from the chaff, the precious from the vile and the clean from the unclean. We may have begun to run the race well, but let us beware of being tripped up or stumbling near the finish line, otherwise we will not receive our full reward.

Caught up in the Atmosphere

In any Christian meeting or conference we must be aware of being caught up in the atmosphere where emotions can override our level of discernment, or where peer pressure or manipulation can lead us to participate in things which we feel uncomfortable with, as we disregard the small still voice of the Holy Spirit. There are a minority who use techniques and methods, which whilst they should not be used, are used to stimulate and move emotions so that we do something or are more prone to do something than if these techniques and methods were not in operation. This is very applicable in regards to soliciting finances, "Give now, hurry!" "Write that cheque (check) and bring it to the front!" These appeals may go directly to the heartstrings, "If you don't give, the ministry will go under…" and / or end in coercion which is plain manipulation, "…You will be responsible!" These appeals often bypass our intelligence, which prompts us to be led of our emotions (or out of fear) rather than of the Spirit.

We should be generous givers, but let us be wise givers who sow into fertile soil being led of the Spirit. Let us allow God to guide us so that we make the right choices when we invest into His Kingdom, building on solid foundations with Jesus Christ at the centre, with ministers of truth and integrity.

What Message do we Give Out?

Millions of churches around the globe are full of people who diligently and faithfully attend Sunday worship and yet are not part of the family of God. They are church-goers with the nickname Christian and they are unregenerate – in heart and lifestyle. But, is it any wonder that thrill seekers turn up at meetings or conferences to have an experience which can tickle their emotions and raise the hairs on the back of their neck? Should we blame these people for their spurious conversions when we have not been preaching the gospel in truth, with Jesus Christ, His shed blood, repentance, the cross and full surrender at the core of the message?

If we preach Christ and Him crucified; the law and grace, the judgment and mercy of God, repentance, sacrifice and full surrender then we will not end up wealthy or popular. Those in Christian ministry who live like Hollywood stars or Premier League footballers should look at their message – is it New Testament Christianity as revealed by John the Baptist, Jesus, Peter and the apostle Paul or another gospel?

Jesus said, "That which is born of the flesh is flesh and that which is born of the Spirit is spirit" (John 3:6). If we work in the flesh our fruit will correspond and souls will be brought into false experience…. If our lives do not convict of sin there is something wrong.[3]

Chapter 27

Deception and Rejection

'And Jesus answering them began to say, "Take heed that no one deceives you. For many will come in My name, saying, 'I am he,' and will deceive many" ' (Mark 13:5-6).

Beware of Deceivers

Jesus said, "Take heed that no one deceives you..." (Matthew 13:5) and even in times of revival we must be on our guard. Those who say that they cannot be deceived, already are! Also, not all signs and miracles are from God. Jesus said, "For false Christs and false prophets will arise and show great signs and wonders, so as to deceive, if possible, even the elect" (Matthew 24:4-5, 24, see also Mark 13:22-23). The apostle Paul wrote: 'I fear, lest somehow, as the serpent deceived Eve by his craftiness, so your minds may be corrupted from the simplicity that is in Christ,' by those who preach another Jesus, another gospel and who have a different spirit (2 Corinthians 11:3-4).

Satan has many followers infiltrating the church, false apostles and false teachers (2 Corinthians 11:13-15) and in times of revival, there is no exception. There are also those who will deny the power of God even in the day of visitation (2 Timothy 3:1-9). Whilst some so-called 'believers' are known as tares, wolves or accursed children (Matthew 7:15, Matthew 13:24-30 and 2 Peter 2:14-15). Jesus warned of false prophets who will come in sheep's clothing but inwardly they are ravenous wolves. By their fruits we will know them (Matthew 7:15-20). Jesus also said, "If you abide in My Word, you are My disciples indeed. And you shall know the truth, and the truth shall make you free" (John 8:31-32).

In 1743, in the midst of the American Great Awakening (1735-1760), Jonathan Edwards published the *Treatise Concerning the Religious Affections* as he identified froth without fruit – stirred emotions, but not changed lives and it was this minority that were bringing the work of God into disrepute.

Warnings from Scripture
- 'Do not be carried about with various and strange doctrines...' (Hebrews 13:9).

- 'Even if we, or an angel from heaven preach any other gospel to you than what we have preached to you, let him be accursed' (Galatians 1:8).
- '…In latter times some will depart from the faith, giving heed to deceiving spirits and doctrines of demons' (1 Timothy 4:1).
- '…There will be false teachers among you, who secretly bring in destructive heresies…many will follow their destructive ways because of whom the way of truth will be blasphemed. By covetousness they will exploit you with deceptive words…and their destruction will not slumber' (2 Peter 2:1-3).
- 'For certain men have crept in unnoticed, who long ago were marked out for this condemnation, ungodly men, who turn the grace of God into licentiousness and deny the only Lord God and our Lord Jesus Christ' (Jude 4).
- The apostle Paul said to the Ephesians, "…After my departure savage wolves will come in among you, not sparing the flock. Also from among yourselves men will rise up, speaking perverse things, to draw away the disciples after themselves" (Acts 20:29-30).
- Jesus said, "Not everyone who says to Me, 'Lord, Lord,' shall enter the Kingdom of heaven, but he who does the will of My Father in heaven" (Matthew 7:21).

The Deceived Revivalist

Less than a year before the armistice of World War I (1914-1918), Spanish flu swept the world. In Basutoland, (modern-day Lesotho), Africa, entire villages were wiped out. The life of the Basuto was at a standstill and travellers were no longer met on the roads. Schools and churches were closed by public order and gatherings were not permitted. Victor Ellenberger wrote: 'Many believed that it was the end of the world and were resigned to their fate…. In many places the natives tried to come together in the open, so intense was the need which they felt of drawing near to God. In that respect, that calamity awakened latent spiritual needs among many Basutos and produced a fairly strong revival.

'One of the agents of that revival was – perhaps in spite of himself – a man…named [Walter] Matita…who had been busy for several years already with a campaign of evangelisation throughout the land, was able, chiefly through speaking to the populace about the resurrection, to move their hearts and to resuscitate numerous conversions…. By mingling the supernatural with the practical, he made out, amongst other things, that he had gone through death; that whilst dead he had been taken up to heaven through innumerable worlds; that an angel had then taught him to read and to write and that finally he had been allowed to appear before Moshesh [the father of Basutoland, who died in 1870], who had expressly charged him to return to earth and to call the Basutos in his name to become converted.'

Matita held many other views, especially in regards to the future 'which he hid from the credulity of his audience; but later, when he threw off the mask and wanted to establish a sect of which he would be head, namely the sect of the 'Followers of Moshesh,' or another, that of the 'Possessed of the Spirit,' recruits for which he reckoned to get among those who had been converted through his appeal and whose names he kept, it happened that the great majority of them refused to follow him and they came to swell the ranks of our churches, 'having given themselves up to God, not to man.'

'Indirectly that man who pretended to be one of us and the movement he inaugurated, proved to be a magic stone for the Church at that critical time, for they made it possible for us to remain united and to victoriously resist an attack *perfidiously launched against our work, [*playing one side against each other] even as deeply as the native pastoral body....'[1]

Whilst Walter Matita began in the faith, somehow, probably gradually, he was led astray, yet the majority of those converted under his ministry stayed true to the faith and that is a testament that those who sat under his preaching were truly born again of the Spirit of God, as they rejected his heresy when it later arose.

A Revivalists Spiritual Bankruptcy

In 1892, there was a revival amongst the Japanese on the Pacific coast of the USA. In 1913, Paget Wilkes, founder of the Japan Evangelistic Band who was no stranger to revivals wrote: 'Some of those who are today the most spiritual leaders in Japan were saved at that time.' Among the new converts 'was a man remarkably converted, whom it was soon evident that God had chosen him as a special instrument.'

This convert from the revival was much used amongst his own people in America, but some years later, he returned home to Japan and was appointed as an English teacher in a large mission school. Paget wrote: 'Almost at once a revival followed; both teacher and students were convicted of sin in no ordinary degree. Many were converted and saved of the Lord.'

After leaving the mission school, this unnamed Japanese revivalist was appointed the pastorate of a country church, where 'he was induced to read books of modern criticism, [also known as higher criticism, where everything in the Bible is questioned] in the hope, we presume, of making himself more intellectually fitted for the task.' He soon lost 'all his old fire and evangelistic zeal…and the result was spiritual bankruptcy.' He shortly afterwards resigned his position and returned to America, having been robbed of the 'solemn fear of God, the quick sensitiveness to sin swiftly disappeared' and he was found to be without 'life and power.'

In 1911, one of Paget's personal friends who himself was a convert of the 1892 Revival who 'had been very intimately acquainted' with the revivalist 'in the early days of his Christian life' visited America for some special meetings. After making inquires as to the whereabouts of his old friend, 'he learnt to his amazement and sorrow that he was keeping a house of shame in the town of ──.' This backslidden revivalist reluctantly met with his old friend through a mutual acquaintance and after being implored told him the story of his downfall which is how we know about it today.

The backslidden revivalist said, "You may pray for me, if you believe in it, but I have given up all that sort of thing long ago." The old friend dropped to his knees and 'poured out his aching heart for this poor deluded and unhappy soul.'[2]

The lessons we can learn is that it is possible for the elect to be deceived (Matthew 24:24) and we must be careful what we fill our minds with. Whilst we are called to give honour to whom honour is due, we should never idolise revivalists or attach too much value to the use of human instruments as they, like ourselves, are human, vulnerable and make mistakes. Lord protect us from deception.

Rejection of Revival

Many Christians reject revivals or claim it to be a demonic delusion, false and counterfeit. Some can cite dozens of reasons for their views. I have included some with rebuttals.
- Unless you use the King James Bible (Authorised Version of 1611) then you cannot have revival! Revivals have taken place before 1611, and amongst non-English speaking congregations across the world. Incidentally a modern '1611 Bible' from 2011 is *not* the same as an original which was printed 400, 250 or even 150 years ago!
- Revivals ended at the death of the apostles, or are no longer for today. Apostasy is growing and ripe! God's Word

is unchanging, God has promised to pour out His Spirit and is not a man that He should lie. Church history also refutes this concept. Jesus will be coming back for a pure and holy bride, without spot or blemish. The worldwide Church *is* growing from strength to strength.
- Revivals are unruly and disruptive, everything should be done decently and in order! Jesus was disruptive when He was on earth and upset the religious people of His day, but the common people heard Him gladly. On the Day of Pentecost, tongues of fire descended on the 120 gathered, they spoke in tongues and people thought they were drunk. When Peter preached, people cried out for salvation – his sermon was disrupted, but souls were saved.
- There are weird people in revival! There are weird people in most churches and bright lights attract bugs.
- People are in the flesh! You can be in the flesh overtly or as an introvert. Resisting, grieving and quenching the Holy Spirit is of the flesh. A dead fellowship is in the flesh! A Church without the Spirit is in the flesh!
- It is a demonic counterfeit! It might possibly be, but what is the fruit? Remember, a kingdom divided against itself cannot stand. Does Satan encourage: repentance, getting sin out of our lives, cross-focussed preaching, worshipping Jesus Christ, zeal for evangelism, world missions, the gifts of the Spirit and more prayer and Bible reading?

Revival of Healing

The controversial Lakeland Outpouring (2008) was a revival of healing under the ministry of Fresh Fire headed by Todd Bentley. The meetings were beamed across the world via God TV who received more than 45,000 emails in regards to the broadcasts and internet web-casts – deemed by some as a media revival. Putting aside the sad circumstances of the outpouring's demise through the personal failings of individuals, the outpouring brought blessing and encouragement amongst the body of Christ, but also friction and division. The evangelical community was divided into camps of opposing forces with their battle swords of words drawn and delivered over the internet.

Due to Lakeland's exposure, many 'revival police' and 'heresy hunters' came to the fore because of this mass televised move of God which was unprecedented in history. This was followed by The Bay of The Holy Spirit Revival (2010) under Nathan Morris and John Kilpatrick. At Lakeland in 2008, there was a mixture of the flesh and sometimes the demonic, as demons manifested through people, which on occasions were incorrectly attributed as an anointing, or from the Holy Spirit. There were various personalities involved, of varying maturity, from both genders and of different ages, some of whom were young in the Lord. No two consecutive nights were the same and there were many different speakers and guests over the three months when Todd Bentley was at the fore. There was too much emphasis on some things and less on others and several high profile Christian leaders have said, "I would have done things differently," but each move of God has lessons that we can learn, if only we take the time to evaluate.

Lakeland exposed to the body of Christ, its hunger for the reality of New Testament Christianity. Many Christians were healed, blessed and refreshed, hundreds were saved, whilst other brethren were revived, refreshed and invigorated. Thousands were trained and encouraged to be witnesses in the highways and byways of their villages and towns at different meetings connected with Lakeland at Ignite Church.

As with any move of God, there will be a prominent leader(s) who if not already, will rise through the ranks and be seen as the spokesperson(s). No revivalist would call themselves sinless but would be the first to acknowledge their imperfections; that they stood and ministered by the grace and mercy of God. Revivals are led by people that are not perfect, some are vulnerable and may have weak areas, whilst with others, their spiritual gifts are far greater than the character of Christ formed in them, as sanctification is an ongoing work. James aptly pointed out: 'We all stumble in many things' (James 3:2) and 'Mercy triumphs over judgment' (James 2:13). Jesus stated, "Whatever you want men to do to you, do also to them" (Matthew 7:12), he "who is without sin" can cast the first stone (John 8:7), and regarding judging, with the measure we use it will be measured back to us (Matthew 7:1-6).

May fallen brothers and sisters in Christ be brought to a place of repentance and restoration (Galatians 6:1). Peter denied the Lord, Thomas doubted Him and Saul persecuted Him, yet all were forgiven and used to advance the Kingdom of God! Imagine if the early Church had cast them aside? It is not recorded that the Church reminded them of their past sins. God does not look on the outward appearance and judge, but He is very interested in the heart, which should be entirely given over to Him. King David greatly sinned, in adultery and murder, but he was a man after God's own heart (Acts 13:22) and was restored (Psalm 51).

Chapter 28

God's Rules and His Laws

'Now faith is the substance of things hoped for, the evidence of things not seen. For by it the elders obtained a good testimony. By faith we understand that the worlds were framed by the Word of God, so that things which are seen were not made of things which are visible' (Hebrews 11:1-3).

The Unusual Workings of God

Some aspects of God's workings seem easier to understand than others. There is a very present danger of trying to keep God in a box by subconsciously defining what He can do, cannot do, and what He will do and will not do. Intellectually and theologically we know God can do anything, but somehow, in our finite minds we limit an infinite God to our own understanding, without even being aware of it until we are in the presence of God in true revival power as the Holy Spirit is moving amongst us.

Some of the things that go on in revival can appear strange and unorthodox, notably the physical phenomena – but then the Bible does have some very unorthodox characters and the Scriptures do reveal strange events. Jacob, the deceiver (later renamed Israel) wrestled with God, Jeremiah wore a wooden yoke for a period of time and Ezekiel ate food by weight and water by measure and lay on his side, paralysed, against a wall as part of an intercession for more than a year. Hosea was called of God to marry a prostitute and Isaiah went naked and barefoot for three and a half years; both these prophets and their intercessions were a sign against Israel. John the Baptist was dressed in camel's hair; he ate locusts and wild honey and to the crowds thundered forth, "Repent" and was the first person in the New Testament to see people confessing their sins (Mark 1:4-6). Jesus overturned the tables of the money changers at the temple, at the beginning and end of His ministry; Peter pronounced to Sapphira that she would drop down dead, just like her husband Ananias, who tested the Spirit of the Lord and lied to God.

The Jews prayed regularly for the coming Messiah, but would not acknowledge or receive Him when He came. Jesus fulfilled what was written about Him in Scripture, yet was still rejected. Do you pray regularly for revival, will you reject it when the Holy Spirit comes in revival power because things may appear different than you perceived it would?

Biblical Paradoxes

The Bible is full of paradoxes, a tenet or proposition contrary to received opinion, and seemingly absurd, but true in fact. For God's thoughts and ways are on a higher plane than ours and therefore may appear impossible or even absurd from our perspective, yet are part of God's wonderful plan.

- We reign by serving (Mark 10:42-44).
- We rest under a yoke (Matthew 11:28-30).
- We see unseen things (2 Corinthians 4:18).
- We triumph by defeat (2 Corinthians 12:7-9).
- We glory in our infirmities (2 Corinthians 12:5).
- We are exalted by being humble (Matthew 23:12).
- We become great by becoming little (Matthew 18:4).
- When we are weak then we are strong (2 Cor. 12:10).
- We possess all things by having nothing (2 Cor. 6:10).
- We live by dying to self (John 12:24-25 & 2 Cor. 4:10-11).
- We conquer by yielding (Matt. 5:5 with Romans 12:20-21).
- If we lose our life for Christ's sake, we will find it (Matthew 16:25). See also Galatians 2:20 and 2 Corinthians 5:15.
- We become free by becoming slaves to God (Romans 6:17-22 with Romans 8:2).

The Law of the Divine

Divine principles are different than those of the world. When God is at work; logic, theories and predetermined rules all have to give way to a higher law – the law of the Divine. God delights in doing the unexpected, the unpredictable and overturning the laws of probability and science, and this frequently happens during times of revival. With God, nothing is impossible (Luke 1:37 and 18:27).

- The children of Israel's garments did not wear out in the wilderness (Deuteronomy 8:4).
- Moses and Israel were fed with manna from heaven for forty years (Exodus 16:4-5, 14-17, 31, 35) and they lacked nothing (Deuteronomy 2:7).
- Joshua prayed for the sun and moon to stand still so that they could finish their battle and get a decisive victory. The sun did not move (the earth's rotation ceased) for about a day and they finished the battle (Joshua 10:11-14).

- The prophet Elijah was fed by ravens with bread and meat and drank from the brook (1 Kings 17:4-6).
- The widow's oil and flour was multiplied which fed Elijah, the widow and her son (1 Kings 17:8-16).
- Elijah was anointed by the hand of God and outran King Ahab's chariot (1 Kings 18:46).
- Elijah was fed by an angel twice (1 Kings 19:4-8).
- Elisha helped a widow who was in debt; a little oil was miraculously multiplied and filled many jars (2 Kings 4:1-7).
- A man brought twenty loaves of bread to feed one hundred men, the man of God told them to eat and they still had some left over (2 Kings 4:42-44).
- An iron axe head fell into the water and under Elisha's anointing it floated to the surface (2 Kings 6:1-7).
- Because of a band of raiders, a dead man was hastily let down into Elisha's tomb and upon touching his bones was brought to life (2 Kings 13:20-21).
- The shadow on the sundial went backwards by ten degrees (2 Kings 20:9-11 and Isaiah 38:7-8).
- The Lord hid Jeremiah and Baruch the scribe from the King of Judah who was unhappy about the prophecies he had given (Jeremiah 36:26).
- Ezekiel was transported in the spirit (Ezekiel 3:10-15).
- Meshach, Shadrach and Abednego were not burnt or singed in the fiery furnace (Daniel 3:8-30).
- Daniel was not attacked in the lion's den (Dan. 6:16-22).
- The feeding of the five and four thousand, the miraculous multiplication of food (Matthew 14:15-21, Matthew 15:32-38 and Matthew 16:8-10).
- Jesus instructed Peter to go fishing and to take the coin out of the fish's mouth which would be enough to pay both their temple taxes (Matthew 17:24-27).
- Jesus turned water into wine (John 2:1-10).
- Lazarus who had been dead for four days and was in his tomb was raised from the dead (John 11:39-44).
- Philip the evangelist was caught away in the Spirit (Divinely transported) to a town called Azotus (Acts 8:39-40).

'Who is wise? Let him understand these things. Who is prudent? Let him know them. For the ways of the Lord are right; the righteous walk in them, but the transgressors stumble in them' (Hosea 14:9).

Chapter 29

Human Emotions

'...Whom having not seen [Jesus] you love. Though now you do not see Him, yet believing, you rejoice with joy inexpressible and full of glory' (1 Peter 1:8).

Human Emotions

God made emotions and if He did not want them expressed then He would have not have created us this way! He would also never have permitted the Psalms, with their exhortation and shouts of praise that can only but move the emotions (Psalm 32:11). It has been said that if a person is void of emotions they are either emotionally bound or have hardness of heart.

During times of joy and happiness, people are known to shout, jump, clap, dance, shed tears or a whole host of other physical responses in their emotional excitement. Whether it is passing your driving test, accepting a proposal of marriage, receiving a letter stating that you've got a promotion, a phone call informing you that you have been accepted into an orchestra, hearing that your wife is pregnant, receiving an answer to a prayer, watching your country win the World Cup or your rugby club beating your rivals etc. Now, if people can get excited about these (and some are more excitable than others) then can we expect anything less, if not more, when God the Holy Spirit turns up and touches lives?

During the triumphal entry into Jerusalem, Jesus refused to silence a 'whole multitude of disciples' who 'began to rejoice and praise with a loud voice' and told the Pharisees that if the people kept quiet 'then the stones would immediately cry out' (Luke 19:37-40). Worship can be exuberant! (Psalm 4:11, 16:11, 47:1, 5).

During revival, when God turns up and His Spirit is poured out from on high; when He comes down and the hills melt like wax before Him; when He pours water on the dry and barren land; when He begins to fill those that thirst after Him and His righteousness, then you can expect the presence of God to externally affect people's bodies in different ways. If physical phenomena happen in the natural, such as when Samuel went to Bethlehem 'and the elders of the town trembled at his coming' (1 Samuel 15:9) then how much more when the Holy Spirit comes and meets with Christians and non-Christians during times of heavenly visitations? I expect all of us have been nervous at a job interview or perhaps before a vital test, but how much more will we tremble in the presence of a holy God when He comes?

When the Holy Spirit comes there can be many physical responses as the human body encounters the tangible presence of God. The Israelites were petrified when God descended on the top of Mount Sinai and the mountain shook and blazed with fire! Moses' face radiated God's glory when he met Him. Hannah in her intense prayer for a child was perceived to be drunk by the undiscerning Eli. The priests who dedicated the temple under King Solomon were unable to perform their duties as the glory of God descended. Isaiah saw his uncleanness before a holy God and cried out, "Woe to me." When Jesus was transfigured before the three disciples, Peter was so dumbstruck that he did not know what to say. John, on the island of Patmos heard a voice as of a trumpet and numerous people throughout the Bible received visions, had dreams or were in a trance as God met with them.

Bodily Reactions to God
- At the burning bush, 'Moses trembled and dared not look' (Acts 7:32 and Exodus 3:1-6). See also Psalm 2:11.
- The Psalmist wrote: 'My flesh trembles in fear of You, and I am afraid of Your judgments' (Psalm 119:120).
- Jeremiah was heartbroken because of the false prophets, "All my bones shake. I am like a drunken man whom wine has overcome, because of the Lord, and because of His holy words" (Jeremiah 23:9).
- In the garden of Gethsemane, when Jesus responded to the soldiers, saying, "I am He," 'they drew back and fell to the ground' (John 18:5-6).
- At the resurrection of Jesus, an angel of the Lord descended from heaven and rolled back the stone to His tomb, 'the guards shook for fear of Him, and became like dead men' (Matthew 28:1-4).
- Peter preached on the Day of Pentecost and was interrupted by the convicted listeners who had been cut to the heart – "What shall we do?" (Acts 2:1-41).

There is More
I have heard it said by well-meaning, godly Christians that when they were converted they received it all, but their shadows' do not heal the sick like the apostle Peter's (Acts 5:15), and their

handkerchiefs or aprons do not carry healing power like the apostle Paul (Acts 19:12-13). There is much more to experience and receive in Jesus' mighty name by the power of the Holy Spirit.

Godly Extremes

During times of revival there are always godly extremes, some will shout to the Lord, while others will be still in His presence, some will stand whilst others will be prostrated before Him. Some will dance, others will kneel. These natural godly emotions, during the same period of time (say within a meeting) will affect each person differently. These feelings and emotions will come and go, but as long as we continually walk in obedience to the Master, the inner experience will remain. God must continually be glorified and after we have met with God, our character and life will be changed – for the better, it will be abiding fruit. 'Serve the Lord with fear, and rejoice with trembling' (Psalm 2:11).

When God meets with a person, He can do a number of things: bring inner healing, show them their sonship, their adoption into the family of God, the fact that they are justified, sanctified, forgiven and made righteous because of what Jesus has done on the cross of Calvary. For many, these concepts are only intellectual and not heart-birthed in the inner man, but especially during revival these doctrines become living. God may refresh a person, renew them, heal them, mend them, bend them, soften them, commission them or reveal more of Himself and anything else He wants to do. It is God coming and meeting with the inner man, Spirit to spirit as God deals with the soul.

May God 'give to you the spirit of wisdom and revelation in the knowledge of Him, the eyes of your understanding being enlightened; that you may know the hope of His calling, what are the riches of the glory of His inheritance in the saints' (Ephesians 1:17-18). May God 'grant you, according to the riches of His glory, to be strengthened with might through His Spirit in the inner man...being rooted and grounded in love, may be able to comprehend with all the saints what is the width and length and depth and height – to know the love of Christ which passes knowledge; that you may be filled with all the fullness of God' (Ephesians 3:16-19).

The Baldhu Schoolmaster – Praising Loudly

After the first Christmas holiday during the Baldhu Revival (1851-1854) in the parish of Kea, near Truro, Cornwall, England, the Baldhu schoolmaster and his wife returned to their post. The

Church of England vicar, Rev. William Haslam wrote: 'They came back full of disdain and prejudiced against the work and even put themselves out of the way to go from house to house, in order to set the people against me and my preaching.'

'The master was particularly set against "excitement" and noise. He said, "It was so very much more reverend to be still in prayer, and orderly in praise; it was not necessary to make such an unseemly uproar!" I had however discovered that *the people who most objected to noise had nothing yet to make a noise about*, and that when they had; they generally made as much or more noise than others. If a house is seen to be on fire, people cannot help making an outcry; which they do not when they only read about it. Witnessing a danger stirs the heart; and when people's eyes are open to see souls in eternal danger, they cannot help being stirred up and crying out....'

'We read that 'the whole multitude of the disciples began to rejoice, and praise God with a loud voice, for all the mighty works that they had seen' (Luke 19:37) and we are told, over and over again, in the Psalms, to 'praise God with a loud voice,' and to 'shout.' When we lift up our voice, the Lord can stir our hearts; and surely the things of the Lord have more right, and ought to have more power, to stir and arouse the soul of man, than a boat race, or a horserace, or a fictitious scene on the stage. I think people would be all the better for letting out their hearts in praise to God. It may be it is trying and exciting to some, but perhaps they are the very ones who need such a stimulus, and this may be the best way to bring it out.'

The schoolmaster still attended the services. One Sunday at the after-service he was on his knees, crying out, "Oh, I fear there is no mercy – the sentence is surely gone forth against me, 'Cut him down! Cut him down!' " and 'then the poor man howled aloud in his distress. The people prayed for him with shouts of thanksgiving, while he threw himself about in agony of mind, and made a great noise, which only drew louder acclamations from the people. In the midst of this tremendous din [noise] he found peace, and rejoiced with the others in unmistakable accents, and as loud as the loudest.' The next Sunday, during the service, the schoolmaster, quickly left church, leaped over a wall and then over a hedge and ran into a field, shouting all the time – it was discovered afterwards that the *Prayer Book* was now full of meaning! See Isaiah 12:6.

Rev. William Haslam wrote: 'There were several revivals in the school while he was there, and many of the children were converted.'[1]

Chapter 30

Handling Physical Phenomena

'Peter, standing up with the eleven, raised his voice and said to them, "...These are not drunk as you suppose, since it is only the third hour of the day. But this is what was spoken by the Prophet Joel, 'And it shall come to pass in the last days, says God that I will pour out of My Spirit on all flesh; your sons and daughters shall prophesy, your young men shall see visions, your old men shall dream dreams. And on My menservants and on My maidservants I will pour out My Spirit in those days' " ' (Acts 2:14-18).

Exercise Sober Judgement
Humans are emotional beings – it is the way we have been designed and in times of revival, or any move of the Holy Spirit, these emotions will be heightened, resulting in wide-ranging physical phenomena, bodily manifestations, some of which may not be as a direct result of the Holy Spirit touching a person's life. It could be of human origin or of demonic origin. Unfortunately in many cases of physical phenomena we may be too quick to judge or presume we know that it is from God or the devil; someone seeking attention or a lack of restraint, but we can always see the *fruit* or *lack of it* within the person's life after the experience and more often that not, this will conclude a correct diagnosis because 'by their fruits you shall know them.' The Bible speaks much of godliness, personal character and putting to death the flesh life, the old man and walking in the newness of the Spirit.

Four Kinds of Physical Phenomena:
1. That which is caused by God's presence on a person.
2. That which is partially Divine and partly emotional.
3. That which is wholly emotional or hysterical.
4. That which is from the devil – demonic manifestations. In the presence of God demons will either be 'playing up' to cause a scene or will be leaving! Read Mark 9:14-27.

Michael Harper writing about the twentieth century Pentecostal Revival wrote: 'There will always be sensuous people looking for cheap thrills and exciting experiences. There will always be those who specialise in the bizarre and unusual and who will be drawn to such a movement...when we move into the supernatural realm we are more likely to be deceived than before. Satan is very cunning, and can even disguise himself as an angel of light.'[1]

With God's help we are called to discern and carefully distinguish between the flesh and the Spirit – we are called to exercise sober judgment. We are called to 'test the spirits' (is it of demonic origin?), not test the phenomena; we can also test the fruit in a person's life. What is their lifestyle like, holy or unholy? Can they declare, "Jesus is Lord" (1 Corinthians 12:13) and acknowledge that He came in the flesh? (1 John 4:1-2 and 2 John 7-11).

It is all too easy to judge another, which we are commanded not to do (Matthew 7:1-5) and we may forget that it is the duty of the pastor or leader to exhort, correct and rebuke the flock (leading to edification via repentance and restoration) and *not us*. They are in spiritual authority and it is *they* who have to give an account to God for those under their care. No one is infallible, and mistakes will be made in areas of judgment especially in regards to physical phenomena, hearsay and half truths during times of revival and whenever the Holy Spirit turns up at a meeting.

We cannot judge a work of God by its phenomena nor by those who are in the flesh. Pastor John Kilpatrick said, "The surest way to stop judging manifestations is for it to happen to you!" Whilst Dave Roberts, editor of *Alpha* magazine wrote: 'Let those who are without carnal [worldly / fleshly] Christians somewhere in their congregation cast the first stone.'

Jonathan Edwards of the eighteenth century rightly noted that 'although the Scripture is full of rules, both how we should judge our own state and also how we should conduct ourselves before others, there are no rules by which to judge emotions.'[2]

The revivals in Kentucky which began in 1800 during the pioneering days of America had perhaps the most 'wildest' (in a positive definition) physical phenomena on record, of shakings, jerking and loud cries, to name some, though undoubtedly, not all was as a direct result of the Holy Spirit touching lives as there is always a minority. See Appendix D.

Division and Divisiveness

All revivals and accompanying phenomena are divisive, but even Jesus, the Prince of Peace, stated that His ministry would cause division, as some members of a household would follow Him whilst others would not (Luke 12:51-53). Not everyone attributed Jesus' ministry as from God (Mark 3:22-29 and John 7:40-43), whilst others hated Him 'without a cause' (John 15:24-25). John the Baptist upset people, calling them to "Repent!"

Stephen F. Olford said, "There is no mistaking it when God starts to work, for men and women are either antagonised by, or attracted to Christ, but never neutralised."

Jonathan Edwards wrote: 'A work of God without stumbling blocks is never to be expected.'

To say that because something causes division it must be evil or wrong is an incorrect assumption and unbiblical. People were divided over Jesus' ministry (John 9:16-34) but He was sinless! The Nazarene 'sect' was 'spoken against everywhere…some were persuaded' and 'others disbelieved' (Acts 28:22-24).

Jesus once said, "Glorify Your name" and a voice came from heaven. Those present were of divided opinion, some said it thundered and others said an angel spoke, but the sign happened for *their* sake (John 12:28-30).

On the Day of Pentecost, thousands heard 'the wonderful works of God' in their own languages, whilst others mocking, said, "They are full of new wine" (Acts 2:1-15).

At Iconium, many Greeks believed the good news, but the 'unbelieving Jews stirred up the Gentiles and *poisoned their minds* against the brethren.' Even after staying there a long time where signs and wonders were performed, the 'city was divided' – to embrace them or stone them?! (Acts 14:1-5).

Imagine; revival comes to a church and is embraced by the leader, but the congregation are divided. Some want to stay with the status quo feeling safe with their familiar services or content in their traditions, whilst others embrace the Lord's will and some stand on the sideline, undecided. Is the leader of the church guilty of divisiveness because he has chosen to go God's way and allowed the Holy Spirit to do what He wants to do? No, the guilt of divisiveness lays on the other side, for those who do not want God to move and *oppose* His workings.

Who can Stand before God

Frequently in revival and times of refreshing, the human body will not be able to stand before the Holy presence of God. Over the centuries various revivalists and witnesses have described this as: 'stricken by God,' 'being overcome,' 'falling,' 'fainting,' 'struck down,' 'sank down,' 'fell over,' 'prostrated,' 'swooning,' 'deprived of their bodily strength,' 'slain in the Spirit' or 'resting in the Spirit.'

Eyewitnesses from different centuries in different countries have recorded these events as: 'swept down in a moment as if a battery of a thousand guns had been opened upon them,' 'cut like grains before a sickle,' 'they fell quicker than they could be cut down by a swordsman;' and 'it was like a field of battle those slain by the Spirit of the Lord.'

Daniel Powell Williams of Penygroes, in Carmarthen, South Wales, UK, was converted on Christmas Day 1904 in Lougher, the birthplace of the Welsh Revival (1904-1905). In reference to the revival he wrote: 'The manifestation of the power was beyond human management. Men and women were mowed down by the axe of God like a forest. The glory was resting for over two years in some localities.'[3]

These writers have also described these same people who have been overcome by the Spirit of God in involuntarily trembling as 'shaking,' 'jerking,' 'shivering,' 'convulsions,' 'agitation of body,' 'rolling around' and 'trembled.' Sometimes people have been labelled as: Quakers, Jumpers, Ranters or Shakers because of the physical phenomena which characterised a movement. Throughout the Bible you will see these physical phenomena and many others scattered throughout the pages of the Holy Bible.[4]

God's Design

In times of revival, the focus should never be on the physical phenomena as a sign or proof of revival, but we should not be alarmed when we witness these events. There is nothing new under the sun and what has been will be. The main focus, within a person's life should be the person's lifestyle – do they bear fruit? Have they confessed and forsaken sin, do they have victory over sin, do they glorify Jesus more and is their life God exalting? Whilst Church history records that during times of revival physical phenomena will happen, to a lesser or greater degree, it is merely peripheral in the greater out-working of God, to be salt and light amidst a wicked and perverse generation.

Dr. James C. L. Carson, a prominent medical practitioner in Coleraine during the 1859 Irish Revival, speaking about the physical phenomena said, "Without doubt, there is a great physical agent, as well as a spiritual one, abroad. The one is, as it were, the hand-maid to the other. They are both specially from God, and are most admirably calculated to work out His great design…. It would be well for those parties who look on physical manifestations as an evil, which should be avoided and repressed, to reconsider their ways. It is an awful thing to be found fighting against God. How dreadful is this presumption which will dare to dictate to the Almighty the way in which He should save sinners!"[5]

Chapter 31

Foolish Excess and the Demonic

'Be sober, be vigilant; because your adversary the devil walks about like a roaring lion, seeking whom he may devour. Resist him, steadfast in the faith...' (1 Peter 4:8-9a).

Excess, Attention-Seekers – FLESH!

Whilst the presence of God affects different people in different ways, we must be aware of foolish excess, attention-seekers and emotional manipulation – the flesh. However, just as important, we are not to resist, quench or grieve the Holy Spirit by our refusal to submit to Him or by being an obstruction in the lives of others. Both outward and inward opposition to the things of God are very dangerous.

There will always be those who fall prey to the latest gimmick or fad and in times of revival or refreshing they may try to jump on the bandwagon and work it up in the flesh. This can be for several reasons: not wanting to be left out, believing it bolsters their spiritual level or plain scoffing or mocking the things of God by imitation. On the other hand there will be those who will stubbornly resist God and what He is doing believing it not to be from Him and these people are inversely fleshly as others are overtly carnal.

Others 'have a zeal for God, but not according to knowledge' (Romans 10:2) – this is also true of Christians who oppose revivals and the moving of the Holy Spirit, who think they are doing Him a favour, as did Saul the persecutor of the Church before his dramatic conversion.

Steve Hill speaking at the Brownsville Revival (1995-2000) in an interview with *Charisma*, stated that by his estimate five percent of what he saw during the revival was fleshly. He said, "You can go to any meeting anywhere and see flesh, if that's what you're looking for. I don't go to these meetings looking for flesh; I go looking for God." Steve concluded, "Am I going to concentrate on five percent? No. You deal with the important situations, but you let God control the revival."[1]

Helen Dyer in reference to the Mukti Revival (1905-1906) in India, wrote: 'The work went on rapidly...Satan was also busy, and tried to counterfeit all he saw. Some who beheld the joy thought they could get it by imitating what they had seen the others do. Yet the work went on, and a spirit of prayer and supplication for a revival in India was poured out like a flood.'[2]

Deliverance from Demons (Exorcism)

In revival or whenever the Holy Spirit moves demons are frightened and may cry out and depart from a person. It is a clash of two worlds, the Kingdom of Light and the kingdom of darkness. Whilst at other times they will publicly manifest (cry out, scream, slither along the floor etc., to cause a scene) and it is the Church's responsibility to bind the strong man (Mark 3:24, 27) and to cast them out in the mighty name of Jesus Christ. In any meeting where God is moving, a person's face may be contorting, but let us not be hasty in our judgment, are the demons manifesting or fleeing? If we reject the Holy Spirit then is it possible that we come under the control or influence of other spirits?

There will be those who demonically manifest, because when the Spirit of God comes down, the demons hate it. These demons need to be commanded to leave in the name of Jesus Christ and a deliverance session can take many hours, often over a period of time. Some people say that as Jesus just spoke a word (which He did *on occasions*) and evil spirits fled, all we have to do is speak a word and they will leave. This has not been my experience, *instant* deliverance; nor of John Wesley nor of most modern-day disciples who obey Jesus' command to preach the gospel and to cast out demons in His name (Mark 16:15-18), some of which can only come out by 'prayer and fasting' (Matthew 17:19-21 and Mark 9:18-29). This is covered alongside related topics of ministry in my book *Discipleship For Everyday Living: Christian Growth.*

During the Argentine Revival (1982-1997), deliverance was *essential* for all new believers along with mass discipleship and being committed to a church of whatever denomination or style took the person's preference. Carlos Annacondia, during some of his campaigns would preach for two months every night and behind the platform there would be a 150-foot tent with yellow and white stripes, which was the "Spiritual intensive care unit" where mass deliverance sessions would be held. Trained workers, "stretcher bearers" would be on the lookout for people manifesting (under the influences of evil spirits / demons) and carry them to the tent where they would pray for them to be delivered. As time went on, mass deliverance sessions were commenced as the strong man was bound, Jesus' name invoked, curses were broken and people were delivered from the evil one.

Chapter 32

Rebellion against the Holy Spirit

'Do not grieve the Holy Spirit of God, by whom you were sealed for the day of redemption' (Ephesians 4:30).

Resisting, Grieving and Quenching the Spirit
We can be just as carnal singing hymns or choruses in a restrained or reluctant manner as in jumping up and down trying to draw attention to ourselves. Resisting the Spirit of God and trying to work up something are both fleshly in nature and wrong. One is outwardly dishonouring to God, the other is inwardly dishonouring to God, both are sinful and neither glorifies the Lord.

Max Warren, in the context of worship during the East African Revival (1930s-1950s) wrote: 'Dancing rhythmic movements and repetitive singing in chorus are spontaneous African expressions of joy.... The appeal of these things in the separatist movement elsewhere should be a warning, lest the traditional sobriety of, for instance, Anglican worship and devotion, too rigidly interpreted, prove too constraining for the rejuvenate spirit of the African. If there is a danger in unrestrained ecstasy, there is also the dullness of decorum.'[1]

If we resist what the Holy Spirit is doing then we are carnal rebels and rebellion is as the sin of witchcraft (1 Samuel 15:23). We are commanded not to 'quench' nor 'grieve' the Holy Spirit (1 Thessalonians 5:19 and Ephesians 4:30) and 'resisting' Him is just as sinful (Acts 7:51), and if we do, then I fail to see how we can call Jesus our Lord, because as the saying goes: 'Either He is Lord of all or He is not Lord at all.' To resist the Holy Spirit is being stiff-necked, rejecting Him and resisting what He wants to do in either our lives or the life of the Church; in effect we are saying, "We know better than God and our judgment is superior!"

To quench the Holy Spirit is like putting water on an open fire, to stop what the Holy Spirit is doing in a meeting, sticking to a routine of religion, our traditions (within our own lives or meetings) and not allowing Him to do what He wants to. To grieve the Holy Spirit, is to go into the flesh, to sin, or to attribute something that is of God as being from the evil one, or to stop what He is doing in a meeting (stopping the meeting, when He is working). To quench or grieve the Holy Spirit both displaces His rightful place within a meeting therefore disenabling Him to glorify Jesus. To attribute a work of God as being from the devil is the unpardonable sin which Jesus warned of, blaspheming the Holy Spirit when His anointing was attributed to beelzebub, the ruler of demons (Matthew 12:24-31).

Do not Harden Your Heart

There is a grave danger when someone hardens his or her heart against the things of God as did Pharaoh, or disbelieve, as according to one's faith it will not be done unto them. See Matthew 9:27-29. This is the rule and not the exception.

The heart is deceitful above all things and desperately wicked (Jeremiah 17:9) and we should be aware of setting up idols in our hearts (Ezekiel 14:1-6). God can also be crushed and grieved by our adulterous heart (Ezekiel 6:9). Those with an evil heart of unbelief will depart from God (Hebrews 3:12) and people do commit sin believing that God cannot see (Ezekiel 8:7-12). We should be aware of having a blasé attitude towards the Word of the Lord, idols and sin (Jeremiah 44:15-17) as it is possible to draw near to God with our lips, yet our hearts can be far from Him (Psalm 81:15 and Isaiah 29:13) and God knows the secrets of the heart (Psalm 44:21). We are told to give God our hearts (Prov. 23:6). He who trusts in his own heart is a fool (Prov. 28:26a).

On occasions God overrides a person's will or intervenes in a dramatic way. Saul of Tarsus (later known as Paul) was struck by God and fell to the floor. He got converted against his will, after seeing the bright light as Jesus confronted him (Acts 9:1-9). Through his misplaced zeal, Saul, believing he was working for God was actually fighting against Him (see Acts 5:38-39 and Acts 23:9), persecuting those who loyally followed Jesus. Saul was persecuting Jesus Himself, but God still had mercy on him. Later on, Paul was persecuted for his faith in Christ and the revivals he saw were accompanied by opposition and riots.

Some aspects of God's activity seem harder to understand than others, but that is no excuse to reject what He is doing or to look down upon those who are having emotional responses, physical phenomena, because of His presence. To try to understand God is beyond comprehension as His ways are not our ways, and His plans are much higher than ours (Isaiah 55:8-9). 'There are many plans in a man's heart, nevertheless the Lord's counsel – that will stand' (Proverbs 19:21). 'The foolishness of a man twists his way, and his heart frets against the Lord' (Proverbs 19:3). Do not fret against God; let Him have His way in your life.

Stephen F. Olford speaking on 'The Price of Revival' at Westminster Chapel, London, in September 1946, said, "It is really pathetic to enter some meeting places and sense the lifelessness and absence of joy among those who gather. It reminds one of the story of a brother who was a real personification of the lack of enthusiasm. He was standing one day outside a certain gospel hall, trying to invite folk into the meeting. He stopped one man and asked him to come in. "No thank you," replied the stranger, "I have enough troubles of my own!"[2]

Dr. Stanley Smith documented the story of the Ruanda Mission which was caught up in revival in 1937, which was the catalyst to the East Africa Revival (1930s-1950s). He wrote: 'They [the Africans] are convinced that the deadliest enemy to the cause of Christ is the nominal Christian and that every born again, blood-bought Christian must be characterised by burning zeal, by purity of life, and by standing as a witness to dying men of a life-giving Christ. Where such signs are missing, they seriously question the reality of the religious profession.'[3]

'Cry out and shout all O inhabitants of Zion, for great is the Holy One of Israel in your midst' (Isaiah 12:6).

Leadership and Discernment

In the Old Testament, there was a man called Elkanah who had two wives, one was barren because the Lord had closed her womb. Hannah, was so desperate for a child and being provoked by Peninnah (Elkanah's other wife), she wept and refused to eat. In Shiloh 'she was in bitterness of soul, and prayed to the Lord and wept in anguish.' She made a vow to God, promising Him that if she gave birth to a son she would give him to the Lord all the days of her life. Hannah spoke only in her heart, her lips moved but no sound came out. Eli the priest thought she was drunk and rebuked her, saying, "How long will you be drunk? Put your wine away from you!" She responded gently, stating that she was not drunk, nor had she drunk any alcohol, but was in a sorrowful spirit and had prayed out of her anguish and grief. Eli was happy with the explanation and stated his desire for God to grant her request. The following year she gave birth to Samuel, who grew up in the house of the Lord and became a mighty prophet and leader of Israel (1 Samuel 1:10-20).

For those within leadership, to pastor a revival need a great level of humility, brokenness and discernment, especially when passing judgment on a situation. But when even the best leaders make mistakes, then how much more those who have lesser experience and maturity? The good news is that in times of revival, under the searchlight of the Holy Spirit, people are highly sensitive to sin, responsive to repentance and forsaking sin and desire to live righteously before a holy God, acknowledging the difference between, 'The holy and the unholy, and causing them to discern between the unclean and the clean' (Ezekiel 44:23). Revival quickens evangelism and aids discipleship, 'Warning every man and teaching every man in all wisdom, that we may present every man perfect in Christ Jesus' (Colossians 1:28).

One worker during the Mukti Revival (1905-1906) in India, wrote: 'There is a very true work of God going on in our midst.... There is much one cannot understand at first, but one grows by His grace into the work and learns to distinguish by the outward signs as well as by the Spirit's inward teaching, the false from the true. Satan counterfeits all that the Lord does, and is working harder to hinder and spoil the work of God, but he is a conquered foe!'[4]

Dr. Michael Brown was approached by a cynic who asked about the youth of the Brownsville Revival (1995-2000) in Florida, America, "whether or not it is possible that some of them are getting in the flesh?" His reply was, "I'm sure it's possible that some of them are getting in the flesh, just as I'm very sure it's probable that ninety-nine percent of people sitting in dead churches are in the flesh the whole time."[5]

Rev. Duncan Campbell in the conclusion to his narrative about the Lewis Revival (1949-1952) wrote: 'One who though mightily used of God, did not escape the bitter opposition of leaders in the Church: "I verily believe revival would have come to —— at that time if prayerful sympathy, instead of carnal criticism had been shown. If only those who opposed had gone to hear for themselves, how different the story might have been today!"'[6]

Pastor John Kilpatrick, during the Brownsville Revival (1995-2000) in America, continually prayed, "Lord please give me wisdom to pastor this thing. Lord, I don't want to be so lenient that I let anything in, but Lord I don't want to be so hard either that I don't let what You're trying to do in – God please give me wisdom. Holy Spirit, help me to walk humbly before You. Holy Spirit, help me to keep my mind on the Lord and to keep my eyes on the Lord, and Holy Spirit, help me not to get distracted with things, where I begin to let the embers grow dim and cold in my life, and Lord, help me not to let the fire go out in this church; Lord, help me...."[7]

Chapter 33

A Variety of Human Personalities

'But when Peter had come to Antioch, I withstood him to his face, because he was to be blamed.... And the rest of the Jews also played the hypocrite with him, so that even Barnabas was carried away with their hypocrisy' (Galatians 2:11, 13).

Prone to make Mistakes

Some people incorrectly assume that because a person makes a mistake, or has a different theological viewpoint than them (on non essential doctrines) then they cannot be used of God. Thank God that despite our imperfections He can use us! We think of lying Abram (renamed Abraham), angry Moses, adulterer and murdering King David, sharp-tongued Peter (who also denied knowing Jesus Christ), doubting Thomas, Saul the persecutor (renamed Paul), John Mark the quitter, Barnabas who was led astray, and Apollos who preached half a gospel. All these men despite their mistakes and character flaws were set on doing the will of God, most with all their heart, mind, soul and strength. Their mistakes were just blips on life's progress chart and they learnt from them, as can we.

The fifteenth century saw reformers such as John Wycliffe of England and John Hus of Bohemia (Czech Republic). The Reformation of the sixteenth century was the most spiritual cataclysmic event that has happened in Europe during the last half a millennia, but all of the sixteenth century reformers had flawed personalities and some held extreme theological views, just like some of us, though naturally this does depend on what side of the fence you sit or stand!

All of the leading reformers (except Erasmus) were distinctly opposed to foreign missions; 'reaching the heathen for Christ' was simply not on the agenda. They stated that the command to go and teach all nations had been carried out by the apostles, 1,500 years previously and therefore was no longer incumbent on them! This was regardless of the fact that vast sways of lands were filled with barbarous and simple tribes. It was only in 1492 that the Americas were discovered, and Australia and New Zealand were not even known. Even in the twenty-first century, there are still people groups who have never ever heard the name of Jesus Christ!

Martin Luther, the German reformer was anti-Semitic, he wanted all Jews to be deported to the Holy Land and their synagogues and books burned. Whilst to the day of his death he stood by the Roman Catholic doctrine of transubstantiation, that during communion the bread and the wine literally becomes the flesh and blood of Jesus Christ. Jonathan Edward's grandfather, Solomon Stoddard of Northampton believed that the Lord's Supper was open for anyone, writing in 1707: it 'is a converting ordinance.' He saw five revivals in his ministry: 1679, 1680, 1683, 1696 and 1712.

Huldrych Zwingli, the German speaking Swiss reformer, authorised the killing by drowning of Anabaptists (a Christian movement loosely organised, but who were not a cult) for those who participated in adult rebaptism. Also, Huldrych Zwingli and Martin Luther did not get along with each other.

John Knox, the Scottish reformer was all for the dispossession of a ruler (a king or queen), by imprisonment, capital punishment or assassination. *If* a ruler went outside of the will of God by disobeying His commands, then he or she forfeited all rights as God's governor and could be justifiably punished by the people. When Knox was living in Frankfurt (Germany) and then in Geneva (Switzerland), some of his comments and views greatly alarmed John Calvin. Yet all these men were Christian giants in their time.

In Geneva, you can see fifteen-foot (3m) stone statues of the reformers along with a large stone memorial to the entire Reformation era. None of us would doubt that they all were men of God who came into the Kingdom for such a time as theirs. The three essential reanimated biblical truths of the Reformation are just as important now, as then within the Protestant Church: 1. The Holy Bible is the final authority on all matters of doctrine and dogma. 2. Justification by faith, salvation is only by faith in the atoning work of Jesus Christ; by grace and not of works (Romans 3:22-25). 3. The priesthood of all believers (1 Peter 2:5-9).

John Calvin gave great emphasis on God's predestined will, that for many who followed this line of thinking to the extreme, it literally relinquished them of any responsibility for their actions. Even John Wesley and George Whitefield, the godly Goliaths of the eighteenth century awakenings disagreed over predestination (Calvinism) versus man's free will (Arminianism) which caused a split in early Methodism and for many years greatly strained their relationship. See Appendix C. If Wesley and Whitefield, along with their respective supporters and followers had taken the advice of Henry Venn (1724-1797) then things may have been different. Venn was a preacher at Huddersfield, England, and refused to be drawn into an argument when the Calvinistic controversy broke out and discouraged such disputes. When once asked whether a certain minister was a Calvinist or Arminian he replied, "I really do not know, he is a sincere disciple of the Lord Jesus Christ, and that is of infinitely more importance than being a disciple of Calvin or Arminius."[1]

During the first few years of George Whitefield's ministry in the 1730s, he was rash and impulsive, and was without financial savvy. Whilst financing an orphanage in Georgia, New England, he got into debt of £1,000 and along with £200 of travelling expenses (debt) was nearly arrested in Britain because of it!

As a wise man once said, "It is an ungracious and ungrateful task to dwell on a man's weaknesses. It is more profitable and more pleasant to turn to the real good that they did." And it is to this that all those previously mentioned are truly remembered for.

Diversity of Views

There is a big danger in building a lot on a little, especially when it is a man-made opinion, preconceived idea or an interpretation and we must be aware of prejudices (personal, nationalistic, racial, denominational or theological) as these can all distort correct biblical doctrine. Even the best teachers will at times make mistakes. As the apostle James wrote: 'We *all stumble in many things.* If anyone does not stumble in word, he is a perfect man...' (James 3:2). Great men and women of God can be working towards the same end whilst using different means and methods; holding different theological views than their contemporaries (or from those in another century) and can still be used of God (even in revival) despite their differences or methods.

In mid seventeenth century England, George Fox founded the Society of Friends, the 'Quakers' and through his preaching of Scriptural truths, more than fifty thousand were converted back to the pure faith in forty years. Quakers believed that baptism was not in accord with the mind of Christ. They believed that no outward form of baptism need be observed, but we could not doubt the commitment of George Fox and his followers towards the work of evangelisation during Puritan England. Nowadays, most Quakers are no longer Christian, having drifted so far from the faith!

Count Zinzendorf saw revival in his community at Herrnhut, (in modern-day Germany) in 1727, which sparked off the Moravian missionary movement. The Moravians greatly influenced John and Charles Wesley, though at the time, these ministers were unconverted. In England they held joint services, but within a few years the Moravians and the Wesley's soon parted company over doctrinal issues; and the Moravians who did not want to be associated with them published this fact in an English newspaper. When Zinzendorf visited America, the Tennents, who were used during the American Great Awakening (1735-1760) wrote tracts opposing him, alongside some other preachers. Yet they were all ministers of God, preached the pure gospel and all saw revival!

Imminent Return of Christ

Jonathan Edwards and Charles Finney, two different revivalists from the eighteenth and nineteenth centuries respectively, both believed that the awakenings they were involved in could lead into the millennial reign; as have many revivalists since. They believed this, the imminent return of Jesus Christ because of what they were seeing as multitudes turned to Christ, year after year, as towns and communities were transformed to the glory of God.

Jesus Christ will return soon, for a pure and holy bride – let us be ready for His return with oil in our lamps, watching and waiting.

Say the Wrong Things

On occasions we all say things that we did not mean to say (Luke 9:33), due to confusion, tiredness, caught of guard or a slip of the tongue etc., or we do not say what we intended to say. In haste or under duress we can speak foolishly (Mark 9:5-6). The Psalmist said, "I believe therefore I spoke…all men are liars" (Psalm 116:10-11) and there is a danger in being hasty with words (Proverbs 29:20). People can sincerely believe what they do, yet still be entirely wrong, see Jeremiah 23:16b, 25-26. A wise person will sift everything they hear or read to see whether it lines up with Scripture and will not major on the minors. Do not disregard or dismiss a person's teaching because you disagree with one sentence – take the best (of their Scriptural teaching) and leave the rest (the fleshly comments), that's maturity. The revivalists through the ages had differing views and theological stances, yet God still used them despite their differences or failings.

Revivalist, John Berridge (1716-1793) of Everton, England, oftentimes over indulged in his humour and declared, "I was born with a fool's cap on." In a letter he wrote: 'Odd things break forth from me as abruptly as croaking from a raven.'

Altered Opinions

People may change their opinions and views over time having made the best possible judgment with the light and understanding that they have. Whilst the Bible declares that 'a double-minded man, [is] unstable in all his ways' (James 1:8) we should not be stubborn like a mule and stick to our principles, when we realise that our views (however honest and sincere) were flawed because the Holy Spirit has since revealed the truth. It is better to admit that we were wrong than to live in the realm of stubborn pride. The Holy Spirit will guide us 'into all truth' (John 16:13), if we allow Him.

John Wesley disdained the idea of lay-preachers, it was repugnant to him and his dislike of them was only overruled by the advice of the one whose counsel he never neglected, his mother, the saintly Susanna Wesley. John Wesley also thought that it was wrong to preach outside of a church building, until he found the doors of many churches closed to him! On Saturday, 31 March 1739, John Wesley met George Whitefield in Bristol, because he had been invited by his friend to take over the successful preaching to the tens of thousands of colliers at Kingswood. The next day Wesley stood in his friend's congregation in the open fields with conflicting feelings. He wrote: 'I could scarce reconcile myself at first to this strange way of preaching in the fields, of which he set an example on Sunday; having been all my life (till very lately) so tenacious of every point relating to decency and order, that I should have thought the saving of souls almost a sin if it had not been done in a church.'[2]

One author from the nineteenth century, writing about the eighteenth century Evangelical Revival (1739-1791) wrote: 'So far was Wesley from being obstinately wedded to his own opinions that he laid himself fairly open to the charge of inconsistency by so frequently modifying them.'[3]

George Whitefield disagreed with the physical prostrations that happened under John Wesley's preaching, but he changed his mind when it happened during his sermons! Wesley on 7 July 1739, spoke to Whitefield 'of those outward signs which had so often accompanied the inward work of God. I found his objections were chiefly grounded on gross misrepresentations of matter of fact,' wrote Wesley in his *Journal*, 'but the next day he had opportunity of informing himself better, for no sooner had he begun to invite all sinners to believe in Christ, than four persons sunk down close to him, almost in the same moment. One of them lay without sense or motion. A second trembled exceedingly. The third had strong convulsions all over his body, but made no noise, unless by groans. The fourth equally convulsed, called upon God, with strong cries and tears. From this time on I trust, we shall all suffer God to carry on His work in the way that pleaseth Him.'[4]

In 1852, evangelist William Booth met Catherine, who shared his views on social reforms but not over the role of women preachers; they married in June 1855. In 1860, Mrs Booth started to preach as she felt compelled by the Spirit of God and could not stay silent any longer, her husband was so impressed by her anointing that his views on women preachers radically changed. The following year revival broke out in Hayle, Cornwall, where 7,000 Cornishmen were converted in just eighteen months during 1861-1862.

Controversy and Contentions

Controversy for the sake of controversy is not a good thing, because 'a brother offended is harder to win than a strong city, and contentions are like the bars of a castle' (Proverbs 18:19). The Holy Bible informs us of many things, which we should not discuss. This is because of the negative effects that can be provoked and manifested through ignorant, unsanctified or stubborn lives. If we desire to see revival in our lives, our church and our country then we must stop being controversial just for the sake of it. We should be generous in our acceptance of others (but not blind to heretics) and we must be aware of the tone of our voice as it may be more inclined to aggravate than to consolidate. But the denunciation of sin (to publicly declare it's wrong or evil) and a clarion call (loud and clear) to "repent," whilst preaching Christ and Him crucified is always controversial for lukewarm Christians (and those outside the Church) as it rocks the boat of complacency and challenges them to forsake sin, and to flee to Christ from the wrath to come.

We should not build our biblical knowledge or faith on one truth only to neglect other truths which are equally important. We can overemphasise or give more prominence to some issues and neglect or underemphasise others. If you take just one part of truth and do not consider the other parts then you will reach a wrong conclusion. Truth out of balance becomes error. There is truth, half truth or error. Truth is found in having firm grounding in the Word of God. Half truth and error can be because of ignorance (Acts 18:24-26), deception (2 Timothy 3:13) or being under the influence of deceiving spirits (1 Timothy 4:1-2). J. Edwin Orr wrote: 'Half the heresies are due to an overemphasis of real truth without the balance of other doctrines in proportion.'

If we know what someone believes and our opinion is contrary, then why bring the same subject to the fore? Why do we want to discuss certain subjects? Is it to learn, to inform or to force our beliefs onto another? 'A fool has no delight in understanding, but in expressing his own heart' (Proverbs 18:2).

Chapter 34

The Tongue and Social Networks

'Finally, all of you be of one mind, having compassion for one another; love as brothers, be tender-hearted, be courteous; not returning evil for evil or reviling for reviling, but on the contrary blessing, knowing that you were called to this, that you may inherit a blessing' (1 Peter 3:8-9).

Doctrine, Discussions and Misunderstandings
  We are called to come together in the 'unity of the faith' (Ephesians 4:11-13), not the unity of *our* doctrine as non-orthodox doctrines vary, whilst the fundamentals of orthodox Christianity are unchanging. Therefore, we should not stand aloof because of denominational nonessentials. Some truths are fundamental whilst others are not as central as we might believe. We should have love one for another so that all men will know that we are His disciples (John 13:34-35). Revival can touch a congregation, yet pass by others in the same village or town when tradition, denominational doctrines (or a refusal to allow the Holy Spirit to move) become more important than the unity of the faith; one in Christ.
  It is possible to believe that some Christians are *wholly* wrong who nevertheless are pleasing to God and would be to us, if we understood them. Under the command of God, Moses summoned the seventy elders of Israel and the Lord descended in a cloud. He took of the Spirit that was on Moses and placed the same Spirit upon the elders and they began to prophesy. Two elders, Elad and Medad remained in the camp, but the Spirit of God came upon them and they prophesied. Joshua, Moses' assistant said, "Moses, my lord, forbid them!" But he replied, "Oh, that all the Lord's people were prophets and that the Lord would put His Spirit on them" (Joshua 11:16-30).
  After the land of Canaan had been taken, two and a half tribes of Israel who had chosen not to settle in the Promised Land, set up an altar (of witness) on the other side of the Jordan River. This was seen as an act of unfaithfulness, following another god, and the tribes of Israel wanted to punish them. Ten tribal rulers spoke to the alleged offenders and when the innocence of the altar was revealed, all the twelve tribes of Israel were able to rejoice together

as war was averted (Joshua 22:11-34). The altar was set up for future generations so that they would not forget that they were one nation, because the River Jordan divided them.

It is possible for Christians to get confused in regards to false doctrine, heresy and heretics, which can lead to contentions because their senses have not been exercised 'to discern good and evil' (Hebrews 5:14). Some hold allegiance to a particular leader, "I am of Paul" or "I am of Apollos" whilst rejecting others (1 Corinthians 1:12-13, 30-31). This causes friction and even division, but our allegiance should always be to Christ and His doctrine.

During the 1859 revival in Wales, unity was manifested amongst several denominations, particularly the non-conformists bodies. 'This unity arose from two main sources; the one, an agreement as to the basic truths of the gospel, and the other, a common, fervent desire for a visitation of the Holy Spirit to glorify Christ as Saviour and Lord. Inasmuch as each denomination based its faith and practice at that time upon God's revealed truth, as found in Holy Scripture, their unity did not involve the violation of any of their distinctive principles, nor the surrender of any essential belief, as these were all common to all. Consequently, their prayer meetings and joint services were eminently useful in furthering the work of the revival, being soundly based on essential, Divinely-revealed truth.'[1]

Wisdom in Words

One of the keys to revival is unity amongst the brethren, albeit only a small group of believers may be praying for a spiritual awakening, but it is impossible to be in unity when we keep having discussions on non-important issues, which only cause division, suspicion or estrangement. The Bible warns us *not* to discuss certain things, as they are unprofitable, unedifying and divisive. They do not make for peace or edify. Things such as: fables and endless genealogies which cause disputes, profane old wives' tales, gossiping, disputes and arguments over words which produces envy, strife, reviling, evil suspicions, and irreverent, sinful, wicked and godless chatter (Ephesians 4:29-30, 1 Timothy 1:4, 1 Timothy 4:7, 1 Timothy 5:13, 1 Timothy 6:4 and 1 Timothy 6:20-21). We are not to strive about words to no profit as it benefits no one and brings ruin to those in earshot. We should shun profane and vain babblings which leads to ungodliness and we should not put up with those who do not endure sound doctrine, having itching ears and who turn aside to fables (2 Timothy 2:14, 16 and 2 Timothy 4:3-4). We are also to disregard Jewish fables and avoid foolish disputes and strivings about the Law (Titus 1:14 and 3:9). We are also warned about grieving the Holy Spirit.

There is a big danger of building a lot on a little especially when that little happens to be a preconceived idea. We are told to warn those who cause divisions and offences and reject them after the second warning and to avoid them (Romans 16:17 and Titus 3:10). We should pursue things that make for peace and edify (Proverbs 25:11-12 and Romans 14:19). Do not answer a fool according to his folly, less he despise the wisdom of your words (see Isaiah 5:20, Proverbs 23:9 and Proverbs 26:4-5).

James Hervey (1714-1758), a minister during the British Great Awakening, in reference to disputes of doubtful disputation wrote: 'If they happen to be started in conversation, I always endeavour to divert the discourse to some more edifying topic. I have often observed them to breed animosity and division, but never knew them to be productive of love and unanimity.'

The Blessing and Judgment of Revival

Revival is not the romantic ideal, which many Christians make it out to be. Just as Jesus came as a babe, He will return as a Judge with a sword in His hand. Revival can be traumatic for Christians within the Church as it really rocks the boat, sifts and shakes. If we are not living right before a holy and just God, when the Refiner comes, the Holy Spirit, He will scorch / chastise before the floods will be poured out! Revival can be a solemn commotion and a Divine disorder all at the same time; with some rejoicing that the Holy Spirit has come whilst others are on their faces before a holy God, weeping and confessing their sins, looking to the cross and pleading for pardon in fear of the wrath to come.

Revival is like a two-edged sword, it is a blessing for many and judgment for a minority. It is 'a sign that is spoken against' for 'the fall and rising of many' because God's presence will reveal the true state of people's hearts (Luke 2:35). The blessing of revival is to cut free and deliver, for the cleansing, purging, sifting, shaking and restoration of the Church, '…do not despise the chastening of the Almighty. For He bruises, but He binds up; He wounds, but His hands make whole' (Job 5:17-18). The judgment of revival is for Christians who are unrepentant and wilfully living in habitual sin, those who continually dishonour the name of the Lord, because judgment always begins at the house of the Lord (1 Peter 4:17). It is the 'Lord [who] kills and makes alive; He brings down to the grave and brings up…He brings low and lifts up' (1 Samuel 2:6-7). The Scriptures declare: 'Utterly slay…begin at My sanctuary'

(Ezekiel 9:6). 'Blow the trumpet in Zion…tremble; for the day of the Lord is coming' (Joel 2:1). God said, "I will come to you quickly and remove your lampstand from its place – unless you repent" (Revelation 2:5). God's grace does wear thin and He does take out individuals and shuts churches! See also 2 Thessalonians 1:8-9.

James Burns from the early twentieth century wrote: 'To the Church, a revival means humiliation, a bitter knowledge of unworthiness…. It comes to scorch before it heals; it comes to condemn ministers and people for their unfaithful witness, for their selfish living, for their neglect of the cross…. That is why a revival has ever been unpopular with large numbers within the Church.'

The paradox of revival is that it unites, but it also upsets others and repels some, but we should not be alarmed at this. Jesus, the Prince of Peace, stated that His ministry would cause division, as some members of a household would follow Him whilst others would not (Luke 12:51-53). Families will be divided over Jesus and His ministry (Matthew 10:34). Not everyone attributed Jesus' ministry as from God (Mark 3:22-29), whilst others hated Him 'without a cause' (John 15:23-25). However, blessed are the unoffended ones (Matthew 11:6).

Dr. Martyn Lloyd-Jones saw a localised revival in his church at Sandfields, Aberavon, near Swansea, Wales, UK, in 1930, though he himself was reluctant to call it revival. As minister of Westminster Chapel, London, UK, he said, "…There has never been anything that has so promoted spiritual unity as revival. But a revival also invariably has another effect, and that is that it creates a new and fresh division. And why does it do so? It does so for this reason, those who have experienced the blessing and the power of God are naturally one and they come together; there are others who dislike it all and who criticise it all and who condemn it all and who are outside it all and the division comes in."

Dr. John White in *When the Spirit Comes With Power* wrote: 'My main theme has to do with the Church's panicky flight at the approach of revival, and the failure to recognise it when God sends it. Revival has dangers. But our fear may lead us to reject what God sends. We must not neglect power because it has dangers.

'The greatest fear in some quarters is that what appears to be the power of God may be nothing more than a massive hoax by the enemy. It is a fear that is paralysing whole segments of the Church, a dread that debilitates [to make very weak and infirm], that causes our hands to hang slack and our feet to lag, at a time when the trumpet calls for advance and attack.'[2]

Chapter 35

Fresh Water or Salt Water

'The tongue is a fire, a world of iniquity. The tongue is so set among our members that it defiles the whole body, and sets on fire the course of nature; and it is set on fire by hell.... Does a spring send forth fresh water and bitter from the same opening? ...No spring can yield both salt and fresh water' (James 3:6, 11-12).

Slander and False Testimony

There is a growing problem within the body of Christ of people who thrive on negativity; some believe it is their ministry to dig up dirt or to throw enough mud till something sticks! Some pass on erroneous information via word of mouth or digital communications without checking out the facts for themselves. Some go so far as to post articles and comments on blogs, websites and social media/ networks for non-Christians to laugh and mock thus repulsing them from the Christ of Christianity. These mediums of communication are uncensored and unaccountable where anybody can voice an opinion, from the unsure and genuine questioning to the mad axe grinder! It is always easier to consider the failures of others and to denounce "their and ministries, mistakes or heresies" (which are often different views of nonessential truths). It makes it more palatable to hide from our own failings and flaws and diverts our attention from the work God has called us to do!

There is a difference between truth and gossip and much of what we call passing on truth, God calls gossip. Many misrepresenting, misquoting or half-truths are perpetuated on the evidence of hearsay and can cause untold harm, and ruin reputations and ministries. Many people are gullible as 'the simple believes every word' (Proverbs 14:15), whereas 'the sons of this world are more shrewd...than the sons of light' (Luke 16:8). When the Lord visited Abraham; after hearing the outcry against Sodom and Gomorrah He *went down to see for Himself* (Genesis 18:21). Leaders should 'inquire, search out and ask diligently' when accusations are brought against others (Deuteronomy 13:4, 17:4 and 19:18).

If you have started a rumour, even unintentionally by passing on erroneous information including posting or leaving comments on social networks then you need to retract it, as difficult as that may be. Inform those to whom you passed it on or entrusted it to and try to counteract the negative. You may need to ask forgiveness to the one wronged. The circle of apology extends to the circle of offence, but a public maligning needs a public retraction, a public apology and may even need a public asking of one's forgiveness which will lead to public reconciliation. In Pyongyang, in modern-day North Korea, an elder's public repentance, confessions and reconciliation led to beginning of the Pyongyang Great Revival (1907-1910) in which 50,000 were converted in its first year!

Accusation and Lies

Some believers assume the worst about those whom they have never met and speak against events or meetings of which they have not attended. Some people have the philosophy based on the adage that, 'where there's smoke there's fire,' but it was this mentality that led to the stoning of Stephen, the first Christian martyr (Acts 6:19-14 and Acts 7:54-59). A similar incident happened more than nine hundred and thirty years prior to Stephen's martyrdom, in the days of Elijah. Naboth the Jezreelite refused to sell his vineyard to King Ahab and began to sulk. Ahab's wife, Jezebel, hatched a plan; she wrote letters in her husband's name, used his seal and sent them to the elders. Naboth was invited to a fast (not a feast!) with the elders and nobles of the city, but was seated between two scoundrels who bore false witness against him. Those present stoned him to death, yet he was innocent of all accusations (1 Kings 21:1-13).

Many inflammatory statements and lies were levied against John the Baptist, the first revivalist of the New Testament, the so-called man with 'a demon' (Matthew 11:18). Jesus was accused of being a glutton, winebibber (drunkard), Samaritan (a cultural insult, see 2 Kings 17:29 and John 4:9) and a madman with a demon (Matthew 11:19, John 8:48-49 and John 10:19-20) who worked miracles by His close association with demons (Matthew 9:32-34). Other biblical figures were accused of various things that were completely untrue and had no foundation in fact: Joseph was accused of adultery with Potiphar's wife, Moses was accused of lording it over the Israelites, Nehemiah was accused of trying to rebel against the king, Jeremiah was accused of trying to defect to the Chaldeans, whilst Daniel was thrown into the lions' den as King Darius had been duped by his advisers into passing a vain law which brought Daniel's allegiance into question. Even the apostle Paul was slanderously reported as saying, "Let us do evil that good may come!" (Romans 3:8).

On numerous occasions religious leaders watched Jesus closely and tried to trap Him by His words or actions, or sent spies so as to accuse, entrap and discredit Him, see Matthew 21:23-27, Mark 3:1-6, Mark 12:1-17, Luke 13:10-17 and Luke 20:20-25. The apostle John stated that because of the pride of Diotrephes he refused to look after the brethren and talks nonsense of them 'with malicious words' (3 John 10). Whilst 'some indeed preached Christ,' so wrote the apostle Paul, out of 'envy and strife' because of 'selfish ambition' and desired to 'add affliction' to his chains (Philippians 1:15-16). 'For where envy and self-seeking exist, confusion and every evil thing are there' (James 3:16).

William Miller saw revival in Dresden, America, in 1831 and other revivals. Due to his lectures on the second coming he was greatly maligned and much untruth was published and spread abroad against him. The editor of the *Gazette and Advertiser* of Williamsburg, Long Island, referred to an interview with William Miller: 'Our curiosity was recently gratified by an introduction to this gentleman, who has probably been an object of more abuse, ridicule and blackguardism [to disparage, scorn or denounce], than any other man living…. When our interview closed, we were left wondering at the cause of the malignant spirit of slander and falsehood with which a man has been assailed, who has spent his time and substance in a course of unceasing toils to persuade men to 'flee from the wrath to come.' '[1]

Howell Harris of Trevecca, Wales, visited John Wesley in Bristol, England, on 18 June 1739. Initially, Harris had been quite reluctant to meet Wesley due to the many evil reports that had been given to him, but said after hearing him preach, "As soon as I heard you preach, I quickly found what spirit you were of. And before you were done, I was so over powered with joy and love that I had much ado [trouble] to walk home."[2]

The Press and Media

It is to the advantage of the press and media to make a story sensational and they will often twist, bend or even fabricate a story so as to increase sales. If unbelievers write maliciously about their own, then how more critically will they write about the family of God and their ministries? See Psalm 56:5, John 15:19 and 2 Timothy 3:12. With 24-hour news, media sound bites, webcasts, social media and video related internet sites, many leaders and their meetings (where excess has occurred) have been edited so as to portray the ministry or its teaching in the worst possible light. But let us all be sensible in our own sphere of work and be wise in all that we do and say. Bible teacher, Charles Stanley said, "Be aware of confusion; what we thought we taught we didn't teach, and what we didn't mean to teach we taught!"

Heresy Hunters and Revival Police

If you follow God there will always be opposition and those who do not appreciate your work in the Lord, and 'if you do not run with them' then they may 'speak evil of you' (1 Peter 4:4). But solace can be found because Jesus said, "Woe to you when *all* men speak well of you..." (Luke 6:26), therefore if you have no opposition, is your ministry of God, are you being effective?

There are a minority of Christians who believe it is *their* ministry to criticise other Christian ministries. Heresy hunters or revival police as they are known, go in search of the negative whilst dismissing the positive. The spirit in which error is pointed out is not done in a spirit of love, to inform and correct but to denounce and condemn. It is also unhelpful when their premise is that the one at fault is a wolf even when the accused confesses Jesus Christ as Lord and adheres to the fundamental doctrines of orthodox Christianity. Francis Frangipane wrote: 'When an attack site fails to list even one good thing about a ministry, you tend to believe their goal is not to discern, but to destroy.'

Winkie Pratney in *Fire on the Horizon* (1999) wrote: 'An embarrassing characteristic of today's awakening is the direct bypassing of critical analysis to allow the Holy Spirit to move at will. This is the manifestation in revivals today that inspires in some religious critics "manifestations" of their own. Self-appointed authorities on revival and cultish behaviour, when faced with admittedly strange phenomena, can themselves behave in most ungracious ways, attacking and slandering the nature and character of the work in question and those involved in it. They make scholarly and detailed reference to the dangers of mindless behaviour and duly quote Scriptures on doing things "decently and in order" (1 Corinthians 14:40). And they broadcast the darkest warnings of the dangers of deception when we turn over our services and Christian meetings to something so patently beyond our control. And almost with exception, *they miss the point.*

'God does what He does without our permission. When He moves, it is always in line with His Word and what He has said and done in history before. This we know from His changeless nature and character. ...God does not have to check in with us to see if we approve first before He does what He wants to do. Revival by its very nature is not under the control of the Church; the Church is to come under the control of God. And the man who thinks His move is always explicable has never really been in it.'[3]

In Acts 18 there was a certain Jew named Apollos, a preacher of Jesus Christ who knew the Scriptures well, the Old Testament. He was fervent in his proclamation of the good news and 'taught accurately the things of the Lord though he knew only the baptism of John.' When Aquila and Priscilla heard, 'they took him aside and explained to him the way of God more accurately' (Acts 18:24-26). Notice that Aquila and Priscilla did not condemn him or label him a heretic for not teaching the whole truth, but privately, 'took him aside' and explained to him the truth 'more accurately.'

Some Christians have condemned Christian workers because of what they did prior to conversion and this is very wrong. Some Christian leaders (or ministries) have retracted statements or beliefs once held, yet some Christians *still* perpetrate these old beliefs or sayings and keep repeating that which has been dealt with. This is also unbiblical. Digging up evil is sin (Proverbs 16:27).

The blood of Christ cleanses from *all* (confessed) sin (1 John 1:9). God has cast them into the depths of the sea (Micah 7:19) and it is as far as the east is from the west (Psalm 103:12). These confessed sins (and forsaken, Prov. 28:13) are not remembered by God, as He chooses to forget as it is covered by the blood of Jesus Christ (Isaiah 43:25) and therefore should not be repeated or posted on websites, email lists, blogs or social networks etc.

Is it possible that many who level accusations against Christian ministries have never built a work that edifies others and are simply envious? See Acts 13:45. Is it also possible that some Christians try to hide their own deficiencies or vent their own frustrations and hurts by pulling down others? Perhaps they do not understand Psalm 133, 'the unity of the brethren' or Jesus' words, "That they may be one just as We are One" (John 17:22). Christian leaders often find that when these people, members of their own congregation are approached in love and gentleness they often espouse (support) their poor spiritual state and seem lost in a haze, and live under shadows of oppression.

James aptly pointed out: 'We all stumble in many things' (James 3:2), so none of us are perfect, yet many point out an issue not in a spirit of love which leads to correction, but in a spirit of condemnation which leads nowhere. Let us never forget that 'mercy triumphs over judgment' (James 2:13) and 'whatever you want men to do to you, do also to them' (Matthew 7:12). Jesus warns us about judging and with the measure we use it will be measured back to us (Matthew 7:1-6). We are told 'to speak evil of no one, to be peaceable, gentle, showing all humility to all men. For we ourselves were once also foolish...living in malice and envy, hateful and hating one another' (Titus 3:2-3). James confirms these words: 'Do not speak evil of one another, brethren' (James 4:11). The apostle Paul set a higher standard in that love 'thinks no evil' (1 Corinthians 13:5) and Jude openly wrote that false teachers 'speak evil of whatever they do not know' (Jude 1:10). The prophet Amos pronounced a warning for those who desired the Day of the Lord; as it will be a day of judgment for those looking for others to be punished, who had not examined themselves, 'it will be darkness and not light...as though a man fled from a lion and a bear met him' (Amos 5:18-20).

Mistakes and Correction

Individual Christians and even those in leadership make mistakes and on occasions fall into or commit sin, as did many of the characters of the Bible. The objective for any fallen brother or sister in the Lord should be for their restoration (after repentance) and not condemnation or gloating (Galatians 6:1-5). Let us be thankful that the early Church did not condemn denying Peter, doubting Thomas, Saul the persecutor, John Mark the quitter or Barnabas when he was led astray for a time. Could it be that there go I, bar the grace of God? If a brother or sister has erred and committed sin, then it is the Church's duty to try and bring the offender to a place of repentance and restoration which is the spirit of Christ, going in search of the lost or straying sheep.

The standard truth for anybody who is guilty must be on the testimony of two or three witnesses (Deuteronomy 19:15-19, 2 Corinthians 13:1 and 1 Timothy 5:19). People need to be treated fairly and graciously and are innocent until proven guilty and not the other way around. Christians should always begin with the bias towards believing the best as love 'thinks no evil' and love 'rejoices in the truth; bears all things, believes all things, hopes all things...love never fails' (1 Corinthians 13:5-8).

According to the New Testament the best qualified to pass judgment on individuals, are those in leadership; like the apostle Paul who wanted to warn the churches he had founded – his flock(s). To name an offender is unwise unless we have the heart of compassion like Jesus and the sanctification and anointing of the apostle Paul. He was at liberty to warn the churches of individuals and to inform about those who had fallen away, as he had pastoral oversight. When Paul had to rebuke individuals or churches, he wrote in spirit of love, 'weeping,' (2 Corinthians 2:4).

Chapter 36

Regeneration and False Converts

'For if he who comes preaches another Jesus whom we have not preached, or if you receive a different spirit which you have not received, or a different gospel which you have not accepted, you may well put up with it' (2 Corinthians 11:4).

Regeneration – Truly Saved

Repentance, a renouncing and turning away from the works of darkness, with faith in the death and resurrection of Jesus Christ is the foundation of salvation – true biblical regeneration, being 'born again' (John 3:3, 7) and passing from 'death to life' (1 John 3:14).

Are you saved – saved from what? From the wrath to come, the lusts of the flesh? Saved from selfishness, greed, impure thoughts, a deceitful heart – saved from what? If the righteous one is scarcely saved (1 Peter 4:18) and those who do not do the will of God are not part of Jesus' family (Matthew 7:21 and Mark 3:35) are you saved? Jesus declared that we are justified and condemned by our words (Matthew 12:37) and our confession of faith in Christ (Romans 10:9-10) is the crux of our faith. If the Lord will say to some, "I never knew you" – to those who even did miracles and cast out demons in His name (Matthew 7:21-23) can you really say you are saved? Jesus said, "Narrow is the gate and difficult is the way which leads to life and there are few who find it" (Matthew 7:14).

The Holy Bible plainly declares that 'whoever calls upon the name of the Lord will be saved' (Acts 2:21 and Romans 10:13), but those who confess with their mouths are also called to profess by their changed lives; that is, 'show forth fruits worthy of repentance' (Matthew 3:8). Genuine disciples of Christ can be differentiated from those who come in sheep's clothing, yet inwardly are ravenous wolves because 'by their fruit you will know them,' because a 'good tree cannot bear bad fruit' (Matthew 7:15-20). Without holiness no man shall see the Lord (Hebrews 12:4) and we are commanded to be holy because He is holy (1 Peter 1:16).

If we abide in God's Word, then we are His disciples and we shall know the truth and it will set us free (John 8:31-32). Also, people will know that we are Jesus' disciples, 'if we have love for one another' (John 13:34-35) and if we 'walk worthy of the Lord, fully pleasing Him' and increase in the knowledge of Him which qualifies us to be 'partakers of the inheritance' (Colossians 1:10-12). By the Word of God and His grace we are able to receive the inheritance, but only 'those who are sanctified' (Acts 20:32).

Some so-called Christians know all about doctrine, but nothing about devotion, they may be living concordances of the Word of God, yet not know the Word who came in the flesh. They may know virtually everything about Christ and religion, yet not know Him in a personal relationship. They go through the motions of Christianity without knowing the Christ of Christianity.

The road to destruction is very broad, but narrow is the gate that leads to eternal life and 'there are few who find it' (Matthew 7:13-14), and 'if the righteous one is scarcely saved' what about the ungodly and habitual sinners? (1 Peter 4:18). Whilst we cannot be plucked out of God's hand (John 10:28) is it possible that we may wander from the path of righteousness and be so entangled in a web of sin that we are unable to break free and thus disinherit ourselves from the family of God? Others are taken captive by the devil to do his will (2 Timothy 2:26) and for some their very conscience has been 'seared with a hot iron,' as they give 'heed to deceiving spirits and doctrines of demons' (1 Timothy 4:1-3), thus rendering them unable to discern between the holy and the unholy, the clean and the unclean (Leviticus 10:10). More often than not they will call 'evil good and good evil; who put darkness for light and light for darkness' and 'put bitter for sweet and sweet for bitter' and woe unto them (Isaiah 5:20), because 'if we sin wilfully after we have received the knowledge of the truth, there no longer remains a sacrifice for sins...' (Hebrews 10:26). '...As they crucify again for themselves the Son of God' (Hebrews 6:6-8).

God knows who His chosen ones are and if we are not wearing the right clothes at the wedding feast we will be caught out and cast out (Matthew 22:11-14). We must accept and live by the Word of God and make Jesus not only our Saviour, but our Lord and Master. Have you?

Charles H. Spurgeon, preaching on the subject of calling (salvation) in March 1859, said, "[Jesus] who hath saved us and called us with a holy calling (2 Timothy 1:9) – many are called, but few are chosen.... It is 'a holy calling, not according to our works, but according to His own purpose and grace which was given us in Christ Jesus before the world began.' This calling forbids all trust in our own doings and conducts us to Christ alone for salvation, but it afterwards purges us from dead works to serve the living and true God. If you are living in sin, you are not called; if you can still continue as you were before your pretended conversion, then it is no conversion at all; that man who is called in his drunkenness will forsake his drunkenness; men may be called in the midst of sin, but they will not continue in it any longer.... Now, by this shall ye know whether ye be called of God or not. If ye continue in sin, if ye walk according to the course of this world, according to the spirit that worketh in the children of disobedience, then ye are still dead in your trespasses and your sins; but as He that hath called you is holy, so must ye be holy. Can ye say, 'Lord, Thou knowest all things, Thou knowest that I desire to keep all Thy commandments and to walk blamelessly in Thy sight. I know my obedience cannot save me, but I long to obey. There is nothing that pains me so much as sin; I desire to be quit and rid of it – Lord help me to be holy?' Is that the panting of thy heart? Is that the tenor of thy life towards God and towards His law? Then, beloved, I have reason to hope that Thou hast been called of God, for it is a holy calling wherewith God doth call His people."[1]

Rocky Ground

Jesus spoke on the parable of the sower; the seed that was scattered being the Word of God. Some fell on the wayside and was trampled underfoot or eaten by birds; some fell on stony ground and sprang up, yet withered because of a lack of soil and moisture; some fell among thorns, it grew, but was choked by the thorns and withered, whilst other seed fell onto good ground, grew and produced a harvest (Matthew 13:1-23, Mark 4:1-34 and Luke 8:4-15). Therefore, according to Jesus, much sowing is needed in sharing the good news and should we be surprised if three quarters of confessions never produce a real harvest? But this does not mean that we sit back on our laurels as we are called to make *disciples*, not favourable statistics or church-goers with the nickname Christian.

In evangelistic campaigns the fall-away rate is very high and only a minute fraction of those who profess Christ become part of a church and are still standing within a few months, let alone years, but in revival this is not the case.

During revival the vast majority of converts stay true to the faith, though there are those who come under conviction of sin, yet for whatever reason they never come to the faith. During the Lewis Revival (1949-1952) in the Outer Hebrides of Scotland, UK, Duncan Campbell stated that seventy-five percent were converted outside of a church building on the moorland, at home and by the side of the road as God's Spirit arrested them!

J. Edwin Orr wrote: 'Those who profess to decide [for Christ] in revival atmosphere show a convincing degree of assurance, for in revival, the Holy Spirit of God does His work unhampered by the usual hindrances of Christians.'[2]

John George Govan, revivalist and founder of The Faith Mission, Scotland, said, "About all work for God, one feels that the all-essential thing is the approval and cooperation of God by the mighty workings of His Spirit. Without that all the plans of man and the varieties of work engaged in will be an utter failure. But if it be in the power of His Spirit, God will use many means and methods for the advancement of His Kingdom."[3]

False Converts and Running after the World

Even during times of revival there are those who pretend to turn to Christ having been under conviction of sin, but do not pass from 'death to life' (1 John 3:14) experiencing the new birth, being 'born again' (John 3:3-21). There are those whose emotions have been stimulated and have had an emotional conversion. Those who during an appeal, put their hand up, maybe even come to the front and repeat a prayer, believe that they are saved and then *carry on as normal*. They may faithfully turn up for the Sunday service (to warm the seats or to do a business deal after the service), or attend the church socials (for the free food and an evening out) and still be unregenerate. Let us not forget that even John Wesley, ordained by the Church of England went to America to convert the Indians and came back realising that he himself was not converted! There were also quite a few Church of England vicars who got converted during the Evangelical Revival (1739-1791), such as John Berridge of Everton, England, and Daniel Rowland of Llangeitho, Wales, whilst William Haslam of Cornwall, England, was an unconverted vicar for nine years, until he saw the light in October 1851. All of these men had been trained in theological studies and ordained by bishops! All of these men looked the part, talked the part yet had not been 'born again' (John 3:3) and had not passed from 'death into life' (John 5:24). After their conversion, all these men saw revival in their ministries, church or parish. During George Whitefield's third visit to America (in the 1740s), as many as twenty ministers were converted in and around the Boston area whilst under the sound of his preaching!

Some 'Christians' are self-deceived and their conversion is only done in pretence; they go through the motions, but are still unregenerate. In Jeremiah's day, Judah ignored Israel's example of what happened to a backsliding nation. The Lord spoke through the prophet Jeremiah saying, "Judah has not turned to Me with *her whole heart, but in pretence*" (Jeremiah 3:10). There are also those who are 'obstinate children' (Isaiah 30:1), NIV, who take no counsel from God, but carry on in their own sinful lifestyle and these are not converted.

Others hear a gospel message of free grace and God's love, but do not hear about their obligations and responsibilities, to forsake sin and the world and to embrace Jesus Christ and the cross! To live unreservedly and wholeheartedly for Jesus Christ with all their heart, soul, mind and strength, now and forever!

It is possible for people to make an intellectual 'head' decision to follow Christ or for Christians to make a fuller commitment to Him, as in full surrender, yet not understand what they have promised, and therefore they are unable to walk into the reality of such a commitment.

Simon, a former sorcerer *believed* the message of salvation and was baptised during the Samaria Revival. He 'continued with Philip' the evangelist, being amazed by the signs and wonders that he saw, yet was only found out when he thought he could buy the impartation of the Holy Spirit! (Acts 8:5-23).

If we look back to the world with longing eyes we are not fit for the Kingdom (Exodus 16:2-3, Numbers 11:4-5 and Luke 9:57-62), but if we turn back to the world, the latter is worse than the beginning (Hebrews 10:36-38 and 2 Peter 2:20-22). We should not be deceived by disobedience, but we are called to enter into the rest of God (Hebrews 3:7-19 and Hebrews 4:1-6, 11). Have you?

James A. Stewart said, "For a Christian redeemed by Calvary's blood to live a worldly life is treason and spiritual suicide."

Thomas Phillips documented the 1859 Welsh Revival. In his rebuttal to the objections that the new converts will backslide, betray religion and bring disgrace on the whole movement, he wrote: 'Suppose this would be found true in part, where would be the marvel? Is not the Kingdom of heaven compared to ten virgins, of whom five were foolish? And to a net cast into the sea, which gathered of every kind? And is not the Christian Church a field in which wheat and tares grow together until harvest? We must be prepared for disappointments – a Judas will appear here – a Demas there – Simon the sorcerer, Diotrephes, and men of kindred spirit will "arise" again. It has been so in former revivals... have we right to expect that the present will be an exception!?'[4]

Tickle my Ears, Tares and Imitators
In the second year of Jesus' ministry, He spoke on the cost of discipleship, that we have to be drawn by the Father to Him and then *committed* to His way. Jesus being the Bread of Life of which we have to eat, *if* we are to partake of eternal life (John 6). It was during this time, the height of His popularity that Jesus revealed the different motives as to why the multitudes followed Him. There is also a parallel between the motives of those who followed Jesus then and now and those who travel to places of revival. Some followed Jesus for the excitement; 'a great multitude followed Him, because they saw His signs which He performed on those who were diseased' (John 6:2). Others followed Him for what they could get from Him, 'you seek Me, not because you saw the signs, but because you ate the loaves and were filled' (John 6:26). But Jesus challenged His followers to identify with Him, 'whoever eats My flesh and drinks My blood has eternal life, and I will raise him up at the last day' (John 6:54). But it was 'from that time many of His disciples went back and walked with Him no more' (John 6:66) though the genuine and true disciples stayed loyal to Jesus.

There are many people who are 'in it' for what *they* can get out of it. Or those who love to hear what God is doing; missionary stories, stories of deliverances, healings and miracles – they love to be entertained by the workings of God in and through people's lives, 'their mouth shows much love, but their hearts pursue their own gain' wrote Ezekiel. 'Indeed you are to them as a very lovely song of one who has a pleasant voice and can play well on an instrument.' The stories excite their emotions, but when you challenge them to a greater commitment or full surrender to God (Romans 12:1, Galatians 2:20 and 2 Corinthians 5:15), 'they hear your words, but they do not do them' (Ezekiel 33:31-33).

There are people who are tares, that is supposed and alleged Christians, who act the part, sound the part and will blend in very well at any church meeting (or even at a Bible College / Seminary, mission or ministry), but it is not until the harvest that they are truly exposed for what they are. Tares and not wheat and they will be burned whilst the wheat will be gathered into God's barn (Matthew 13:24-30). Jude notes false teachers who were so well disguised that they even participated in the 'love feasts,' but only ministered for their own financial gain. Being 'clouds without rain, carried about by the winds; late autumn trees, twice dead, pulled up by the roots; raging waves of the sea, foaming up their shame; wandering stars for whom is reserved the blackness of darkness for ever' (Jude 12-13). See also 1 John 2:18-19.

Chapter 37

The Devil's Deception

'Examine yourselves as to whether you are in the faith. Prove yourselves. Do you not know yourselves that Jesus Christ is in you? – Unless indeed you are disqualified' (2 Corinthians 13:5).

True and False Repentance
There is a state of true and false repentance. True repentance is confessing (Leviticus 5:5) and forsaking one's sin before God and asking His forgiveness for those sins (Proverbs 28:13 and 1 John 1:9). Ephesians 4:31 tell us 'to put away' bitterness, wrath, anger, clamour, evil speaking and malice. Colossians 3:5 tells us to 'put to death' fleshly passions, fornication, evil desire and covetousness whilst Galatians 6:19-21 lists a whole host of sins, 'the works of the flesh' and that 'those who practice such things will not inherit the Kingdom of God.' The following two verses list the fruit of the Spirit (nine of, which are manifested through love) which exemplify all true Christians and states 'those who are Christ's have crucified the flesh with its passion and desires. If we live in the Spirit, let us also walk in the Spirit' (Galatians 5:22-25). And most are very familiar with Jesus' saying about being "salt and light" (Matthew 5:15-16) which follows after The Beatitudes.

False repentance is getting emotionally charged, often shedding tears (because we have been caught or found-out or are under conviction of sin) yet still carry on how we were before. Esau despised and sold his birthright, yet he later sought repentance with tears but he could not find it (Hebrews 12:15-17). Esau was not truly repentant, but grieved because he lost out on that which should have been his; a large inheritance. The rich young ruler, who obeyed the commandments and desired to inherit eternal life became sorrowful, not because he could not inherit it, but because he did not want to give away his own inheritance to the poor and truly follow Jesus. It was this "one thing" which stopped him from having treasure in heaven (Luke 18:18-27).

The Samaritans 'feared the Lord yet served their own gods' (2 Kings 17:32-33). The people of Judah 'worship and swear oaths by the Lord, but who also swear by Milcom' (Zephaniah 1:5). In Jesus' day, 'even among the rulers, many believed in Him, but because of the Pharisees they did not confess Him lest they be put out of the synagogue for they loved the praise of men more than the praise of God' (John 12:42-43). James rightly noted: 'A double-minded man, [is] unstable in all his ways' (James 1:8).

From 1927 to 1937, revival swept across China, but especially in the Northern Provinces. Rev. Olav Espegren, president of the Norwegian Lutheran Mission who ministered in south-western Honan and north Hupeh, wrote a report for the year 1933. It is dated 24 January 1934. He emphasised the great need for pastoral care of those who have "come through," but also noted that defections were among such as had simulated repentance, but had not really come through. Otherwise his impression was that very few of the newly saved fell away.[1]

In 1743, in the midst of the American Great Awakening (1735-1760) Jonathan Edwards published the *Treatise Concerning the Religious Affections*. The second chapter concerns false signs of true religious affections. He noted:
- That enthusiasm can quickly end, just like the Israelites deliverance through the Red Sea, who habitually complained in the wilderness.
- People have been enlightened as in Hebrews 6:4-5, but are unacquainted with the better things that 'accompany salvation' (verse 9).
- A counterfeit love of which the apostle Paul alludes to in Ephesians 6:24, 'grace be with all those that love our Lord Jesus Christ in *sincerity*. Amen.' [See also 1 Jn. 2:18-19].
- Godly sorrow without a change of character, such as: Pharaoh and the ten plagues, "I have sinned," yet carried on defying God (Exodus 9:27). King Saul who wept before David whom he tried to kill at least three times (1 Samuel 24:16-17, 26:21). King Ahab humbled himself (1 Kings 21:27) but carried on in sin and the dogs licked up his blood (1 Kings 22:37-38). The children of Israel in the wilderness who tested God ten times and still doubted Him (Numbers 14, especially verse 22).

Categories of Alleged Christians
- A Non-Christian: One who thinks that he or she is a Christian, yet have not put real faith in Jesus Christ's atoning death for the forgiveness of one's sins. At the end times, unrighteous people will follow the deceptions of the devil (2 Thessalonians 2:7-12).

- A Premature Christian: One who does not live the life, who constantly, deliberately and habitually sins (John 14:15, 21, Hebrews 6:1-6 and Hebrews 10:26-31).
- A Young Christian: One who gets led astray. Simon (who had previously practised sorcery) wanted to buy the power of the impartation of the Holy Spirit. Peter denounced him and called him to repent as his heart was not right in the sight of God, being poisoned by bitterness and bound by iniquity (Acts 8:9-13, 18-23).
- A Naïve Christian: One who has been taken captive by the devil to do his will (2 Timothy 2:26) or one who has been deceived by another (2 Timothy 3:1-6).
- A Religious Christian: One who outwardly appears right before God, but in the heart, he or she is looking for the praise and adoration of man. The Pharisees were full of hypocrisy and lawlessness (Matthew 23:1-7, 13-15, Matthew 23:23-33 and Luke 11:42-44).
- A Traditional Christian: One who believes that his or her devotion to tradition is more important than his or her relationship to God (Matthew 23:16-22 and Mark 7:6-13). Often doctrine comes before devotion.
- An Apostate Christian: One who upon seeing lawlessness abound, allows his or her love for Christ to grow cold (Matthew 24:10-12 and 2 Thessalonians 2:3-4).
- A "Manipulated" Christian: The elect who after seeing deceiving signs and wonders follow after a false Christ or a false prophet (Matthew 24:23-26).

Prevention of Deception

Many people believe what they want to believe, that which they are comfortable with. Some look for teachers to teach them what they want to hear. Others seek those who will not teach what they do not want to hear and that is why several cults were founded two centuries ago with their aversion to hell and eternal torment.

Some captains of the army asked the prophet Jeremiah for a word from the Lord, but when it came they rejected it. They stated that Jeremiah had spoken falsely (Jeremiah chapters 42-43). Some hear what they want to hear and will follow their own deceptive heart (2 Timothy 4:3-4). Jesus preached on total commitment, however hard the cost, but many turned back and followed Him no more (John 6:44-66). Jesus said, "Take heed that you do not be deceived..." (Luke 21:8). We should dig deep from the Word of God and have firm solid foundations in sound biblical doctrine. Most people do not decide to be deceived (or to deceive others), even in the midst of revival, but it is a process that happens over time, a gradual process, rather than a sudden single event. We must all take heed as to who or what we are listening to, and who or what is influencing our knowledge of God and Christianity. We are all called to intelligently judge the message we hear and the person who brings it. For Christians, only the Holy Bible (God's objective Word) can truly judge our personal experiences (subjective feelings), thoughts, attitudes, doctrine and interpretation of Scripture, along with any preconceived ideas. *Discipleship For Everyday Living: Christian Growth* by the author is recommended reading to understand this in further detail.

Test the Spirits
　The Bible tells us to 'test the spirits' (1 John 4:1) and warns us of: tares, wolves, accursed children, hirelings and false: prophets, teachers and apostles. Not all those who profess the name of Jesus Christ are genuine and loyal to the King and His cause. They have a variety of motives for teaching or preaching about Him and His message whilst cloaking their sermons or discussions in Christian verbiage, with phrases from Scripture interspersed.
　'For I fear, lest somehow, as the serpent deceived Eve by his craftiness, so your minds may be corrupted from the simplicity that is in Christ (2 Corinthians 11:3).
　During the Azusa Street Revival (1906-1909) in Los Angeles, California, America, all sorts of people would turn up at the meetings. The church held three services a day, had an open pulpit (made from two boxes), and a variety of people came to the front to speak or to share. Those in the flesh often fumbled their words or became flustered and sat down, whilst at other times Pastor William Seymour used to put his hand on their shoulder and gently tell them that this was a different type of meeting, where the Holy Spirit was in charge (and then they would sit down).
　Some teachers, preachers, apostles or prophets are just out and out false, whilst others are lopsided in their teaching, focusing more on some aspects rather than others which are equally or if not more important. The apostle Paul wrote: 'The Lord knows those who are His' (2 Timothy 2:19), but often we don't. Life does not consist in the abundance of our possessions, but of our wealth in Christ, the unsearchable riches of Christ. Let us keep focused on Christ and be like the Bereans who didn't believe something just because someone said so, but 'searched the Scriptures daily to find out whether these things were so' (Acts 17:11).

Chapter 38

You Shall Know the Truth

Jesus said to those Jews who believed in Him, "If you abide in My Word, you are My disciples indeed. And you shall know the truth and the truth shall make you free" (John 8:31-32).

Share the Good News
You may not be an evangelist, but we are all called to evangelise and if Jesus has changed you, then He can change anyone! We should be preaching the gospel in season and out of season, Christ and Him crucified (1 Corinthians 2:2), blood-bought redemption (and atonement) that purchased salvation for mankind at the ultimate cost, through repentance and faith in Him by the grace and mercy of God. We should always be prepared to share our testimony and preach the unsearchable riches of Christ Jesus. The apostle Paul was not ashamed of the gospel, knowing it is the power of God to salvation (Romans 1:16). Outside of Jesus Christ there is no other name by which we must be saved (Acts 4:12), and those who reject Jesus Christ stand condemned (John 3:18).

'Deliver those who are drawn towards death, and hold back those stumbling to slaughter. If you say, "Surely we did not know this," does not He who weighs the heart consider it? He who keeps your soul, does He not know it? And will He not render to each man according to his deeds?' (Proverbs 24:11-12).

Simply Believism Versus Blood-Bought Redemption
Rev. Duncan Campbell gave the following address at a meeting for ministers, at Oxford and Manchester, England, in the early 1950s, "...It has been said that 'the Kingdom of God is not going to be advanced by our churches becoming filled with men, but by men in our churches becoming filled with God.' Today, we have a Christianity made easy as an accommodation to an age that is unwilling to face the implications of Calvary, and the gospel of 'simply believism' has produced a harvest of professions which have done untold harm to the cause of Christ."[1]

The apostle Paul did not shun to declare the whole counsel of God. We must preach: Jesus Christ who was crucified for our sins; the cross, the blood, repentance, new life in Christ, the judgment to come, hell and the lake of fire for those who refuse to depart from iniquity, for those who do not believe and those who reject Jesus Christ as their Lord and Saviour (John 3:18-20, 2 Thessalonians 1:8-9, Revelation 20:11-15 and Revelation 21:8).

The law (the Ten Commandments) is our schoolmaster that brings us to Christ, because we can see with greater clarity how we have transgressed the moral law. If you have lied you are a liar, if you have stolen, you are a thief etc., it brings conviction of sin by the Holy Spirit and our conscience condemns us. We are guilty before a holy and just God who demands an account of that which is past. Once we preach the law it makes the judgment (hell) seem reasonable, and just (as for every action there is a consequence – sowing and reaping) – if I break the law of the land, I will be punished for it, how much more when I break God's perfect law of liberty? After the law which prepares the heart then we can preach grace. 'The wages of sin is death, but the gift of God is eternal life in Christ Jesus our Lord' (Romans 6:23).

Never forget that a Christ-less, cross-less, blood-less message will result in spine-less, defence-less and power-less church goers with the nickname Christian. For too long, premature Christians (what the Scriptures call: tares, goats or accursed children) have been birthed who have no real knowledge of salvation or of God and soon become entangled by the cares of this life, the deceitfulness of riches, or they fall away under trials and tribulations. Other writers call them 'spurious Christians,' 'dummy Christians' or 'adulterous' or 'false converts.' Jonathan Goforth of China, called those with a 'give me' attitude 'rice Christians' as some people are offered inducements to come to Jesus.

We should not preach a false gospel message of 'easy believism,' 'self-improvement,' 'self-centredness' and 'self-indulgence,' or 'come to Jesus and all your problems will go away,' or 'come to Jesus and receive financial benefits from God.' Whilst there are many benefits in Christ Jesus (of peace and joy, acceptance in Christ, being part of the family of God, having a lighter yoke etc.), we should preach the entire gospel, not just a 'pick and mix' gospel and declare that each individual has to take up their own cross daily and follow Him, and that those who live godly in Christ Jesus will suffer persecution.

'Now after John was put in prison, Jesus came to Galilee, preaching the gospel of the Kingdom of God, and saying, "The time is fulfilled, and the Kingdom of God is at hand. Repent, and believe the gospel" ' (Mark 1:14-15).

Chapter 39

Analysing Revivals

'O Lord, though our iniquities testify against us, do it for Your name's sake; for our backslidings are many, we have sinned against You' (Jeremiah 14:7).

We need revival so that: God can be glorified and vindicated amongst the people, Jesus is exalted, the Holy Spirit is given His rightful place within the Church; the Church can get right with God and become revived, backsliders restored and that multitudes can drawn by the Spirit of God into a saving knowledge of Jesus Christ.

If you have seen revival or read extensively about revival, it makes it a whole lot easier to see the wheat from the chaff, the true from the false, the genuine from the counterfeit, but we should be able to make wise judgments and discern by its fruit, or lack of it, see Matthew 7:15-20.

Looking Back

The problem with analysing revivals and it is something that needs to be done, is that it is often better understood by a future generation. Revival can only be lived in the present but is best understood in retrospect – looking back, able to see the bigger picture. We are all too prone to subconsciously view past revivals through rose-coloured glasses, yet tend to put contemporary revivals under a high-powered microscope.

Dr. Michael Brown said, "We tend to sanitise past revivals and demonise present revivals." Revivalist James A. Stewart, thirty-three years after he saw his first revival in Latvia in 1931, wrote: 'Oh, beloved, it is only when revival is a matter of history that it may gain the subject of applause.'

Max Warren in *Revival An Enquiry* (1954) wrote: 'One of the uses of history is to present a mirror in which we can recognise ourselves not in outward lineaments [a distinctive feature] of those things which are peculiar to the fashion of our age, but in those fundamentals of our human nature which do not change. In this sense any revival movement which looks at history only to shrink from its lessons, is like the man in the Epistle of St. James who, seeing himself in a glass, goes away and at once forgets what he looked like, and so in a very true sense of the word loses himself.'

Dr. Martyn Lloyd-Jones said, "Read the history of the past to discover its lessons…there is nothing quite so foolish as ignoring the past."

Historian, E. H. Carr said, "You cannot look forward intelligently into the future unless you are also prepared to look back attentively into the past."

Frank Bartleman, the chronicler of the Azusa Street Revival (1906-1909) in America, said, "In order to understand what God is going to do, we must understand what He once did."

In regards to revival, let us not be like the fool who has no delight in understanding, but in expressing his own heart (Proverbs 18:2). Nor like the man who answers a matter before he hears it as it is folly and shame to him (Proverbs 18:13), but let us pray that the Lord will give us understanding in all things (2 Timothy 2:7).

Recent or Present Moves of God

When evaluating recent or present moves of God, it is best to start with a bias of believing the best (1 Corinthians 13:7) and treating the leader(s) as a brother or sister in the Lord rather than wolves or tares – then examine the evidence. This is not to say we immediately leave our brains at the door or disregard the warnings in Scripture, but we must not jump to rash conclusions or base our conclusion on the opinions of others, hearsay, third-hand evidence or our own denominational bias or prejudices. We must examine the facts to see what is what and look for the fruit, changed lives and characters – or is there a lack of it? Is there "too much emphasis on charisma and not enough on character," as the Anglican vicar Mark Stibbe said. Because bearing fruit (John 15:1-11) is preferable than moving in the gifts (whilst participating in sin) because the Corinthians were rebuked by the apostle Paul for this very reason! (1 Corinthians 5-6 and 1 Corinthians 11-14).

We should handle any negative issues or concerns in a spirit of love and grace, but especially towards those who disagree with us and who may have valid points especially in relation to a present move of the Holy Spirit (as some may believe it is counterfeit).

We may not like the person at the front, at the fore of the revival, he or she may dress or look different than ourselves and we may be guilty of judging them. By their: appearance, size, style of suit or dress, by the vehicle they drive, their home, the denomination they are associated with or their association with fellow Christian workers whom we may not approve of. But what do they teach or preach? Is it Christ and Him crucified, the cross (1 Cor. 3:11), or is it a merely a happy knees up of soulish delight and entertainment, scattered with Christian phrases? Is another gospel being preached (2 Cor. 11:4) and have people been taken captive by the devil to do his will? (2 Timothy 2:6). These issues are covered in earlier chapters and are worth re-reading: Divine or Demonic – True and False (21), False and Counterfeit Revival (23), The Dangers of Revival (24), Wisdom and Discernment (26), Deception and Rejection (27) and Foolish Excess and the Demonic (31).

We should be aware of the working of the Holy Spirit during times of revival without denouncing a genuine move God as counterfeit or unholy. On the other hand, we do not want to be deceived by the false or led astray by the demonic.

We cannot dismiss revival because of its small negative aspects no more than we would dismiss a Sunday service where negative apathy is often present. We take the best and leave the rest and should never throw out the baby with the bath water; rejecting the majority because of a negative minority is not maturity, nor should we paddle in polluted waters! Also, "Bright lights attract bugs," said Steve Hill frequently during the Brownsville Revival (1995-2000) "And they probably come from *your* church," was his witty reply!

"The crow cannot imitate the dove," said Frank Bartleman from the Azusa Street Revival (1906-1909) but the devilish crow will try to deceive and draw people away from the Holy Spirit who descended onto Jesus as a dove at His baptism (Matthew 3:16). The devil does not help us to love God, our fellowman or to crucify the flesh. In addition, he certainly does not encourage us to live holy lives or to read the Bible and pray more.

A Mixture Within Revival

We should not blame God for the devil's hindrances or be annoyed with God when people scream out or roll on the floor under conviction of sin! Strange things happen in revival. Let God be God; He does things His way because He knows best. The presence of God always testifies to the world that its works are evil (John 7:7 and John 16:8) and non-Christians and lukewarm believers will be offended with the presence of God!

When God comes and descends on a meeting, in church or on a community, He comes to revive and transform and for many it can be a truly emotional experience of jubilation and joy; or terror and fear for others – the Refiner has to do His sifting and shaking first, sometimes quite literally! See Appendix D.

In revival, in the midst of the presence of God, there can be a mixture of the flesh or the demonic and any combination, working in and through those who are not fully sanctified and surrendered to the Lord. Be it, the leader at the fore, assistants, elders and deacons, church members and especially those who have come in off the street, as they have heard that something is happening. As in any group of people there will be mixed ages of maturity in the Lord, from babes in Christ to those who take solid foods (1 Corinthians 3:2) as well as the curious, seekers, fad-lovers and those who turn up for mischief! When God touches people's lives, we often do not know their circumstances or whether they are even converted at all. To judge hastily would be unwise as the measure we use; it will be measured back to us (Matthew 7:2). The Kingdom of God and the kingdom of the devil are at conflict with each other and during a move of God there are power clashes and manifestations – Divine and demonic. Will you denounce the good because of some bad? Separate the precious from the vile, do not lump the devil's dross and God's ore together as one. They are separate and need to be separated. 'For no other foundation can anyone lay than that which is laid, which is Jesus Christ…and the fire will test each one's work…' (1 Corinthians 3:11, 13).

Rejecting or Missing Revival

Some Christians who have actively sought for and prayed for a revival will reject it when God sends it; because the effects and results were different than what they had anticipated. Rejecting revival is rejecting the Holy Spirit – rejecting God Himself! The Pharisees and Sadducees missed the day of visitation when the Messiah (Jesus Christ) came, yet they had the Scriptures which foretold His life (John 5:39-40) and they got upset with those who embraced Him! (Luke 19:42-44). God can also bless one church, yet bypass another in the same town! We all need to be careful that we do not miss the day of visitation (1 Peter 2:12b), when the showers of blessing fall (Ezekiel 34:26), the former and the latter rain (Joel 2:23). Let us not be too hesitant to move into the River of God. Some at first may appear paralysed, unable to roll up their trouser legs and paddle, let alone wade, but like in Ezekiel's day, the river flows from the temple and only in steps may we walk into the river. Up to our ankles, then our knees, and up to our waist until we are immersed in the River of God which is life giving, refreshing and reviving and brings healing to the nations (Ezekiel 47 and Revelation 22:1-5). However let us not frolic in the River of God and neglect our duty, "Go into all the world, and preach the gospel to every creature," said Jesus (Mark 16:15). See also Matthew 28:18-20, Luke 24:47-49, John 20:21-23 and Acts 1:8.

Chapter 40

Self and Full Surrender

'The night is far spent, the day is at hand. Therefore let us cast off the works of darkness, and let us put on the armour of light. Let us walk properly, as in the day.... Put on the Lord Jesus Christ, and make no provision for the flesh, to fulfill its lusts' (Rom. 13:12-14).

The Greatest Enemy
Many Christians are happy with the status quo and attending church is just a ritual. There are also many church-goers with the nickname Christian, those who have never been born again, let alone, fully surrendered, nor matured in the Lord and thus are not disciples, which Jesus commanded all those who followed Him to make, "Go therefore and make disciples..." (Matthew 28:19). Jesus declared in the preceding verse, "All authority has been given to Me," yet all too often many who have made a profession of faith, live and act as if He has no authority and thus by their lack of witness and inaction deny Him. They are Christians 'who are at ease in Zion' (Amos 6:1), the 'complacent ones' (Isaiah 32:9-15). Like the tribes of Gilead, Dan and Asher the 'curse' of 'Meroz' is pronounced against them by the Lord 'because they did not come to the help of the Lord...' in the work He has now delegated to the Church (Judges 5:17, 23).

Full Surrender
The greatest enemy to each individual is self – self that has not surrendered to God – we have not offered our bodies as 'living sacrifices' which is merely our reasonable service (Romans 12:1), nor taken up our cross daily and followed the Master. All too often it is not Thy will be done, but *my will* be done. The apostle Paul wrote: 'He [Jesus] died for all, that those who live should no longer live for themselves, but for Him who died for them and rose again' (2 Corinthians 5:15). Self must be crucified and dethroned. If we truly desire to see our lives changed in personal revival – which always precedes local or national revival, then we must die to self.
'For I through the law died to the law that I might live to God. I have been crucified with Christ; it is no longer I who live, but Christ lives in me; and the life which I now live in the flesh I live by faith in

the Son of God, who loved me and gave Himself for me' (Galatians 2:19-20). We are not our own as we have been bought at a great price and should glorify God (1 Corinthians 6:19-20).

If you confess that Jesus Christ is Lord then you must allow Him to be in *full* control, being led of the Spirit. Full and unconditional surrender to the will of God; putting to death the old man and exchanging your life for His; a giving of yourself to be entirely at His disposal and to hate the things of the world so that they have no hold over you (1 John 2:15-17); so that you can live entirely for the glory of God and to be led of the Holy Spirit.

The apostle Paul wrote: '...Shall we continue in sin that grace may abound? Certainly not! How shall we who died to sin live any longer in it? ...Therefore we were buried with Him through baptism into death, that just as Christ was raised from the dead by the glory of the Father, even so we should also walk in newness of life. ...knowing this, that our old man was crucified with Him, that the body of sin might be done away with, that we should no longer be slaves of sin' (Romans 6:1-2, 4, 6).

One preacher said, "The great hindrance to God pouring out His Spirit in Pentecostal power on many a convention of God's people is simply a refusal on their part to be broken."

Nicky Cruz wrote: 'For too long Christians have conformed to the world. We have allowed the world not only to *affect* us but to completely *infect* us. To take over our hearts and minds and keep us in bondage to sin, even though we convince ourselves that we're free.'[1]

G. D. Watson (1845-1924) was a Wesleyan Methodist minister and evangelist. He wrote: 'If God has called you to be truly like Jesus in all your spirit, He will draw you into a life of crucifixion and humility. He will put on you such demands of obedience that you will not be allowed to follow other Christians. In many ways, He seems to let other good people do things which He will not let you do. Others who seem to be very religious and useful may push themselves, pull wires, and scheme to carry out their plans, but you cannot. If you attempt it, you will meet with such failure and rebuke from the Lord as to make you sorely penitent.

'Others can brag about themselves, their work, their successes, their writings, but the Holy Spirit will not allow you to do any such thing. If you begin to do so, He will lead you into some deep mortification that will make you despise yourself and all your good works.

'Others will be allowed to succeed in making great sums of money, or having a legacy left to them, or in having luxuries, but

God may supply you only on a day-to-day basis, because He wants you to have something far better than gold, a helpless dependence on Him and His unseen treasury.

'The Lord may let others be honoured and put forward while keeping you hidden in obscurity because He wants to produce some choice, fragrant fruit for His coming glory, which can only be produced in the shade. God may let others be great, but keep you small. He will let others do a work for Him and get the credit, but He will make you work and toil on without knowing how much you are doing. Then, to make your work still more precious, He will let others get the credit for the work which you have done; this is to teach you the message of the cross, humility, and something of the value of being cloaked with His nature.

'The Holy Spirit will put a strict watch on you, and with a jealous love rebuke you for careless words and feelings, or for wasting your time [doing various things] which other Christians never seem distressed over. So make up your mind that God is an infinite Sovereign and has a right to do as He pleases with His own, and that He may not explain to you a thousand things which may puzzle your reason in His dealings with you.

'God will take you at your word; if you absolutely sell yourself to be His slave, He will wrap you up in a jealous love and let other people say and do many things that you cannot. Settle it forever; you are to deal directly with the Holy Spirit, He is to have the privilege of tying your tongue or chaining your hand or closing your eyes in ways which others are not dealt with. However, know this great secret of the Kingdom: When you are so completely possessed with the Living God that you are, in your secret heart, pleased and delighted over this peculiar, personal, private, jealous guardianship and management of the Holy Spirit over your life, you will have found the vestibule of heaven, the high calling of God.'[2]

In March 1962, Rev. Geoffrey R. King gave the presidential address at the Annual Assembly of the London Baptist Association. He said, "There can be no quickening of the power of the Holy Spirit in church, home or individual life unless and until we deal faithfully with sin. In the New Testament, the Church was separated from the world and was thus able to reach the world. Vain the lifeboat when the sea gets into it. Only in separation can it be a means of saving. Consider what I say."[3]

In the context of God reviving the Church, Bible teacher, Derek Prince, speaking on Isaiah 40:3-4, preparing the way of the Lord, said, "You and I are going to have to determine whether we will be channels for His glory or mountains that hold it out?"

Chapter 41

Personal Revival

'Love does no harm to its neighbour; therefore love is the fulfilment of the law...knowing the time, that now it is high time to awake out of sleep for our salvation is nearer than when we first believed. The night is far spent; the day is at hand...let us put on the armour of light. Let us walk properly as in the day...' (Romans 13:10-13).

Personal Revival
It has been stated on many occasions that individuals can always have their own personal revival, a reviving of oneself – by getting the sin out of their lives. The story is told of a man who stood on a beach and drew a circle around his feet and then prayed, "Lord send revival, but start the work in me."

'He who covers his sin will not prosper, but whoever confesses *and forsakes them* will have mercy' (Proverbs 28:13).

Somebody once went up to Gipsy Smith whilst he was in America and asked, whilst naming a habit, "Is this sin?" Smith responded, "I dare not say so!" Smith retelling the incident to an audience a few days after the event, said, "There are commandments in the Bible, and it takes me all my time to keep them. Why do you ask me that question? If the habit is a doubtful one – if the doing of it rests upon your conscience – take the question to Christ and in the light of His purity and holiness, decide the matter once and for all. Anything that comes between you and God is wrong, no matter what it is. If it comes between you and God, it must go. In the light of that statement you can settle your whole life. God said, 'Thou shalt have none other gods before Me.' He must have the place of the throne in your heart and in your home He will not share your devotion with another. He is a jealous God. He gave you everything in life worth having and He demands from you your best in return. Nothing else will satisfy Him. He demands a whole surrender."[1]

Oh, God, "Send revival, and start the work in me," should be our cry to our heavenly Father, whose will should be done on earth, as it is in heaven. "I must decrease and He must increase" (John 3:30), should also be our declaration, repeating the words of John the Baptist, the first revivalist of the New Testament.

One man with God can become a deliverer of a nation – Elijah stood before the four hundred and fifty prophets of Baal and four hundred prophets of Asherah. Once the altar was prepared, a complete offering was given, Elijah called upon his God, the fire fell and the people fell on their faces, crying out, "The Lord, He is God! The Lord, He is God!" and then the rain fell which came and healed the barren land! (1 Kings 18). Make sure that you are in a right standing relationship with the Living God and then call upon Him, "Lord send revival, but start the work in me!" From the past we can draw faith for the present and hope for the future.

Evan Roberts of the Welsh Revival (1904-1905), in his latter years wrote: 'The baptism of the Holy Spirit is the essence of revival, for revival comes from knowledge of the Holy Spirit and the way of co-working with Him which enables Him to work in revival power. The primary condition of revival is therefore that believers should individually know the baptism of the Holy Ghost.'[2]

God does not give the Spirit by measure (John 3:34) and has promised to give the Holy Spirit to those that ask Him (Luke 11:13). It is the responsibility of each and every believer to be endued with power from on high (Acts 1:8), but He only gives the Holy Spirit to those who obey Him (Acts 5:32). Do you obey God? Have you been endued with power from on high?

The Holy Spirit
- God has given the Holy Spirit to those who obey Him – not the disobedient (Acts 5:32).
- Your heavenly Father will give the Holy Spirit to those who ask – have you? (Luke 11:13).
- The Holy Spirit will not come and fill dirty vessels (Isaiah 52:11b). Be holy because God is holy (1 Peter 1:16).
- Grieve not the Holy Spirit (Ephesians 4:30-31).
- Do not resist the Holy Spirit (Acts 7:51 and Proverbs 29:1).
- Do not quench the Holy Spirit (1 Thessalonians 5:19-20).
- Be filled with the Holy Spirit – are you? (Ephesians 5:18).

Maynard James wrote: 'The Holy Spirit is He who speaks, guides, teaches, reveals and convicts (John 14-16). The apostle Paul said that the Spirit could be grieved and quenched (Ephesians 4:30 and 1 Thessalonians 5:19) [as well as resisted Acts 7:51] and Saint Peter declared that professing Christians could "tempt" the Holy Ghost and even lie to Him (Acts 5:3, 9). Every child of God is commanded to be filled with the Spirit and to walk in the Spirit (Ephesians 5:18 and Galatians 5:16).'[3]

Oswald J. Smith in *The Enduement of Power* (1933) wrote: 'No sooner have I dealt with sin than I am compelled to deal with self. And so must you. God insists on having first place. Where then do you stand in relation to His will? Have you really surrendered all to Jesus Christ? Do you recognise Him alone as your Lord and Master? Are you willing to go, where He wants you to go, to do what He wants you to do, and to be what He wants you to be? Have you still a will of your own, or is God's will yours and is it your supreme delight to please Him? Who holds the reins of your life? Who controls your actions? In your choices and decisions, is God the dictator? Or are you? Are you sold out to Jesus Christ?'[4]

Healing evangelist, Fred F. Bosworth wrote: 'God's work of quickening or increasing the Divine life in our spirit, soul and body is hindered or limited when we are anything less than *full* of the Spirit. Jesus said that He came, not only that we might have life, but that we might have it "more abundantly." '[5]

A Quaker revivalist, Stephen Crisp (1628-1692) was preaching on being justified by Christ, but went on to declare, "If a man hope[s] to be saved by Christ, he must be ruled by Him. It is contrary to all manner of reason that the devil should rule a man and Christ be his Saviour."[6]

Missionary to Tibet, Geoffrey T. Bull wrote: 'We speak of the Holy Spirit as a gift of God to the believer in Christ.... It is not so much our possessing the Spirit, as the Spirit possessing us. On acceptance of Christ the believer is born of the Spirit, yet it may be but slowly that He will obtain full sovereignty of the heart and will.'[7] But this begins with a choice, to choose to die to self and to offer one's body as a living sacrifice (Romans 12:1), have you?

As a student at Spurgeon's College, London, England, William Fetler of Russia, (later known as Basil Malof through his writings), read a tract on the Holy Spirit by Charles Inwood, a prominent Keswick speaker. Fetler said, "For the first time in my life I realised that the gift of the Holy Spirit had to be treated not only historically, but also experimentally; and that often our theological knowledge falls short of our theological practice. And then and there I prayed. By simple faith I claimed the promise of the Father. It meant breaking with every known sin. It meant full surrender to the Lord. It meant death and resurrection with the Saviour. The subsequent ministry in Russia proved the reality of that experience in London. Faith became the substance of things hoped for. God was faithful to His promise, showing that He is a rewarder of them that diligently seek Him."[8]

Chapter 42

Pathway to Revival

'For thus says the High and Lofty One who inhabits eternity, whose name is Holy, "I dwell in the high and holy place, with him who has a contrite and humble spirit, to revive the spirit of the humble and to revive the heart of the contrite ones" ' (Isaiah 57:15).

Before we can look at the pathway to revival, which follows on from full surrender and being filled with the Holy Spirit, we need to pause and reflect – why is there no revival and what can we do about it? There are hundreds of reasons as to why there is no revival, but the responsibility lies with us, individual members of the body of Christ, the Church, those who choose not to forsake sin, nor press in and plead for God to come and heal our land. As someone once said, "The hindrances to revivals are the sins of the individuals."

Leonard Ravenhill said, "I offer it as my considered judgment that the main reason why we do not have heaven-born, Spirit-operated revival in our day is that we are content to live without it."

J. Edwin Orr wrote: 'If we are not positively channels through which the Spirit pours revival blessing on others, then we are hindrances to the work of God. There is no neutral position. Let us face the question squarely. Let there be no evasion.'[1]

Playing with Sin

J. Edwin Orr wrote: 'The greatest hindrance to revival is *sin*.... There are sins of the flesh – impurity of thought, impurity of words, impurity of deed. There are sins of that unruly member, the tongue – lying, deceit, spiteful talk. How many fall into pride; and then hypocrisy. Sometimes there is a heavy burden upon our consciences, some deceit, some theft; some disgrace.... There is lack of love...prayerlessness...and now to deal with the greatest hindrance of all. We may have sinned in a hundred ways, and we may confess our sins; but lack of faith can rob us of victory... unbelief – what a terrible snare.... Unbelief is sin, (Hebrews 3:12 and Romans 4:20)...Faith is the victory. Unbelief is defeat.... Are you praying for revival? Are you revived? Lord, send revival and start the work in me!'[2]

Stephen F. Olford speaking on 'The Price of Revival' at Westminster Chapel, London, in September 1946, said, "We must face up to the dishonesties of life. Think, for a moment of the dishonesties of lying – that is, any species of designed deception. How many times a day do we lie, in thought, word or deed? Then there is the dishonesty of hypocrisy, pretending to be what we are not, in our prayers, confessions, messages and the like. Another serious dishonesty is that of thieving, or robbing God, by misspent money and squandered hours, which God gave us to serve Him in the winning of souls.... Also, am I out of place, or out of adjustment to the will of God – in relation to my personal life? Family life? Church life? Social life? Business life? Re-creative life?.... If we are out of adjustment at any one point, let the Christ of Gethsemane teach us to pray, 'Thy will be done.' These are heavy demands, but they constitute what is entailed in seeing revival. Indeed this is the price of revival!"[3]

John D. Drysdale wrote: 'The greatest hindrance to deep, permanent, and spreading revival are carnality and worldliness in ministers and church members.... There are many others in our churches who are a decided hindrance to revival; the great army of non-effectives; the well-behaved, do-nothing people, who take up pew room on Sundays (at least once a day) but are never seen at a prayer meeting, or the open-air meeting; nor are they particularly interested in the evangelisation of the heathen. Such people weigh heavily upon the heart of spiritual ministers; they are the devil's instruments of discouragement.'[4]

Rev. Douglas Brown was used in the East Anglia Revival (1921-1922) in England and the Fishermen's Revival (1922) in Scotland. He said, "If you have men in your pulpits who doubt the Bible, the deity of Christ, the atonement, the great fundamentals of your faith, you can't get revival."[5]

Octavius Winslow wrote: 'If a child of God restrains prayer, he opens the door to the departure of every grace and to the admission of every sin.... It should be remembered by every professing man, that there is a great difference between prayer and praying; we mean, between the formal observance of the duty and the spiritual character of the observance.'[6]

Charles G. Finney was a great American revivalist of the 1820s-1860s. His greatest work was his *Lectures on Revival* (also known as *Revival of Religion*) which was written from experience and practical observation during times of revivals across America. Finney knew that the way to help promote revival was to break up one's 'fallow ground for it is time to seek the Lord, till He comes and rains righteousness on you' (Hosea 10:12). He noted many hindrances to seeing revival:

- Ingratitude, want of love towards God, neglect of the Bible, unbelief, neglect of prayer, neglect of the means of grace (silly and futile excuses as to why you cannot attend religious meetings).
- Performing Christian duties, such as prayer and Bible reading in a worldly frame of mind, in such carelessness that you cannot remember what you prayed or read.
- A lack of love for fellow believers and no concern for the unconverted.
- Neglect of family duties (setting a bad example before them, not reading the Bible to your children, or praying with and for them).
- Neglect of watchfulness over your own life, sinning before the world, the church and before God!
- Neglect to watch over the brethren, unconcerned for their state of soul, not reproving (rebuking) them in love over their lukewarm attitude or blatant sin.
- Neglect of self-denial in any areas especially in regards to serving the Lord.
- Worldly mindedness, pride, slander, censoriousness (a bitter spirit), envy, levity (lack of respect for God). Lying, cheating, hypocrisy or bad temper. Finney's definition of lying was: any calculated deceit; if you try to convey an impression contrary to the truth, you lie.
- Robbing God, in time, money (tithes and offerings), misapplying your talents and power of mind, wasting your precious resources (on smoking, drinking, opulent living, excessive waste / poor stewardship etc.).
- Hindering others from being useful, wasting their time (especially the minister), destroying fellow believer's confidence, playing into Satan's hand – repent and confess immediately.
- Taking sides against another Christian when a non-believer bad mouths / speaks evil of them.
- Neglecting the claims of world mission; being focussed only on their own field of labour, their own church, their own circle of ministry.
- A dishonouring of the Sabbath and or fighting against the Temperance Reformation (a group who were against alcohol consumption).

During the Ruanda Revival (1937-1950s), at one mission station; two missionaries had been for a long time estranged from one another. During the 1937 Easter Convention, the Holy Spirit showed one of the missionaries her guilt and she went and apologised to her fellow labourer. The two were immediately reconciled and went straight away to a meeting which was attended by a large number of village evangelists. They testified of what God had done for them. A. C. Stanley Smith wrote: 'It seemed as though their simple but costly testimony opened the floodgates of Divine power.... The striking fact was not how much missionaries can help the work of God, but how much they can hinder it.'[7]

J. Edwin Orr, in response to the question, "Why is it that God does not hear our prayers for revival?" wrote: 'Because of your inconsistencies.... Is the Almighty (I ask it reverently) deaf to His pleading people? Or are God's people deaf to a pleading God? Which? – I know which. Hypocrisy and humbug make the so-called prayers for revival so much hot air.... Stop and think a moment. The lack of revival in *your* district, in *your* church, in *your own* life is due not to God's failure, but to yours. Dare you tell me that God denies revival to a heart that is willing to pay the price?'[8]

During the Welsh Revival (1904-1905), in Anglesey, Caernarfon and Bala, Evan Roberts repeated the challenge *to witness in every possible form*. He said, "It will not do for us to go to heaven by ourselves. We must be on fire, friends, for saving others. To be workers, will draw heaven down and will draw others to heaven. Without readiness to work, the spirit of prayer will not come."[9]

Do you Desire Revival Enough to…

W. P. Nicholson was preaching on the subject of 'Revival' from Psalm 85:6, 'Wilt Thou not revive us again; that Thy people may rejoice in Thee.' He said…

- Do you desire a revival enough to pray earnestly and constantly for it?
- Do you desire revival enough to search your heart and ask God to cast out all that is displeasing to Him?
- Do you desire revival enough to attend meetings for prayer and take part in them, even at the sacrifice of pride, comfort and conveniences?
- Do you desire revival enough to seek opportunities to speak and pray with the unconverted?

- Do you desire a revival so earnestly as to continue labouring and praying for it, even if the answer is delayed?[10]

Sins of Omission and Commission
Sins of omission and commission – the former is passive sin (neglecting that which should be done) and the latter is active, doing that which ought *not* be done. A minister once wrote: 'Our offences are innumerable, including sins of omission as well as of commission, for our comparatively best thoughts, words, and actions have come immeasurably short of the standard of the Divine law. 'We have left undone that which we ought to have done' as well as 'done that which we ought not to have done.' Our offences are aggravated, committed against knowledge and instruction, against the love and grace, no less than against the law and holiness of God.'[11]

William Booth-Clibborn wrote: 'The secret of Christian repentance is to confess every sin individually, both sins of commission and the greater and the many more sins of omission.'[12]

Evan Roberts of the Welsh Revival (1904-1905) stated that there were four conditions for revival, which he frequently emphasised:
1. Is there any sin in your past with which you have not honestly dealt with, or not confessed to God? On your knees at once. Your past must be put away and cleansed.
2. Is there anything in your life that is doubtful – anything which you cannot decide is good or evil? Away with it. There must not be a trace of a cloud between you and God. Have you forgiven everybody, EVERYBODY? If not, don't expect forgiveness for your sins. Better to offend ten thousand friends than grieve the Spirit of God, or quench Him.
3. Do what the Holy Spirit prompts without hesitation or fear. Obedience, prompt, implicit, unquestioning obedience at whatever cost.
4. Make a public confession of Christ as personal Saviour. Profession and confession are vastly different. Multitudes are guilty of long and loud profession. Confession of Christ as Lord has to do with His workings in your life TODAY!

'…Who is then willing to consecrate himself this day to the Lord?' (1 Chronicles 29:5b).

Chapter 43

Steps Towards Revival

Jesus said, "…I will build My Church, and the gates of hades [hell] shall not prevail against it" (Matthew 16:18b).

Why we Need Revival:
1. God must be glorified, Jesus must be exalted and the Holy Spirit needs to be given His rightful place within the Church.
2. The Church needs to be revived. It must be swept free and cleansed from sin. If revival does not start in the Church then it cannot move outside the Church amongst the graceless.
3. The graceless need to receive the grace of God, sinners need to be surrendered to Him and in times of revival they are drawn as if by an unseen hand to call upon the name of the Lord and to turn from their wicked ways. A community, society or nation can be transformed to the praise and glory of God.

Without revival the Church is lost in itself, its programmes, its routines, its religious rituals and trappings which are not effective in reaching out to the lost and hurting, and worst of all, the Church is not reflecting a true biblical representation of New Testament Christianity. Jesus is not being lifted up (in testimony, through evangelism and honoured) and therefore He cannot draw all men to Himself.

The Church in general is weak, frequently stagnant, and all too often dishonouring to the Lord by the lifestyles of its members, which causes the heathen to blaspheme the name of God. Jesus said, "Why do you call Me, 'Lord, Lord,' and do not do the things which I say?" (Luke 6:46).

The Scriptures Declare…
There has been much written within this book, verified by Scripture (and accounts from Church history), but the Word of God is always central and our final authority. In the Bible, what does it say (Galatians 4:30a) about: revival, Divine visitations, the Holy Spirit and meeting God, coupled with the conditions for Christians to live correctly before God and man?
- 'For the Word of the Lord is right and all His work is done in truth' (Psalm 33:4).

- God said, "For I will pour water on him who is thirsty, and floods on the dry ground; I will pour My Spirit on your descendants, and My blessing on your offspring" (Isaiah 44:3).

Preparing for Revival

We need revival because it pertains to the glory of God and the honour of His name – the Church should be better, and society can be better. To see revival we must first get our own lives in order. Then with clean hands and a pure heart we can plead God's covenant promises so that the Spirit will be poured out on those who are thirsty, the Church will be revived and He will come and heal our land as floods are poured out – God will be glorified amongst the nations; Jesus will be lifted high, drawing all men to Himself, the Holy Spirit will have His way in the Church and the desert will bloom once again.

- 'Justice is turned back, and righteousness stand afar off; for truth is fallen in the street, and equity cannot enter. So truth fails, and he who departs from evil makes himself a prey' (Isaiah 59:14-15).
- 'It is time for You to act, O Lord, for they have regarded Your law as void' (Psalm 119:126).
- 'Gentiles…glorify God in the day of visitation' (1 Pet. 2:12).
- '…To confirm the promise made to the fathers and that the Gentiles might glorify God in His mercy' (Rom. 15:8b-9a).

The Fear of the Lord

- 'Behold the eyes of the Lord is on those who fear Him, on those who hope in mercy' (Psalm 33:18).
- 'The fear of the Lord is the beginning of knowledge…' (Proverbs 1:7a).
- 'The fear of the Lord is the beginning of wisdom and knowledge of the Holy One is understanding' (Proverbs 9:10).
- 'The fear of the Lord is to hate evil' (Proverbs 8:13a).
- Jesus said, "But I will show you whom you should fear: Fear Him who, after He has killed, has power to cast into hell; yes I say, fear Him!" (Luke 12:5).

Holiness – Dealing with Sin

- 'Let the wicked forsake his way, and the unrighteous man his thoughts, let him return to the Lord, and He will have

- mercy on him; and to our God, for He will abundantly pardon' (Isaiah 55:7).
- 'Depart from me, all you workers of iniquity; for the Lord has heard the voice of My weeping. The Lord has heard my supplication; the Lord will receive my prayer' (Psalm 6:8-9).
- 'Cry aloud, spare not; lift up your voice like a trumpet; tell My people their transgression and the house of Jacob their sins' (Isaiah 58:1).
- 'Let the words of my mouth and the meditation of my heart be acceptable in Your sight, O Lord, my strength and my Redeemer' (Psalm 19:14).
- 'Search me, O God, and know my heart; try me, and know my anxieties; and see if there is any wicked way in me, and lead me in the way everlasting' (Psalm 139:23-24).
- '...O Lord, revive Thy work in the midst of the years, in the midst of the years make known; in wrath remember mercy' (Habakkuk 3:2).
- 'For the time is come that judgment must begin at the house of the Lord...' (1 Peter 4:17a).

George Jeffreys held large Healing and Revival Campaigns across Britain for seventeen years (up to 1932) and saw tens of thousands of converts and thousands of miracles. In 1932, he wrote: 'How true it is that when the Church compromises with the world and diverts from the pathway of holiness, the power of God is withdrawn. It has been so from the beginning. The Creator withdrew from the first man because of transgression, the glory of God was withdrawn from the Temple in the land because of the backsliding people. Today the community of the Church that mixes with the world and does not stand for separation from it, need not expect an outpouring of the Holy Ghost.'[1]

The Former and the Latter Rain
- 'He shall come down like rain upon the mown grass, like showers that water the earth' (Psalm 72:6).
- '...Let us now fear the Lord our God, who gives rain, both the former and the latter, in its season. He reserves for us the appointed weeks of the harvest' (Jeremiah 5:24).
- Thus says the Lord God, "...I will cause showers to come down in their season, there shall be showers of blessing" (Ezekiel 34:26).

- 'Let us pursue knowledge of the Lord. His going forth is established as the morning; He will come to us like the rain, like the latter and the former rain to the earth' (Hosea 6:3).
- 'Be glad you children of Zion, and rejoice in the Lord your God; for He has given you the former rain faithfully, and He will cause the rain to come down for you – the former rain and the latter rain in the first month. The threshing floors shall be full of wheat, and the vats shall overflow with new wine and oil. So I will restore to you the years that the swarming locust have eaten…' (Joel 2:23-25a).
- 'Sow for yourselves righteousness; reap in mercy; break up your fallow ground, for it is time to seek the Lord, till He comes and rains righteousness on you' (Hosea 10:12).
- 'Let us not grow weary while doing good, for in due season *we shall reap* if we do not lose heart' (Galatians 6:9).

Basic Principles to Answered Prayer

If you want your prayers to go higher than the ceiling, into the throne room of God and be effective then:
- Pray according to God's will (Matt. 6:10 and 1 Jn. 5:14-15).
- Pray with unselfish and right motives (James 4:3).
- Confess and forsake sin, in order to pray with clean hands and a pure heart (Psalm 24:4, Psalm 66:17-19, Proverbs 28:13 and 1 John 3:21-22).
- Pray in Jesus' victory for God's glory (John 14:13-14).
- We must be in right relationships with others and have good fellowship (Matthew 5:23-24, 6:12 and 1 Peter 3:7).
- There needs to be unity based on the Holy Spirit's anointing, but not compromise (Psalm 133, John chapters 13 and 15).
- Be persistent in your prayers (Luke 11:8 and Luke 18:1-8).

Crying out to God
- 'He does not forget the cry of the humble' (Psalm 9:12b).
- 'The righteous cry out, and the Lord hears, and delivers them from all their troubles. The Lord is near to those who have a broken heart, and saves such as have a contrite spirit. Many are the afflictions of the righteous, but the Lord delivers him out of them all' (Psalm 34:17-19).
- 'Their heart cried out to the Lord, O wall of the daughter of Zion, let tears run down like a river day and night; give

yourself no relief; give your eyes no rest. Arise, cry out in the night, at the beginning of the watches; pour out your heart like water before the face of the Lord. Lift your hands towards Him for the life of your children…' (Lam. 2:18-19).
- 'Through the Lord's mercies we are not consumed, because His compassions fail not. They are new every morning; great is Your faithfulness. "The Lord is my portion," says my soul, "therefore I hope in Him!" The Lord is good to those who wait for Him, to the soul who seeks Him' (Lamentations 3:22-25).
- 'Gird yourselves and lament you priests; wail, you who minister before the altar, come lie all night in sackcloth you who minister to my God' (Joel 1:13).
- 'Turn to Me with all your heart, with fasting, with weeping, and with mourning. So rend your heart, and not your garments; return to the Lord your God; for He is gracious and merciful, slow to anger, and of great kindness, and He relents from doing harm' (Joel 2:12-13).
- 'Blow the trumpet in Zion, consecrate a fast, call a sacred assembly; gather the people, sanctify the congregation, assemble the elders, gather the children and the nursing babes…. Let the priests, who minister to the Lord weep between the porch and the altar; let them say, "Spare your people, O Lord, and do not give Your heritage to reproach …why should they say among the people 'where is their God?' " ' (Joel 2:15-17).
- 'Those who sow in tears shall reap in joy. He who continually goes forth weeping, bearing seed for sowing, shall doubtless come again with rejoicing, bringing his sheaves with him' (Psalm 126:5-6).
- 'Let us therefore come boldly to the throne of grace, that we may obtain mercy and find grace to help in our time of need' (Hebrews 4:16).
- '…As soon as Zion travailed she gave birth to her children' (Isaiah 66:8b).

God's Concern and Our Prayers
- Daniel prayed, "O Lord, listen! O Lord, forgive! O Lord, listen and act! Do not delay for Your own sake, my God, for Your city and Your people are called by Your name" (Daniel 9:19).

- God said to Jonah, "Should I not pity Nineveh, that great city…who cannot discern between their right hand and their left?" (Jonah 4:11).
- 'O Lord, though our iniquities testify against us, do it for Your name's sake; for our backslidings are many; we have sinned against You' (Jeremiah 14:7).

Pray for a floodtide of the Holy Spirit to come and cleanse and wash our land in the blood of Jesus Christ; to revive saints and to save sinners, to glorify God, to exalt Jesus Christ and to allow the Holy Spirit to have His way in the Church – to touch the Church and to transform the community. See Appendix E.

Three centuries ago, a missionary in the West of America respecting his people wrote: 'We are obediently waiting, anxiously looking, fervently praying, confidently hoping, and everyday living, for a revival of the work of God in our charge.'

May the church be awakened and arise and call upon our God – for He shall surely come! He will rend the heavens and pour out His Spirit for His great name's sake. The glory of the Lord will be GREATER in the latter days than the former. The world will sit up and take notice. The Church will be revived, sinners will be saved, the backslider will be restored and GLORY will be stamped on the lintels of the houses of the Lord. God will be glorified, Jesus will be exalted and will arise with healing in His wings, whilst the Holy Spirit will accomplish His work through surrendered vessels. That the manifold wisdom of God might be made known by the Church to the principalities and powers in the heavenly places (Ephesians 3:10), according to the eternal purposes which He accomplished in Christ Jesus our Lord, in whom we have boldness and access with confidence through faith in Him.

God said, "If My people who are called by My name, shall humble themselves, and pray, and seek My face, and turn from their wicked ways; then I will hear from heaven, and will forgive their sin, and will heal their land" (2 Chronicles 7:14).

'Tell ye your children of it, and let your children tell their children, and their children another generation' (Joel 1:3).

'Our God shall come…' (Psalm 50:3).

Thank you for reading this book, please write a short (or long) review on your favourite review site, and give a shout-out on social media – thank you.

Appendix A

Revival Memorabilia and Products

Christian Memorabilia
If memorabilia is for sale within a church building or is connected in any way to a revival, some Christians assume that it is not a move of God, but merely a money making venture, but this is largely unfounded and untrue. The history of Christian memorabilia has a long and varied history. Anniversary dates connected with popular Christians such as missionary explorer, Dr. David Livingstone, as well as Christian institutions like the Baptist Missionary Society and the British and Foreign Bible Society, alongside denominations or local chapels and churches have had their own memorabilia produced. This includes porcelain, medallions, magic lantern slides, postcards, posters, bookmarks and teacloths (drying up cloths) etc.

In addition, there are Christian museums and historical places of interest connected with many men of God including: John Bunyan, John and Charles Wesley, William Carey, Billy Bray, Dr. David Livingstone, D. L. Moody, General William Booth of the Salvation Army and Smith Wigglesworth, who had the gift of healing.

Methodist Memorabilia
During and after the Evangelical Revival (1739-1791) which is also known as the British Great Awakening or the Methodist Revival, on anniversary dates connected with John and Charles Wesleys' birth, conversion, death, year of the awakening, and the foundation of the Methodist Society; memorabilia was produced or minted. Items such as: busts (head and shoulder sculpture), complete figurines, statuettes, mugs, plates and medallions, some of which are more than two centuries old and can command high prices.

In May 2007, the author visited the first Methodist Chapel in the world, The New Room founded in 1739 in Bristol, England. It is also known as John Wesley's Chapel. In the preacher's rooms upstairs, where Methodist preachers were lodged, (the stables are outside); apart from seeing Wesley's cassock, the bed that he slept in when visiting, his chair, the desk that he wrote at, a lock of his hair, numerous paintings and Methodist history etc., there was a plethora of revival memorabilia from the eighteenth and nineteenth centuries.

In the nineteenth century, there were at least sixty potters in Staffordshire who made porcelain figures and busts of John Wesley of various sizes – about twenty were on show in The New Room. On display were medallions, handkerchiefs, thimbles, cups, saucers, mugs, plates, jugs and many other Wesley revival memorabilia (Wesley-mania), items manufactured from the eighteenth century.

Wesley's Cottage at Trewint, Altarnun, Cornwall, UK, is believed to be the smallest Methodist Chapel in the world. It was the first place in Cornwall to accept Methodism when John Nelson and John Downes arrived on 29 August 1743 and were taken into the cottage of Digory and Elizabeth Isbell's for refreshment. Inside, you can also purchase your own modern reproduced John Wesley thimble, bone china plate or mug. On display, there was a wooden cross, made from wood from the home where Susanna Wesley (the mother of John and Charles) was born in 1669!

On the second floor, there are many items of revival memorabilia on display, which had been contributed from around the globe; including a small doll-sized effigy of John Nelson behind a pulpit encapsulated in a glass dome ornamental case. Behind two glass cabinets were plates (including an octagon shaped plate), porcelain figurine of Wesley in a pulpit, busts of John Wesley (the rarest Wesley busts can sell for £1,000s), a teapot, large drinking cup, milk jug, John Wesley's first edition *Journal* (1769) and John Nelson's first edition *Journal* (1767), hymn books and other interesting items, all connected to John Wesley and Methodism.

On Saturday, 26 March 1785, Easter weekend, John Wesley, stayed at Ambrose Foley's house at Quinton, (twenty miles from Northampton), England. In gratitude to his hosts and their warm hospitality, Wesley presented to Mr and Mrs Foley, a tea-service. The 1890 edition of *Wesley His Own Biography, Selections From The Journals* with 450 illustrations shows that the teacups and saucers had an oriental design (Chinese). The teapot's sides depict the face and shoulders of John Wesley (who was centred) with the inscription 'The Rev. John Wesley A.M.' with fifteen other Methodist preachers (and their surnames) encircling him with biblical scenes in the background. Thus, John Wesley had no qualms with memorabilia. On the death of John Wesley in March 1791, everyone at his funeral was given a biscuit with a portrait of Wesley engraved on it![1]

In October 2008, an 1841 Staffordshire mug commemorating the fiftieth anniversary of the death of John Wesley sold for £127 (approximately $216) and was in fine original condition. Whilst a chipped Wesley mug from 1839 was listed in October 2012 at £85 ($136), plus £8.50 ($13.60) P&P but did not sell.

Inside the Moffat Homestead at the Moffat Mission in Kuruman, South Africa, amongst various artefacts is a 3" (7.6cm) statuette of John Wesley from 1839 (the year of the Centenary Celebrations). The display card noted: '…Moffat was greatly influenced by the movement and was on leave in England at that time.' Thus Moffat who saw revival in 1829 at the mission, probably purchased this very item. A John Wesley medallion, minted in 1839 sold for just £21 ($33.60) in October 2012; because Wesley's nose had been rubbed away!

Billy Bray Memorabilia

Three Eyes Chapel, Kerley Downs, near Truro, in the parish of Kea, Cornwall, England, had been built by the revivalist, Billy Bray in around 1835 and at a later date was enlarged. Its walls are adorned with Billy Bray (1794-1868) memorabilia, photos and achievements from his life including a Centenary Celebration poster of his life, 1794-1894, which had been originally collated (before being printed as a poster) from photographs and a few postcards, which were evidently produced. On sale were Billy Bray mugs, thimbles, bookmarks, a postcard of his grave (at Baldhu Church, less than one mile away), books about his life and even printed tea towels (dish drying cloths).

Fulton Street Revival Memorabilia

At the end of September 2007, the Christian Broadcasting Network reported on the 150th anniversary of the Fulton Street Revival (1857-1859) which led to the America's last great awakening. They spoke to Pastor Ted Lavigne of Kissimme, Florida, USA, who owns the world's largest collection of memorabilia from the 1857 revival, including rare photos, a studio viewer and a portrait of Jeremiah Lanphier.

Welsh Revival Memorabilia

For the Centenary Celebrations of the Welsh Revival (1904-1905) revival memorabilia had been collated and was on display in the school room of Moriah Chapel in Lougher, South Wales, UK; the precise location where revival broke out on 31 October 1904. For the celebrations special porcelain plates were commissioned and on sale. On display were other revival related items: including books, revival hymnbooks, paper cuttings, photocopies, postcards and porcelain. Cotton handkerchiefs with the face of Evan Roberts were also manufactured during the revival, as was a Staffordshire figurine similar to the busts of other revivalists.

The revival postcards were of Evan Roberts, his brother and some of the women helpers, which had been printed during the revival by the *Western Mail* newspaper. On 4 November 1904, Evan Roberts wrote to the editor of the *Sunday Companion* asking for a quotation for a visible representation of his visions on printed postcards, which would give the message wider circulation.

On an internet auction website the *starting* bids for Welsh Revival postcards range from £1-20 ($1.6-32) with an exchange rate of £1 to $1.6 U.S. dollars (summer 2012). In June 2012, a Welsh Revival (1904-1905) postcard of Evan Roberts in Bala, amongst a crowd of people (and you could not see Evan Roberts) on a large field during an open-air meeting sold for £82 ($131). In July 2012, a large face and shoulders postcard of Evan Roberts sold for £52 ($83), though £5-15 ($8-24) per postcard plus postage £1 ($1.60) is more common.

On display within a locked cabinet in Moriah was a white mug with Evan Roberts' face and shoulders emblazoned on it. A. B. Jones and Sons, Grafton Works, Longton, Staffordshire, produced cups and saucers with the face of Evan Roberts on them. The Grafton backstamp was used from 1900-1913. The starting price for the pair was £47 ($94) in the summer of 2007.

What Purpose Does Revival Memorabilia Serve?

There are many and varied reasons as to why some revivalists, those who are involved in the revival, the church, its members or associated ministries (and even entrepreneurs) produce revival memorabilia. It could be books, porcelain (the least common now), printed or recorded sermons; teaching tapes/CDs, videos/DVDs (the most popular) of the services or even bumper stickers, badges, greeting cards and T-shirts (quite common in the West).

In the past, churches which have experienced revival have sold their Christian products during these times of blessing within the location of the revival, such as the church foyer. Since the mid 1990s, but especially in the subsequent decade into the twenty-first century, ministry websites became very popular outlets for worldwide customers to purchase revival memorabilia.

- Books, tapes, CDs and DVDs (documented services) provide a faithful account of what has happened.
- People want to know about moves of God; how it started, who was involved etc., what does it look like, and where there is a demand, the need should be met.
- If the revivalist does not write about the revival then someone will. A book is sometimes written by the revivalist to explain truth from fiction, to address misunderstandings and state the facts.
- There is always a demand for a revivalist to retell their experiences, years or even decades after the event. They cannot be in two places at once and a book can meet the demand.
- Books and DVDs etc. help fire-up those who are not yet on fire and praying for revival. A person on the other side of the world could be given a book or DVD and his or her life could be transformed as they read or see the wonderful workings of God.
- Revival books and DVDs add fuel to those who are already passionate for revival and increase one's faith. They help stimulate a person to press in deeper for the things of God.
- The profits from items sold, if directed back into the church where revival has broken out, will assist in paying additional staff wages, increased utility bills (drinking fountain, toilet flushes x 1,000s!, electricity or gas for heating, air-conditioning and lighting) that inevitably occur when multitudes descend on your church building; prematurely ageing carpets and seating etc.

- If people travel halfway round the world to a revival location (which is not cheap), then they want to have physical mementoes (which are cheap in comparison to their plane ticket and accommodation) which they can share with their friends, family and local church.
- Christian T-shirts are living evangelism. At the Brownsville Revival (1995-2000) there was a stall in the car park (parking lot) where you could buy Christian T-shirts, two of which had printed on them, 'Run to the Mercy Seat' and the 'Pensacola Outpouring,' which was run by a Christian entrepreneur. Inside the church foyer and semi-circular hallway, the Brownsville Church and ministries relating to the team, sold books, videos of every service, tapes, music CDs, badges and a red bumper sticker, 'Yes Lord We Will Ride With You.' With the Lakeland Outpouring (2008), Christian T-shirts, 'Come and Get Some' were on sale within two months. Also a Christian artist who had been inspired by a specific Lakeland meeting in connection with Israel was selling hand painted greeting cards on an internet auction website.

Christian Products

Some believers strongly object to Christians making money, especially during times of revival with Christian products, but is it not fair to say that a worker is worthy of his wage? Does not the schoolteacher as well as the shelf-stacker get a wage for the hours they have worked? Revival products such as Christian: books, music, DVDs etc., edify and build up the body of Christ, to bring to a full stature and knowledge of Christ. Also, if a lay worker (like A. Lindsay Glegg) is in secular employment in order to pay the bills and feed the family, is it so wrong that a Christian worker (like the apostle Paul) supplements or earns an income in order to survive? Those within Christian ministry also have bills to pay and not all Christian workers get a guaranteed salary, or even a wage. Jesus had a team of faithful supporters to meet His and the disciples needs (Luke 8:1-3). The apostle Paul on occasions reverted to his trade as a tentmaker in order to live (Acts 18:1-3) because he never wanted to be a financial burden to anyone. Did he sell the tents, or give them away for free? It could be asked, was tent making the most effective use of the apostle Paul's time? If he had more support would he have planted more churches and written more letters?

Let us not be upset over Christian products that are sold during times of revival (or from ministries outside of revival) as they can encourage, build up and stimulate us in the most holy faith, and that investment can last a lifetime. On the other hand, do not profit just to make a profit. Revivals cease and most have little lasting financial benefit as the expenditure and wear and tear is exacerbated and accelerated.

Appendix B

Why Revivals are Chronicled

In the eighteenth century, revivalists such as Rev. James Robe of Scotland, Jonathan Edwards of America, John and Charles Wesley of Great Britain, George Whitefield of Great Britain and America and John Nelson of England, wrote journals or documented accounts about the revivals which they were involved in (including revival sermons) which were published in their lifetime and beyond. Jonathan Goforth of China and Manchuria, Paget Wilkes of Japan, Marie Monsen of China, and Duncan Campbell of Scotland, to name but four, all wrote about the revivals they were involved in. Since 1995, revival articles have found themselves reported on media websites and blogs, but more recently, on social networking/media sites.

Imagine if nobody ever chronicled a revival – the volumes of Church history would be greatly diminished and a large portion of God's blessing and the heritage of the Church would be unknown to future generations. Many valuable and important lessons would be lost, yet known only in eternity. Little detail is known about the Shotts Revival (1630) in Scotland, under John Livingston because it was never documented at the time. The omission of our forefathers to transmit a full and circumstantial account of the revival is not only our generation's loss, but all generations.

What if Doctor Luke had not chronicled the book of Acts? We would have lost eighteen accounts of revival from Church history. The history of the Christian Church would be incomplete and it would have taken a completely different course. Doctor Luke wrote: 'It seemed good to me also, having perfect understanding of all things from the very first, to write to you an orderly account, most excellent Theophilus that you may know the certainty of those things in which you were instructed' (Luke 1:3-4).

The apostle Paul wrote to the church at Corinth: 'All these things [from the Old Testament] happened to them as examples, and they were written for our admonition...' (1 Corinthians 10:11). The psalmists wrote: 'This will be written for the generation to come, that a people yet to be created may praise the Lord' (Psalm 102:18) and 'One generation shall praise Your works to another and shall declare Your mighty acts' (Psalm 145:4).

In 1875, a letter appeared in *The Royal Cornwall Gazette* (17 April), written to the editor, complaining that Billy Bray had an unmarked grave, and asking, why had no monument been erected? Others who also wanted to honour Billy Bray shared the writer's sentiments. A monument was officially proposed in 1878 (the year of the 15th edition of *The King's Son*, F. W. Bourne's life of Billy Bray), and was built in 1880 from some of its profits and by subscription as a sign of gratitude of the Bible Christian Society. However, the precise last resting place of Billy Bray's wife, Joey, is unknown. She is interred at Baldhu Church graveyard and Billy who died four years later in 1868 possibly lay beside her – though the monument erected to the memory of Billy Bray does not state this. Everyone connected with Joey knew the burial plot at the time and therefore did not deem it necessary to put facts to paper. Facts are lost when not recorded.

In 1742, Rev. James Robe desired to 'publish about a sheet once a week or a fortnight' on the account of the Kilsyth and Cambuslang Revivals (1742). '…To serve the truth and the interest of religion and to satisfy the longing curiosity of those who are giving Zion's King no rest until He makes His Jerusalem a praise in the midst of the earth…' These sheets were collated and later published under the title *When the Wind Blows*.

Rev. James Robe continued: 'Praise to our God, for these His mighty acts are not to be confined to the present generation, wherein they appear. Posterity shall reap the benefit of them and it is our duty to transmit the history of them to posterity, that they may reap the greater benefit by them and praise the Lord more distinctly for them. It would be a contempt of these wonderful works which God hath made to be had in remembrance, if they should be buried in oblivion, so as not to be known by those who live in after ages. One generation shall praise His works together and declare His mighty acts.'[1]

Why Revivalists Write

- There is a demand to know about revivals and not everyone is able to travel to a revival. Where there is a need for the story to be told, it will be met by one person or another. If the revivalist does not write about their work then somebody else will. I think it is better that those who have paid the price, profit from it than those who are just out to make a profit!
- They may be called of the Holy Spirit to write an account of the workings of God in heaven-sent revival. An account of revival will glorify God and exalt Jesus Christ.
- A book can explain fact from fiction as rumours can circulate. A book by the revivalist is the wheat that distinguishes it from the verbal chaff. Books written by an eyewitness or a faithful researcher / historian provide a faithful account which is beneficial not only for the present, but for future generations.
- Revival books add fuel to the flames of those who are already passionate to see revival in their life, church or nation.
- Royalties from the sale of books if directed back into the church or mission organisation connected to the revival, assists in paying

the bills and wages of people. It can also finance more labourers to go into the harvest field and fulfil the Great Commission.
- Most Christian authors see their work as a ministry, a calling from God and contrary to popular belief, most see little financial reward. The publisher and retailer often receive the lion's share.

Spread the Facts – Promote Revival

In May 1905, evangelist / journalist, Frank Bartleman, who would become the chronicler of the Azusa Street Revival (1906-1909) was given the book *The Great Revival In Wales* by S. B. Shaw. The Welsh Revival began on 31 October 1904, so within seven months a book had already been printed. After reading it, Bartleman who was already involved in active Christian work resolved to give up his secular employment and became a channel in which the burden for revival could come upon him. After receiving 5,000 copies of the pamphlet, *The Revival in Wales* by G. Campbell Morgan, he began to distribute them. He wrote: '[It] spread the fire in the churches wonderfully' and 'they had a wonderful quickening influence.' He also began to sell S. B. Shaw's book amongst the churches that he spoke at and 'God wonderfully used it to promote faith for a revival spirit.'[2]

Appendix C

Contentions of the Evangelical Revival (1739-1791)

The Evangelical Revival (1739-1791), spanning seven decades and two generations inevitably had varying views and opinions on a variety of subjects which included personality clashes between the numerous revivalists themselves who came from different denominations and were at varying levels of maturity and sanctification.

Archibald W. Harrison in his book *The Evangelical Revival And Christian Reunion* wrote: 'The Revival was singularly rich in men and women of strong character, whose temperament did not always blend harmoniously. Even the wisest and best may sometimes be difficult. The leaders of the Revival suffered much from detraction and misrepresentation.... But when the mist of controversy had passed away their fine qualities appeared.'[1]

John Wesley with his strong affirmations led him to separate from the Moravians and Calvinists because what he saw clearly he proclaimed freely. He was never willing to surrender a truth of tested validity and he tested religious experience consistently by the standard of the New Testament. John Wesley often attacked principles, though not necessarily the person who held or promoted them. The controversy of 'Election' and 'Free Grace' was at the infancy of the revival, and thus its labourers lacked the wisdom of which only years can bring.

They were also more prone to strong rebuttals of that which they held dear to themselves as important truths and gave harsh denunciations for those who disagreed and tried to undermine them.[2]

The main blight on the history of the Evangelical Revival was the doctrines of 'Election' (Calvinism) as preached by Whitefield, versus 'Free Grace' (Arminianism) as preached by John and Charles Wesley. This led to two camps being birthed within Methodism. Yet these men of God were striving for the same goal, to preach Christ and to see men turn back to God, and regardless of their theology, God brought about revival wherever they went.

At the end of March 1741, John Wesley went to hear George Whitefield preach, having heard much of his unkind behaviour since his return from Georgia, New England, America, though this debate had been going on in private between the Wesley's, Whitefield, the Moravians and their close associates for over a year. Wesley in his *Journal* wrote: 'He told me, he and I preach two different gospels; and therefore, he not only would not join with, or give me the right hand of fellowship, but was resolved to publicly preach against me and my brother, wheresoever he preached at all.'

George Whitefield then wrote a letter to John Wesley which had been printed without either party consenting and was distributed in great numbers. The Methodists foolishly decided to embrace one and denounce the other, so the Societies were divided. Whitefield then printed a letter that he had written in answer to John Wesley's *Sermon on Free Grace*. Wesley in his *Journal* wrote: 'It was quite imprudent to publish it at all, being only the putting of weapons into their hands who loved neither the one nor the other.' Wesley stated that if Whitefield wanted to write anything then he should not have called his name into question. They met in May 1742 when they were summoned before the Archbishop of Canterbury and the Bishop of London.[3]

In August 1743, John Wesley tried to arrange a conference, where he and his brother would be present along with George Whitefield and the Moravians. He was even prepared to make concessions for the sake of peace; but as Whitefield and the Moravians refused to take part, the conference was not held.[4]

Within a decade, the friendship between Wesley and Whitefield had been healed, as Wesley on 28 January 1750 wrote in his *Journal:* 'I read prayers and Mr Whitefield preached. How wise is God in giving different talents to different preachers.'[5] Whitefield died on 30 September 1770, in America. John Wesley was informed on 10 November and preached a memorial sermon in London, England, on 18 November by the request of the executors of Whitefield's will.[6]

John Wesley, ordained by the Church of England, never wanted to start a new denomination, though as the decades rolled on it was inevitable that it would happen, but not in his lifetime. When his

Societies were formed he made sure that the meetings never clashed with the parish church timetable and he enjoyed celebrating the Feasts Days which are part of the Church of England's calendar. But John Wesley set apart Dr. Thomas Coke (who did not become a Methodist until 1776) as 'a superintendent' which could be construed as consecrating himself to be a bishop, thus informally beginning the extended framework of a new denomination.

Appendix D

Kentucky Revivals (1800s) – Physical Phenomena

The revivals in Kentucky, America, began in 1800 during the frontier days as settlers pushed further West and had some of the most 'wildest' (in a positive definition) physical phenomena on record. Undoubtedly not all was as a direct result of God's presence, the Holy Spirit touching lives, as there is always a minority who are under demonic activity. The author disagrees with the manifestation of involuntary barking, believing it to be of demonic origin even though the author from 1808 stated that it was a humbling process. In the Bible, dogs are disdained (2 Sam. 16:9, Ps. 22:20 and 59:6, 14-15).

Barton Stone was the protégé of James McGreedy and both were Presbyterian ministers. Both were used during the Red River Revival (1800) in Kentucky. In May 1801, Barton Stone, who had been preaching at the Cane Ridge Meeting House in Bourbon County, Kentucky, called for a camp meeting at Cane Ridge. In August he called another and 20,000 people turned up for what had been billed as a six day camp and thus sprang the Cane Ridge Revival (1801).

James B. Finley, a convert of Cane Ridge who later became a Methodist circuit rider wrote: 'The noise was like the roar of Niagra. The vast sea of human beings seemed to be agitated as if by a storm. I counted seven ministers all preaching at one time, some on stumps, others in wagons and one standing in a tree.... Some of the people were singing, others praying, some crying for mercy...while others were shouting most vociferously. While witnessing these scenes, a peculiarly-strange sensation such as I had never felt before came over me. My heart beat tumultuously, my knees trembled, my lips quivered and I felt as though I must fall to the ground. A strange supernatural power seemed to pervade the entire mass of minds there collected.' Finley got on a log for a better view 'of the surging sea of humanity...it was indescribable. At one time I saw at least five hundred swept down in a moment as if a battery of a thousand guns had been opened upon them and then immediately followed shrieks and shouts that rent the heaven.'[1]

Peter Cartwright, a Methodist circuit rider, estimated that he had preached 14,600 sermons and received into the Church at least

10,000 adults and baptised nearly as many children. In his *Autobiography* he noted the 'jerks' that came as he preached on those who heard the Word of the Lord or as they sang, 'convulsive jerking all over, which they could not by any possibility avoid and the more they resisted the more they jerked…. I have seen more than five hundred persons at one time jerking in my large congregation.' In regard to the *proud* gentlemen and young ladies present, Cartwright noted for the ladies that as the jerks began, 'their fine bonnets, caps and combs fly; and so sudden would be the jerking of the head that their long hair would crack almost as loud as a wagoner's whip.'[2] This phenomena produced no injuries. However, one man cursed the jerks and all religion and swore he would drink the jerks to death with whisky. He jerked at such a rate that he could not get the bottle to his mouth and a very violent jerk snapped his neck as an allusion to Proverbs 29:1![3]

Peter Cartwright wrote: 'I always looked upon the jerks as a judgment sent from God, first, to bring sinners to repentance, and secondly, to show professors that God can work with or without means and that He could work over and above means and do whatsoever seemeth [to] Him good, to the glory of His grace and the salvation of the world.'[4]

Appendix E

What to Pray For

We must be careful that whilst praying for revival we do not forget other important prayers that we are commanded or encouraged to pray. The Holy Bible reveals that we should be praying for many things on a consistent basis:
- For the nations (Psalm 2:8).
- For the peace of Jerusalem (Psalm 122:6).
- For the persecuted Church (Hebrews 13:3).
- For the harvest (Matthew 9:38 and John 4:34-38).
- For fruitfulness as we abide in Him (John 15:1-17).
- To receive the Holy Spirit (Luke 11:11-13 and Acts 1:8).
- For our leaders and those in authority (1 Timothy 2:1-2).
- For the greater gifts of the Holy Spirit (1 Corinthians 12:31).
- For people to be saved (2 Peter 3:9, 1 Tim. 2:4 & Ezekiel 22:30).
- Lest we enter into temptation, we should all watch and pray (Matthew 26:41). See also Luke 21:36.

www.ByFaith.co.uk

www.RevivalNow.co.uk

www.MissionsNow.co.uk

Sources and Notes

Preface
1. *In Search of Revival* by Stuart Bell, Revival Press, 1998, page 7.

Chapter 1
1. Dr. Martyn Lloyd-Jones speaking on the centenary of the 1859 revival, at Westminster Chapel, London, boxed cassette, tape one.
2. *The Price of Revival* by John D. Drysdale, C. Tinling & Co., Ltd, 1946, page 25.
3. See *Global Revival – Worldwide Outpourings* by Mathew Backholer, ByFaith Media, 2010, appendix B.
4. *Opened Windows – The Church and Revival* by James A. Stewart, Marshal, Morgan & Scott (MM&S), 1958, page 80.
5. Ibid. pages 73 and 75.
6. Ibid. page 73.

Chapter 2
1. *Opened Windows – The Church and Revival* by James A. Stewart, MM&S, 1958, page 19.
2. *From Death Into Life* by Rev. William Haslam, Jarold & Sons, 1880, 1904, page 174.
3. *Revival For Survival* by Dr. Fred Barlow, Sword of the Lord Publishers, 1973, p.64.
4. *The Fire of God's Presence* by Owen Murphy and John Wesley Adams, Ambassador Press, 2003, page 13.
5. *This Is That*, Out of Africa Publishers, c.1997, pages 64-65.
6. *The History of Revivals of Religion* by William E. Allen (revival series No. 7), Revival Publishing Co., 1951, page 4.

Chapter 3
1. The revival at Nineveh is quite unique, in that God did not come to revive His people first (the Israelites), but He came to give life to those who were dead in trespasses and sins, the Assyrians.

Chapter 4
1. The Scripture is in the context of judgment, but before God can heal and bind up, He often has to discipline His children and judgment has begun at the house of the Lord! See 1 Peter 4:17.
2. This Scripture is in the context of the Messiah's reign but can still be prayed for God to come by His Spirit to meet with His people.

Chapter 5
1. *When the Wind Blows, The Kilsyth and Cambuslang Revivals* by Rev. James Robe, Ambassador Productions LTD, 1985, page 189.
2. *Narrative of Remarkable Conversion and Revival Incidents – Great Awakening of 1857-'8* by William C. Conant, Derby & Jackson, 1859, pages 43-44.
3. *The Half Can Never Be Told*, published by the World Wide Revival Prayer Movement, 1927, page 68.
4. *The Shantung Revival* by Mary K. Crawford, The China Baptist Publication Society, 1933, pages 34-35.
5. *Good News in Bad Times* by J. Edwin Orr, Zondervan Publishing House, 1953, page 258.

Chapter 6
1. *Opened Windows – The Church and Revival* by James A. Stewart, MM&S, 1958, pages 35 and 89.
2. *This Is The Victory 10,000 Miles of Miracle in America* by J. Edwin Orr, MM&S, 1936, pages 73-74. The student was called 'Tut' from the Evangelical Theological College, Dallas, America.

3. *Opened Windows – The Church and Revival* by James A. Stewart, MM&S, 1958, page 44.
4. *Can God – ? 10,000 Miles of Miracle in Britain* by J. Edwin Orr, MM&S, 1934, p.121.
5. *This Is The Victory 10,000 Miles of Miracle in America* by J. Edwin Orr, MM&S, 1936, pages 127-128.
6. *All Your Need 10,000 Miles of Miracle Through Australia and New Zealand* by J. Edwin Orr, MM&S, 1936, page 123.
7. *Revival An Enquiry* by Max Warren, SCM Press LTD, 1954, pages 105-106.
8. *Opened Windows – The Church and Revival* by James A. Stewart, MM&S, 1958, page 92.
9. *Meat For Men, Revival Sermons* by Leonard Ravenhill, Bethany House Publishers, 1961, 1989, page 19.
10. *Rend the Heavens!* by Geoffrey R. King, booklet, 1962, page 15.
11. *Great Revivals* by Colin Whittaker, MM&S, 1984, pages 105-106.
12. *Power No. 2 – Heavenly Power in Wales* – paper, editor, Wm. E. Allen, page 2.
13. See *How Christianity Made the Modern World* by Paul Backholer, ByFaith Media, 2009.

Chapter 7
1. *United Evangelical Action* (Oct. 1970) as cited in *Azusa Street & Beyond* edited by Grant McClung, Bridge-Logos, 2006, page 98.
2. *Revival Sermons In Outline* by eminent pastors and evangelists edited by Rev. C. Perren, Fleming H. Revell Company, 1894, pages 18 and 20.
3. *Memoirs of John Smith*, 1822, as cited in *Missionary Joys in Japan* by Paget Wilkes, Morgan & Scott, 1913, page 225.

Chapter 8
1. *Can God – ? 10,000 Miles of Miracle in Britain* by J. Edwin Orr, MM&S, 1934, p.113.
2. *Thirsting For God* by Eva Stuart Watt, MM&S, 1936, page 152.
3. *In the Day of Thy Power* by Arthur Wallis, CLC, 1956, page 15.

Chapter 12
1. *Road to Revival – The Story of the Ruanda* Mission by A. C. Stanley Smith, Church Missionary Society, 1946, page 49.   2. Ibid. page 104.
3. *Hill Ablaze* by Bill Butler, Hodder & Stoughton, 1976, pages 91-92.
4. *From Death Into Life* by Rev. William Haslam, Jarold & Sons, 1880, 1904, page 257.

Chapter 13
1. *One Divine Moment – The Asbury Revival* by Robert E. Coleman, Editor, Fleming H. Revell Company, 1970, page 24.
2. *This Is The Victory 10,000 Miles of Miracle in America* by J. Edwin Orr, MM&S, 1936, pages 74-75.
3. *Revival Fire – 150 Years of Revivals* by Mathew Backholer, ByFaith Media, 2010, pages 91-92.

Chapter 14
1. *Handbook of Revivals For the Use of Winners of Souls* by Henry. C. Fish, James H. Earle, 1874, pages 13-14.

Chapter 15
1. *Children in Revival – 300 Years of God's Work in Scotland* by Harry Sprange, Christian Focus Publications, 2002, page 256.
2. *China in Revival* by Gustav Carlberg, 1935, chapter five.
3. Dr. Martyn Lloyd-Jones speaking on the centenary of the 1859 revival, tape ten.
4. *The 'Toronto' Blessing* by Dave Roberts, Kingsway Publications, 1994, page 145.
5. Ibid. page 158.

6. See *Clash of Tongues with Glimpses of Revival* by Hugh B. Black, New Dawn Books, 1988, page 150 and *Revival Personal Encounters* by Hugh Black, New Dawn Books, 1993, pages 73-75.
7. *As At The Beginning, The Twentieth Century Pentecostal Revival* by Michael Harper, Hodder and Stoughton, 1965, page 59.
8. *Prove Me Now! 10,000 Miles of Miracle to Moscow* by J. Edwin Orr, MM&S, 1935, page 31.

Chapter 17
1. *China in Revival* by Gustav Carlberg, 1935, chapter five.
2. *The Korean Pentecost & The Sufferings Which Followed* by William Blair & Bruce Hunt, The Banner of Truth Trust, 1977, page 74.

Chapter 18
1. The soul and body are interlinked. See *Discipleship For Everyday Living* by Mathew Backholer, ByFaith Media, 2011, chapter 43.
2. Carol and John Arnott from Toronto Airport Christian Fellowship, interviewed on *The 700 Club* by Pat Robertson for the Christian Broadcasting Network (CBN), Sep. 2008.

Chapter 19
1. Aired on the *God Channel* on 24 June 2008.
2. Based on a page written by William Cooper of Boston, New England, in November 1741, as found in the Preface to *The Distinguishing Marks of a Work of the Spirit of God* by Jonathan Edwards, 1741.

Chapter 20
1. John Wesley, an ordained clergyman never wanted to form another denomination. Methodist class meetings were deliberately set at different times to the local Church of England services and its members were expected to attend them both. It was only after his death in 1791 that the Methodist denomination was officially formed. Father Daniel, a converted Copt monk saw revival in Egypt in 1991 when 20,000 Copts in El-Minya, became born again. He encouraged his people not to leave the church of their fathers but to be the light from within it. Father Daniel was excommunicated from the Coptic Church and for a period of time was in hiding. In 2008, he was an AoG pastor in Cairo, Egypt. The year 2011 saw the Arab Spring (uprising) in Egypt and other North African countries and in several Middle East countries.
2. *Road to Revival – The Story of the Ruanda Mission* by A. C. Stanley Smith, Church Missionary Society, 1946, page 112.
3. *China in Revival* by Gustav Carlsberg, 1936, chapter five.
4. *China in Revival* by Gustav Carlsberg, 1936, chapter four.

Chapter 21
1. *The 59 Revival* by Ian R. K. Paisley, Ravenhill Free Presbyterian Church, 1958, 1969, page 175.
2. *Road to Revival – The Story of the Ruanda Mission* by A. C. Stanley Smith, Church Missionary Society, 1946, page 104.
3. See *Revival Fire – 150 Years of Revivals* by Mathew Backholer, 2010, ByFaith Media, pages 49-62.
4. *Road to Revival – The Story of the Ruanda Mission* by A. C. Stanley Smith, Church Missionary Society, 1946, pages 96-97.
5. *Missionary Band A Record And Appeal,* London: Morgan and Scott, 1887, pages 53-54.
6. *The Price of Revival* by John D. Drysdale, C. Tinling & Co., Ltd, 1946, page 101.

Chapter 22
1. See *Discipleship For Everyday Living: Christian Growth* by Mathew Backholer, ByFaith Media, 2011, chapter 48.

Chapter 23
1. Adapted from *Revival Fires and Awakenings* by Mathew Backholer, ByFaith Media, 2006, 2010, 2012, pages 139-143.
2. *Handbook of Revivals For the Use of Winners of Souls* by Henry. C. Fish, James H. Earle, 1874, pages 21-22.

Chapter 24
1. *Manifestations & Prophetic Symbolism In a Move of the Spirit* by John Arnott, New Wine Ministries, 2008, pages 22, 26 and 28.
2. *Overcome By The Spirit* by Francis McNutt, Eagle, 1990, 1991, Great Britain edition, back cover.
3. Part of a prophecy given to Michael Backholer, 15 July 2012 – as found on www.ProphecyNow.co.uk, titled 'The Lord's Paratroopers (Theocratic Intervention).'

Chapter 26
1. *Thomas Birch Freeman, Missionary Pioneer to Ashanti, Dahomey & Egba* by J. Milum, London, 1894, page 148.
2. www.desiringgod.org/ResourceLibrary/sermons/bydate/1990/711_Are_Signs_and_Wonders_for_Today/
3. *The Revival We Need* by Oswald J. Smith, Marshal Morgan & Scott, 1940, page 83.

Chapter 27
1. *A Century of Mission work in Basutoland 1833-1933* by V. Ellenberger, Morija Sesuto Book Depot, 1938, pages 320-323 and 348.
2. *Missionary Joys in Japan* by Paget Wilkes, Morgan & Scott, 1913, pages 314-315.

Chapter 29
1. *From Death Into Life* by Rev. William Haslam, Jarold & Sons, 1880, 1904, pp.81-83.

Chapter 30
1. *As At The Beginning, The Twentieth Century Pentecostal Revival* by Michael Harper, Hodder and Stoughton, 1965, pages 114 and 117.
2. *Religious Affection* by Jonathan Edwards, edited by Dr. James M. Houston, 1984, 1996, page 40.
3. *The Prophetical Ministry* or (*The Voice Gifts*) *in the Church*, 1931, pages 98-99, as cited in *The Welsh Revival of 1904* by Eifion Evans, Evangelical Press of Wales, 1969, 1987, pages 193-194.
4. See *Overcome By The Spirit* by Francis McNutt, 1991.
5. *The 59 Revival* by Ian R. K. Paisley, Ravenhill Free Presbyterian Church, 1958, 1969, page 174.

Chapter 31
1. *Charisma Reports The Brownsville Revival* by Marcia Ford, Creation House, 1997, pages 124-125.
2. *Pandita Ramabai, A Great Life In Indian Lessons* by Helen S. Dyer, Pickering & Inglis, c.1922, page 102.

Chapter 32
1. *Revival An Enquiry* by Max Warren, SCM Press LTD, 1954, page 65.
2. *Revival In Our Time*, Edited by Fredk A. Tatford, The Paternoster Press, 1947, p.60.
3. *Road to Revival – The Story of the Ruanda Mission* by A. C. Stanley Smith, Church Missionary Society, 1946, page 82.
4. *Pandita Ramabai, A Great Life In Indian Lessons* by Helen S. Dyer, Pickering & Inglis, circa 1922, pages 102-103.
5. *Revival, Not An Option* by Dr. Michael Brown, 1997, teaching tape.
6. *The Lewis Awakening 1949-1953* by Duncan Campbell, The Faith Mission, 1954, page 30.

7. *Where Lions Feed* by John Kilpatrick, teaching tape, c.1997.

Chapter 33
1. *The Evangelical Revival in The Eighteenth Century* by J. H. Overton, London, Green, and CO., 1891, page 69.
2. *The Life of John Wesley* by Telford, The Epworth Press, 1886, 1929, pages 119-120.
3. *The Evangelical Revival In The Eighteenth Century* by J. H. Overton, London, Green, and CO., 1891, page 17.
4. *Wesley His Own Biography, Selections From The Journals*, Charles H. Kelly, 1890, page 111.

Chapter 34
1. *Revival comes to Wales The story of the 1859 Revival in Wales* by Eifion Evans, Evangelical Press of Wales, 1995, pages 101-102.
2. *When the Spirit Comes With Power* by Dr. John White, Hodder & Stoughton, 1989, page 137.

Chapter 35
1. *The Advance Guard of Missions* by Clifford G. Howell, Pacific Press Publishing Assn., 1912, page 336.
2. *Wesley His Own Biography, Selections From The Journals*, Charles H. Kelly, 1890, page 109.
3. *Fire on the Horizon* by Winkie Pratney, 1999, Renew Books, pages 169-170.

Chapter 36
1. *Revival Year Sermons – C. H. Spurgeon, Preached in the Surrey Music Hall 1859*, The Banner of Truth Trust, 1959, pages 73-74.
2. *If Ye Abide 10,000 Miles of Miracle In South Africa* by J. Edwin Orr, MM&S, 1936, page 104.
3. *Spirit of Revival* by I. R. Govan, The Faith Mission, 1938, 1978, page 89.
4. *The Welsh Revival – Its Origin and Development* by Thomas Phillips, 1860, 1989, 2002, Banner of Truth Trust, page 133.

Chapter 37
1. *China in Revival* by Gustav Carlberg, chapter five.

Chapter 38
1. *The Lewis Awakening 1949-1953* by Duncan Campbell, The Faith Mission, 1954, page 31.

Chapter 40
1. *Soul Obsession* by Nicky Cruz, Hodder and Stoughton, 2005, page 126.
2. Book source unknown, though in the public domain.
3. *Rend the Heavens!* by Geoffrey R. King, booklet, 1962, page 12.

Chapter 41
1. *Real Religion – Revival Sermons Delivered During His Twentieth Visit to America* by Gipsy Smith, Hodder and Stoughton, 1922, page 122.
2. *Great Revivals* by Colin Whittaker, MM&S, 1984, page 92.
3. *I Believe In the Holy Ghost* by Maynard James, Bethany Fellowship, Inc.,1965, 1969 (British edition), page 18.
4. *The Enduement of Power* by Oswald J. Smith, MM&S, 1933, 1937, page 40.
5. *Christ the Healer* by F. F. Bosworth, Chosen, 1924, 2008, page 163.
6. *Annals of The Early Friends* by Frances Anne Budge, Henry Longstreth, Philadelphia, 1900, page 134.
7. *When Iron Gates Yield* by Geoffrey T. Bull, Hodder and Stoughton, 1955, 1965, pages 98-99.

8. *The Enduement of Power* by Oswald J. Smith, MM&S, 1933, 1937, page 81.

Chapter 42
1. *Prove Me Now! 10,000 Miles of Miracle to Moscow* by J. Edwin Orr, MM&S, 1935, page 113.
2. *Prove Me Now! 10,000 Miles of Miracle to Moscow* by J. Edwin Orr, MM&S, 1935, pages 116-119.
3. *Revival in our Time*, Edited by Fredrik A. Tatford, The Paternoster Press, 1947, pages 62-63.
4. *The Price of Revival* by John D. Drysdale, C. Tinling & Co., Ltd, 1946, pages 30-31.
5. *Spirit of Revival* by I. R. Govan, Faith Mission, 1978, page 181.
6. *Personal Declension and Revival of Religion in the Soul* by Octavius Winslow, Banner of Truth, 1841, 2000, pages 102-103.
7. *Road to Revival – The Story of the Ruanda Mission* by A. C. Stanley Smith, Church Missionary Society, 1946, pages 74-75.
8. *All Your Need 10,000 Miles of Miracle Through Australia and New Zealand* by J. Edwin Orr, MM&S, 1936, pages 123-124.
9. *An Instrument of Revival – The Complete Life of Evan Roberts 1878-1951* by Brynmor Pierce Jones, Bridge Publishing, 1995, page 145.
10. *The Evangelist – His Ministry and Message* by W. P. Nicholson, Marshal Morgan & Scott, c.1940, page 37.
11. *The Churchman's Monthly Penny Magazine*, c.1845, page 101.
12. *The Baptism in the Holy Spirit – A Personal Testimony* by William Booth-Clibborn, Ryder Printing Co., 1929, 1936, page 29.

Chapter 43
1. *Healing Rays* by George Jeffreys, Elim Publishing, 1932, page 118.

Appendix A
1. *John Wesley's London Chapels* by J. Henry Martin, The Epworth Press, 1946, p.41.

Appendix B
1. *When the Wind Blows* by Rev. James Robe, Ambassador Productions LTD, 1985, pages 35-36.
2. *Another Wave of Revival* by Frank Bartleman, (*Another Wave Rolls In,* 1962), Whitaker House, 1982, pages 11-12 and 20.

Appendix C
1. *The Evangelical Revival And Christian Reunion* by Archibald W. Harrison, The Epworth Press, 1942, page 89.
2. Ibid. page 75.
3. *Wesley His Own Biography, Selections From The Journals*, Charles H. Kelly, 1890, pages 139 and 157.
4. *The Life of John Wesley* by John Telford, The Epworth Press, 1929, page 144.
5. *Wesley His Own Biography, Selections From The Journals*, Charles H. Kelly, 1890, page 238.
6. Ibid. page 374. Facts from appendix A (1-5) from *Revival Fires and Awakenings* by Mathew Backholer, ByFaith, 2009, 2012, chapter three.

Appendix D
1. *Exploring Evangelism* by Mendel Taylor as cited in *Revival* by Winkie Pratney, Whitaker House, 1983, pages 114-115.
2. *Catch the Fire, the Toronto Blessing* by Guy Chevreau, Marshal Pickering, 1994, pages 214-215.
3. *Handbook of Revivals* by Henry. C. Fish, James H. Earle, 1874, page 19.
4. *Autobiography of Peter Cartwright the Backwood Preacher* edited by W. P. Strickland, Granson and Curts, c.1900, page 51.

ByFaith Media Books

Revival Fires and Awakenings, Thirty-Six Visitations of the Holy Spirit: A Call to Holiness, Prayer and Intercession for the Nations by Mathew Backholer. Also available as a hardback.

Understanding Revival and Addressing the Issues it Provokes: So that we Can Intelligently Cooperate with the Holy Spirit During Times of Revivals and Awakenings by Mathew Backholer.

Global Revival, Worldwide Outpourings, Forty-Three Visitations of the Holy Spirit: The Great Commission by Mathew Backholer.

Revival Answers, True and False Revivals: Genuine or Counterfeit, Do Not Be Deceived by Mathew Backholer.

Reformation to Revival, 500 Years of God's Glory: Sixty Revivals, Awakenings and Heaven-Sent Visitation of the Holy Spirit by Mathew Backholer.

Revival Fire, 150 Years of Revivals, Spiritual Awakenings and Moves of the Holy Spirit: Days of Heaven on Earth by M. Backholer

Discipleship For Everyday Living, Christian Growth: Following Jesus Christ And Making Disciples by Mathew Backholer.

Extreme Faith, On Fire Christianity: Hearing from God and Moving in His Grace, Strength and Power by Mathew Backholer.

Short-Term Missions, A Christian Guide to STMs: For Leaders, Pastors, Churches, Students, STM Teams…by Mathew Backholer.

How to Plan, Prepare and Successfully Complete Your Short-Term Mission by Mathew Backholer.

Budget Travel, A Guide to Travelling on a Shoestring: Explore the World: A Discount Overseas Adventure Trip by M. Backholer.

Prophecy Now, Prophetic Words and Divine Revelations: For You, the Church and the Nations by Michael Backholer.

Holy Spirit Power, Knowing the Voice, Guidance and Person of the Holy Spirit by Paul Backholer.

How Christianity Made the Modern World, The Legacy of Christian Liberty: How the Bible Inspired Freedom, Shaped Western Civilization, Revolutionized Human Rights…by Paul Backholer.

Britain A Christian Country: A Nation Defined by Christianity and the Bible & the Social Changes that Challenge...by P. Backholer.

Celtic Christianity & the First Christian Kings in Britain: From St. Patrick and St. Columba to King Ethelbert...by Paul Backholer.

Heaven – A Journey to Paradise and the Heavenly City by Paul Backholer. What will heaven be like? Experience it now!

Jesus Today, Daily Devotional, 100 Days with Jesus Christ: 2 Minutes a Day of Christian Bible Inspiration by Paul Backholer.

The Baptism of Fire: Personal Revival, Renewal and the Anointing for Supernatural Living by Paul Backholer.

Glimpses of Glory, Revelations in the Realms of God: Beyond the Veil in the Heavenly Abode by Paul Backholer.

The Holy Spirit in a Man: Spiritual Warfare, Intercession, Faith, Healings and Miracles in the Modern World by R. B. Watchman.

Tares and Weeds in your Church: Trouble & Deception in God's House, The End Time Overcomers by R. B. Watchman.

Samuel, Son and Successor of Rees Howells: Director of the Bible College of Wales – A Biography by Richard Maton. With 113 black & white photos in the paperback and hardback editions.

Samuel Rees Howells: A Life of Intercession by Richard Maton. With 39 black & white photos in the paperback and hardback editions.

The Exodus Evidence In Pictures, The Bible's Exodus: The Hunt for Ancient Israel in Egypt, the Red Sea, the Exodus Route and Mount Sinai by Paul Backholer. 100+ full colour photos.

The Ark of the Covenant – Investigating the Ten Leading Claims by Paul Backholer. 80+ colour photos.

Lost Treasures of the Bible: Exploration and Pictorial Travel Adventure of Biblical Archaeology by Paul Backholer. (160+ images).

Social Media
www.facebook.com/ByFaithMedia
www.instagram.com/ByFaithMedia
www.youtube.com/ByFaithMedia
www.twitter.com/ByFaithMedia

www.ByFaithBooks.co.uk

ByFaith Media DVDs

Great Christian Revivals on DVD is an inspirational and uplifting account of some of the greatest revivals in Church history. Filmed in England, Scotland and Wales and drawing upon archive information, including historic photos, computer animation and depictions, the stories of the Welsh Revival (1904-1905), the Hebridean Revival (1949-1952) and the Evangelical Revival (1739-1791) are brought to life in this moving 72-minutes documentary.

ByFaith – World Mission DVD is an 85-minute compelling reality TV documentary that reveals the real experiences of a backpacking style Christian short-term mission in Asia, Europe and North Africa. Filmed over three years, *ByFaith – World Mission* is the very best of ByFaith TV – season one.

Israel in Egypt – The Exodus Mystery on 1 DVD. A four year quest searching for Joseph, Moses and the Hebrew slaves in Egypt. Join Paul and Mathew as they hunt through ancient relics and explore the mystery of the biblical exodus, hunt for the Red Sea and climb Mt. Sinai. Discover the first reference to Israel outside of the Bible, uncover depictions of people with multicolour coats, encounter the Egyptian records of slaves making bricks and find lost cities. 110 minutes. The best of *ByFaith – In Search of the Exodus*.

ByFaith – Quest for the Ark of the Covenant on 1 DVD. Join two adventurers on their quest for the Ark, beginning at Mount Sinai where it was made, to Pharaoh Tutankhamun's tomb, where Egyptian treasures evoke the majesty of the Ark. The quest proceeds onto the trail of Pharaoh Shishak, who raided Jerusalem. The mission continues up the River Nile to find a lost temple, with clues to a mysterious civilisation. Crossing through the Sahara Desert, the investigators enter the underground rock churches of Ethiopia, find a forgotten civilisation and examine the enigma of the final resting place of the Ark itself. 100+ minutes.

www.ByFaithDVDs.co.uk

www.ingramcontent.com/pod-product-compliance
Lightning Source LLC
Chambersburg PA
CBHW060512100426
42743CB00009B/1288